This book is designed to assist sea-going personnel in their understanding of the safe operation, testing and maintenance of ships electrical equipment and services.

The publication also supports a series of eight film/video cassettes (with the same chapter titles) which examine practical electrical maintenance and fault-finding procedures on board various ship types.

Further details of the film/video cassettes can be obtained from the producers:

Videotel Productions,
84 Newman Street,
London W1P 3LD,
U.K.

Telephone: +44 207 299 1800
Fax: +44 207 299 1818
E-mail: mail@videotelmail.com
Website: http://www.videotel.co.uk

Videotel Productions and Witherby Publishers would like to thank the following organisations for their contribution and assistance in the production of Practical Marine Electrical Knowledge:

South Tyneside College
P & O Cruises (UK) Ltd.
Atlantic Power
PGS Offshore Technology
BP Shipping Ltd.
Shell Tankers (UK) Ltd.
Mobil Shipping Co. Ltd.
Lothian Shipping
R & B Switchgear Services Ltd.
The Institute of Marine Engineers
International Maritime Organisation (IMO)

We wish to thank the following authors and publishers for permission to use some of the illustrations in this book:
M.L. Lewis, Electrical Installation Technology 2 (Hutchinson)
M. Neidle, Electrical Installations and Regulations (Macmillan)
M. Neidle, Basic Electrical Installation Principles (Macmillan)

Preface

This book describes up-to-date electrical practice employed in international shipping. The chapters have the same titles as *eight* electrical training videos within a series also entitled Practical Marine Electrical Knowledge. The content of the book has been designed to be complete in itself but is also arranged to give training support to the practical video material. It has been particularly written to assist marine engineer and electrical officer personnel in their understanding of electrical systems, equipment and its maintenance.

A ship's electrical power system is explained in terms of its main and emergency generation plant and the distribution network. Electrical safety and safe working practice is stressed throughout. The types and significance of circuit faults are examined together with the various forms of protection methods and switchgear operation.

An appreciation of generator construction and its control is followed by a guide to its protection and maintenance. Motor and starter construction, operation and protection are explained. A survey of variable speed control methods for motors applicable to ships is also included.

A wide range of ancillary electrical services for ships lighting, catering, refrigeration, air-conditioning, laundry equipment and cathodic protection are described together with battery support, care and maintenance.

The special design and maintenance for electrical equipment used in potentially hazardous areas is reviewed in relation to oil, gas and chemical tankers. Various explosion-protected (Ex) methods are outlined along with electrical testing in hazardous areas.

Specific parts of the electrical network together with its correct operation and safety, including UMS requirements, are examined in relation to the standards to be met for a successful electrical survey by a classification society.

The application and operation of electrical propulsion for ships is explained, together with high voltage practice, safety procedures and testing methods.

About the author:

Dennis Hall has a long experience with the marine industry. His initial training in shipbuilding was followed by practical experience in the merchant navy as an electrical officer. This was followed by design and inspection work for large power industrial electrical systems around the world. Further experience and knowledge was acquired in the Royal Navy where he was introduced to the requirements and effective delivery methods for the training of engineering personnel. At South Tyneside College, as lecturer and manager, his cumulative knowledge has been very usefully applied to the training of merchant navy electrical and engineering candidates from cadet to senior officer level. As Head of Electrical Power Systems at the college, he has examined many ship types and visited many marine colleges in Europe, USA and Japan in his drive to meet the training and education needs of the marine industry.

Contents

Page

Chapter One
Ships' Electrical Systems, Safety and Maintenance

1.0. Introduction

An overview of a ship's electrical system is presented and describes various types of circuit diagrams used in electrical work. Electrical calculations, safety precautions, circuit diagrams and testing methods are outlined together with a description of general electrical maintenance and fault finding techniques.

1.1. Ships' Electrical System

Auxiliary services on board ship range from engine room pumps, compressors and fans, deck winches and windlasses, to general lighting, catering and air conditioning. Electrical power is used to drive the majority of these auxiliary services. The electrical power system on board ship is designed to provide a secure supply to all loads with adequate built-in protection for the equipment and operating personnel.

The general scheme of a ship's electrical power system is common to nearly all ships.

The *main* a.c. generators (sometimes called alternators) produce the electrical power. It is supplied to the main switchboard and then distributed to the various auxiliary services comprising the electrical load. An *emergency generator* and *emergency switchboard* maintain supplies in the event of a main power failure.

Compare this general layout in Fig. 1.1 with the system on your ship. Note the great similarities and also note the differences – all ships' systems differ in some respect.

The generators may be driven by a diesel engine, by a steam or gas turbine, or by the main propulsion engine as a *shaft* generator. The type of prime mover is determined by the design of the ship and by economic factors.

The combined power rating of the generators is determined by the overall demand of the ship's electrical load.

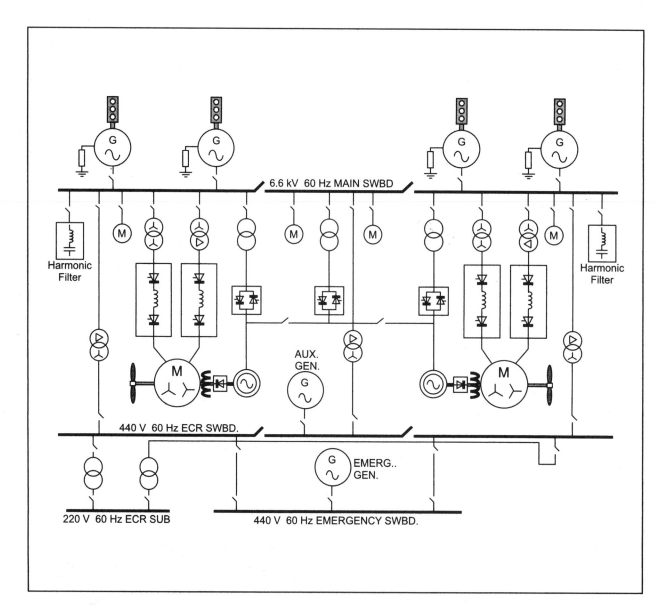

Fig. 1.1 Electric power system.

Large passenger ships usually have four large generators rated at 10 MW or more to supply the electric propulsion motors and the extensive hotel services on board. A cargo ship may have two main generators typically rated from 350 to 1000 kW which are sufficient to supply the engine room auxiliaries while at sea and the winches or cranes for handling cargo while in port. The limited load required during an emergency requires that an emergency generator may be rated from about 10 kW for a small coaster to about 300 kW or more for a cargo liner. The shipbuilder must estimate the number and power rating of the required generators by assessing the power demand of the load for all situations whether at sea or in port.

Electrical power on board ship is commonly generated at 440 V, 60 Hz (sometimes 380 V, 50 Hz). Ships with a very large electrical power demand will require generators that operate at a *high voltage* (3.3 kV, 6.6 kV or 11 kV) to limit the size of normal load current *and* the prospective fault current.

The British Standard (BS) and International Electrotechnical Commission (IEC) definition of *low voltage* is 50 V a.c. to 1000 V a.c. (the IEC give this definition to harmonise British and European standards).

Lighting and other low power ancillary services usually operate at 110 V or 220 V, single-phase a.c. Transformers are used to reduce the 440 V system voltage to these lower voltage levels.

Where portable equipment is to be used in dangerous, hot and damp locations, it is advisable to operate at 55 V or even 24 V supplied again by a step-down transformer. Occasionally, transformers are also used to step-up voltages, e.g. supplying a large 3.3 kV bow thruster motor from a 440 V switchboard supply.

Batteries for various essential services operate at 12 V or 24 V d.c. but sometimes higher voltages are used if such loads require a large power supply.

1.2. Circuit Calculations

The following gives a brief revision of d.c. and a.c. circuits and calculations.

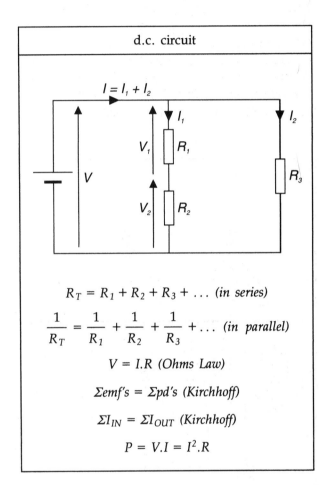

d.c. circuit

$$R_T = R_1 + R_2 + R_3 + \ldots \text{ (in series)}$$

$$\frac{1}{R_T} = \frac{1}{R_1} + \frac{1}{R_2} + \frac{1}{R_3} + \ldots \text{ (in parallel)}$$

$$V = I.R \text{ (Ohms Law)}$$

$$\Sigma emf's = \Sigma pd's \text{ (Kirchhoff)}$$

$$\Sigma I_{IN} = \Sigma I_{OUT} \text{ (Kirchhoff)}$$

$$P = V.I = I^2.R$$

Example:
Using the above circuit with a 110 V d.c. supply and $R_1 = 6\ \Omega$, $R_2 = 5\ \Omega$, $R_3 = 5.5\ \Omega$: Calculate all currents, supply power and p.d. across the 6 Ω resistor.

Determine as,
$I_1 = 110/(6 + 5) = \underline{10\ A}$ *and* $I_2 = 110/5.5 = \underline{20\ A}$
so supply current is $I = 30\ A$.
Supply power is $P = V.I = 110 . 30 = \underline{3.3\ kW}$
[check with $P = \Sigma(I^2R)]$
p.d. across 6 Ω resistor is $I_1.6 = 10 . 6 = \underline{60\ V}$

Single phase a.c. circuit

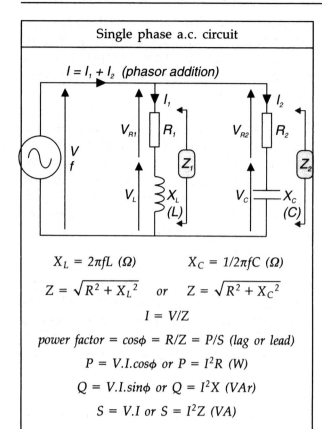

$I = I_1 + I_2$ *(phasor addition)*

$$X_L = 2\pi f L \ (\Omega) \qquad X_C = 1/2\pi f C \ (\Omega)$$

$$Z = \sqrt{R^2 + X_L^2} \quad or \quad Z = \sqrt{R^2 + X_C^2}$$

$$I = V/Z$$

power factor $= \cos\phi = R/Z = P/S$ *(lag or lead)*

$$P = V.I.\cos\phi \ or \ P = I^2R \ (W)$$

$$Q = V.I.\sin\phi \ or \ Q = I^2X \ (VAr)$$

$$S = V.I \ or \ S = I^2Z \ (VA)$$

three phase a.c. circuit

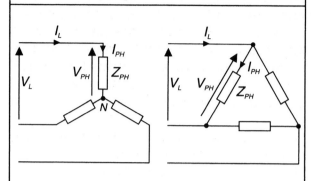

$$V_L = \sqrt{3}.V_{PH} \ and \ I_L = I_{PH} \ (in \ STAR)$$

$$V_L = V_{PH} \ and \ I_L = \sqrt{3}.I_{PH} \ (in \ DELTA)$$

$$P_{PH} = V_{PH}.I_{PH}.\cos\phi = I_{PH}^2.R$$

Balanced 3-phase: $P = \sqrt{3}.V_L.I_L.\cos\phi$

Example:
Using the above circuit with a
220 V, 60 Hz a.c. supply and $R_1 = 6 \ \Omega$,
$R_2 = 5 \ \Omega$, $L = 0.1$ H, $C = 100 \ \mu$F:
Calculate all currents, supply power, overall
power factor and p.d. across the 6 Ω resistor.

Determine as,

$X_L = 2.\pi.f.L = 37.7 \ \Omega$ *and* $X_C = 1/2.\pi.f.C = 26.5 \ \Omega$
Then $Z_1 = 38.2 \ \Omega$ *at* $81°$ *(lagging)*
and $Z_2 = 27 \ \Omega$ *at* $79.3°$ *(leading)*
So, $I_1 = 220/38.2 = \underline{5.76 \ A}$ *lagging V by* $81°$
and $l_2 = 220/27 = \underline{8.15 \ A}$ *leading V by* $79.3°$
The total supply current is the <u>*phasor*</u> *sum of*
I_1 *and* I_2
which must be resolved into "in-phase"
(horizontal) and "quadrature" (vertical)
components before adding,
the result (for you to check) is $I = \underline{3.34 \ A}$
at $43.8°$ *leading*
Supply Power is $P = 220 . 3.34 . \cos43.8° = \underline{531 \ W}$
[check with $P = \Sigma(I^2R)]$
Overall power factor is $\cos43.8° = \underline{0.72 \ leading}$
p.d. across 6 $\Omega = I_1 . 6 = 5.76 . 6 = \underline{34.56 \ V}$

Example:
Using the above circuit with a
440 V, 3-phase, 60 Hz a.c. supply
and $Z_{PH} = 10 \ \Omega$ at p.f. = 0.8 lagging
(balanced load)
Calculate phase and line currents and supply
power when connected as:
(a) STAR and (b) DELTA

Determine as,

(a) in Star, $V_{PH} = 440/\sqrt{3} = 254$ *V*
so $I_{PH} = 254/10 = \underline{25.4 \ A}$
and $I_L = I_{PH} = \underline{25.4 \ A}$ *also*
$P = \sqrt{3} . 440 . 25.4 . 0.8 = \underline{15.49 \ kW}$
(b) in Delta, $V_{PH} = V_L = 440$ *V*
so $I_{PH} = 440/10 = \underline{44 \ A}$
and $I_L = \sqrt{3}.44 = \underline{76.2 \ A}$
$P = \sqrt{3} . 440 . 76.2 . 0.8 = \underline{46.46 \ kW}$
(notice this power is three times the
value in star)

1.3 Electrical Diagrams

There are various types of diagram
which attempt to show how an electrical

circuit operates. Symbols are used to represent the various items of equipment. The shipbuilder provides a complete set of ships' electrical diagrams. It is important that you study these diagrams to be able to read and understand them competently, and to use them as an aid in locating electrical faults.

A *block diagram* shows in simplified form the main inter-relationships of the elements in a system, and how the system works or may be operated. Such diagrams are often used to depict control systems and other complex relationships. The block diagram in Fig. 1.2 describes the main functions of an overcurrent relay (OCR) used for protection. Its *circuit diagram* shows one way of realising the overall OCR function.

Diagrams like this state the function of each block but usually do not give any information about the components in each block or how the blocks are actually interconnected.

A *system diagram*, as in Fig. 1.3, shows the main features of a system and its bounds, without necessarily showing cause-to-effect. Its main use is to illustrate the ways of operating the system. Detail is omitted in order to make the diagram as clear as possible, and so, easily understood.

A *circuit diagram* shows, *in full*, the functioning of a circuit. All essential parts and connections are depicted by means of graphical symbols arranged to show the operation as clearly as possible but

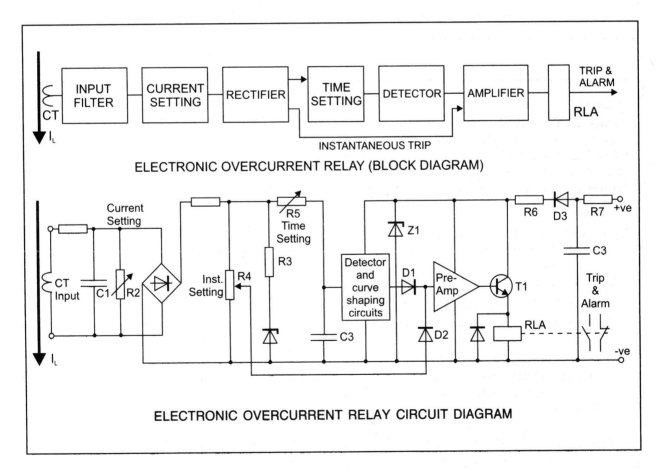

Fig. 1.2 Block and circuit diagrams.

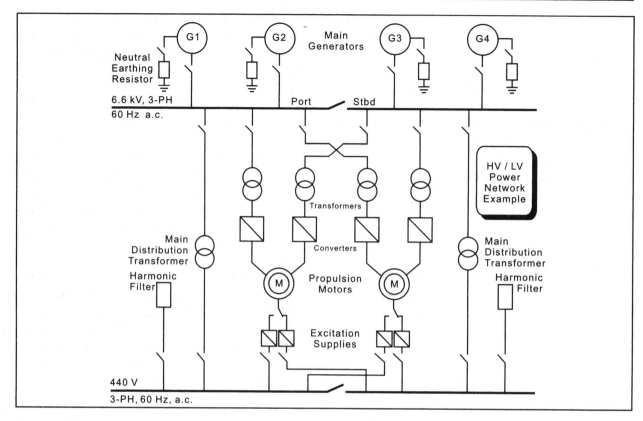

Fig. 1.3 Power system diagram.

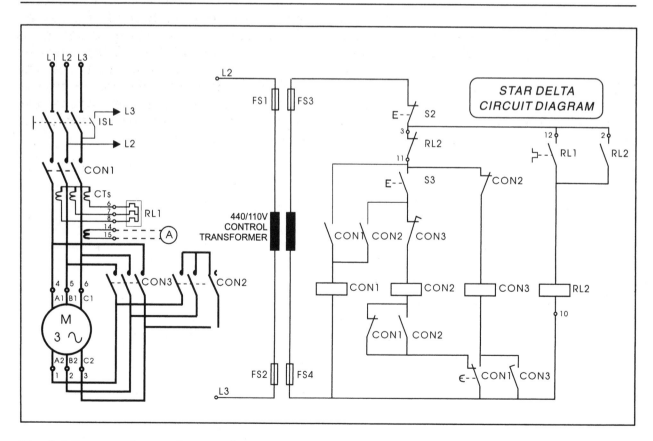

Fig. 1.4 Power and control circuit diagram.

without regard to the physical layout of the various items, their parts or connections.

The electrical connections in Fig. 1.4 for a motor starter are clearly shown in the simplest possible way. A most important point is that no attempt is made to show the moving contacts of a relay or contactor alongside the coil that operates them (where they are actually physically located). Instead, the coil and its related contacts are identified by a common number or letter. Although there are international agreements as to the symbol to be used to represent electrical components you must be prepared to meet various different symbols representing the same component.

The use of a circuit diagram is to enable the reader to understand the operation of the circuit, to follow each sequence in the operation from the moment of initiating the operation (e.g. by pressing a *start* button) to the final act (e.g. starting of the motor). If the equipment fails to operate correctly, the reader can follow the sequence of operations until he comes to the operation that has failed. The components involved in that faulty operation can then be examined to locate the suspect item. There is no need to examine other components that are known to function correctly and have no influence on the fault, so the work is simplified. A circuit diagram is an essential tool for *fault finding*.

A *wiring diagram* shows the detailed connections between components or items of equipment, and in some cases the routeing of these connections. An equipment wiring diagram shows the components in their approximate positions occupied within the actual enclosure. The component may be shown complete (e.g. a contactor coil together with all the contacts it drives) or may be simply represented by a block with the necessary terminals clearly marked. A different thickness of line can be used to differentiate between power and control circuit connections. The wiring diagram in Fig. 1.5 is of the same starter shown for the circuit diagram of Fig. 1.4.

A wiring diagram may be of a fairly simple circuit, but its layout makes it quite difficult to use and to understand the sequential operation of the circuit. The purpose of a wiring diagram is mainly to instruct the wiring installer how to construct and connect the equipment. It is of little use in trouble shooting apart from identifying the exact position of suspect components, terminals and wires.

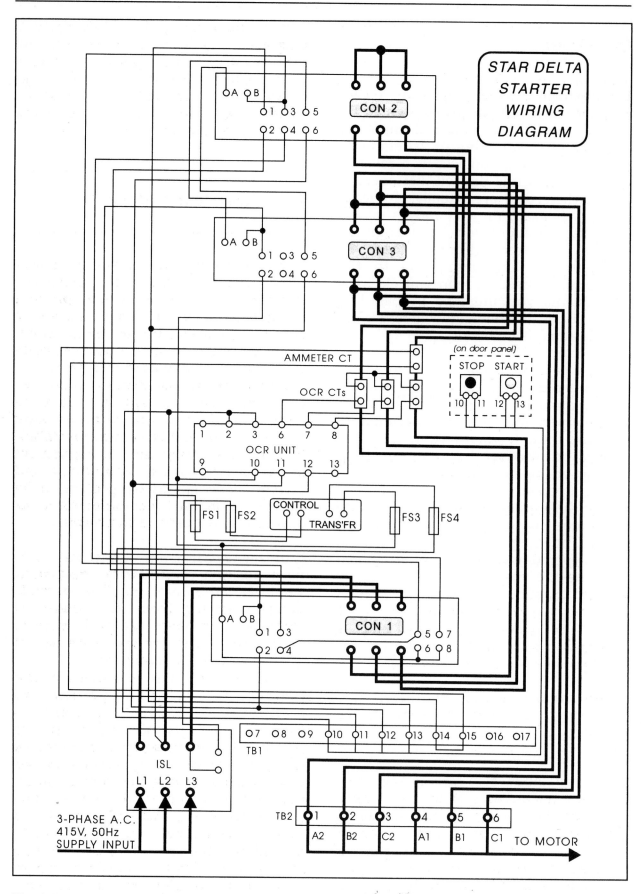

Fig. 1.5 Power and control wiring diagram.

QUESTION

What are you to do if difficulties arise in locating a fault on an item of equipment and only a *wiring diagram* is available?

ANSWER

It may well save time and trouble to convert the wiring diagram into a much simpler and more useful *circuit diagram*. When converting a wiring diagram into a circuit diagram certain basic rules and conventions should be followed.

- Every sequence should be drawn from left to right and from top to bottom (where possible).

- Each stage should be in order of occurrence from left to right.

- All contacts and components which are in series should be drawn in a straight line (where possible) with the component they control.

- All contacts and components which are in parallel should be drawn side by side and at the same level to emphasise their parallel function.

- All major components operating at bus-bar voltage should be drawn at the same level (or aligned horizontally) to help identify the required components quickly.

- All contacts should be shown *open* or *closed* as in their *normal* or de-energised condition.

There are other conventions but these cover the main points of good systematic diagrams. *Block, system, circuit and wiring diagrams* are the main types in general use for electrical work. Other types of diagram are sometimes used to give information for which the basic types are unsuitable (e.g. a pictorial view of a component).

You should study the ship's electrical diagrams to gain an understanding of equipment operation prior to carrying out maintenance or fault finding. Diagrams should be regarded as an essential tool when carrying out work on electrical equipment.

1.4. Electrical Safety

Large power equipment and processes utilise high forces. Electrical, mechanical, thermal and chemical changes produce the desired operation. Very high values of voltage, current, power, temperature, force, pressure etc. create the possibility of danger in an engineering system.

To minimise the safety risk to personnel and equipment a system must be designed and manufactured to the latest high standards and be correctly installed. During its working life the equipment must be continuously monitored and correctly maintained by professionally qualified personnel who understand its operation and safety requirements.

Before attempting any electrical work, there are some basic safety precautions you must bear in mind. The possible dangers arising from the misuse of electrical equipment are well known. Electric shock and fire can cause loss of life and damage to equipment.

Regulations exist to control the construction, installation, operation and maintenance of electrical equipment so that danger is eliminated as far as possible. Minimum acceptable standards of safety are issued by various bodies including national governments, international governmental conventions (e.g. SOLAS), national and international standards associations (e.g. BS and IEC), learned societies (e.g. IEE), classification societies (e.g. Lloyds), etc. Where danger arises it is usually due to accident, neglect or some other contravention of the regulations.

Ships' staff must operate equipment in a safe manner and maintain it in a safe condition at all times. Failure to do so will cause danger with serious consequences arising. Keep in mind an essential list of *DO's* and *DO NOT's* when working with electrical equipment:

✔ *DO* get to know the ship's electrical system and equipment. Study the ship's diagrams to pinpoint the location of switches and protection devices supplying distribution boards and essential items of equipment. Write down this information in a note book. Become familiar with the *normal* indications on switchboard instruments so that abnormal operation can be quickly detected.

✔ *DO* operate equipment according to the manufacturer's recommendations.

✔ *DO* maintain equipment according to the manufacturer's recommendations or the shipowner's maintenance procedures.

✔ *DO* ensure that all guards, covers and doors are securely fitted and that all bolts and fixings are in place and tight.

✔ *DO* inform the Officer of the Watch before shutting down equipment for maintenance.

✔ *DO* switch off and lock-off supplies, remove fuses, and display warning notices before removing covers of equipment for maintenance.

✔ *DO* confirm that circuits are *DEAD* (by using an approved voltage tester) before touching conductors and terminals.

✘ *DO NOT* touch live conductors under any pretext

✘ *DO NOT* touch rotating parts.

✘ *DO NOT* leave live conductors or rotating parts exposed.

✘ *DO NOT* overload equipment.

✘ *DO NOT* neglect or abuse equipment.

You should think *SAFETY* at all times and so develop a *safety conscious attitude*. This may well save your life and the lives of others. Most accidents occur due to a momentary loss of concentration or attempts to short-circuit standard safety procedures.
      DO NOT let this happen to YOU.

1.5 Electric Shock

Nearly everyone has experienced an electric shock at some time. At best it is an unpleasant experience, at worst it is fatal.

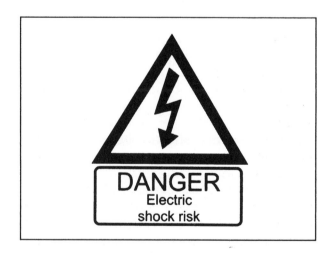

Fig. 1.6 Electrical safety warning.

Anyone who has access to live electrical equipment must be fully aware of *first-aid* and *safety procedures* related to electric shock as described in relevant safety acts. Copies of these safety procedures should be displayed on board ship. Electric shock is due to the flow of current through your body. This is often from hand to hand or from hand to foot. A shock current as low as 15 mA a.c. or d.c. may be fatal. Obviously the size of shock current is related to the applied voltage and your body resistance. Unfortunately, your body resistance goes down as the applied voltage goes up. This means that the shock current is further increased at high voltages. The size of your body resistance also depends on other factors such as your state of health, the degree of contact with live wires and the perspiration or dampness on your skin. Typical dry full-contact body resistance is about 5000 Ω at 25 V falling to about 2000 Ω at 250 V.

QUESTION

What would the equivalent shock current levels be at 25 V and 250 V?

ANSWER

5 mA and 125 mA.

Voltages of about 60 V and below are regarded as reasonably safe for portable hand tools. This is why special step-down *isolating* transformers are used with portable tools and handlamps. These transformers supply the tool or lamp at 110 V a.c. but because the secondary winding is centre-tapped to earth, the maximum shock voltage to earth is 55 V a.c.

Electric shock is often accompanied by falling, which may cause additional physical injury and require first-aid action. If the shock victim is unconscious, resuscitation must take priority over first aid methods. Check the resuscitation techniques described on the electric shock posters displayed on your ship.

1.6. Insulation Resistance

All electrical equipment has insulation. The purpose of the insulation is to keep electric currents in the conductors and to prevent contact with live wires. The electrical resistance of insulation must be very high (MΩ) to prevent current *leaking* away from conductors. Insulation resistance is measured between:

- Conductors and Earth

- Conductors.

The insulation resistance includes the resistance of the insulation material and also the resistance of any surface deposits of dirt, oil, moisture, etc. Surface deposits can reduce the insulation resistance.

The flow of leakage currents through such surface deposits is called tracking which is also affected by the *creepage and clearance* distances between terminals as shown in Fig. 1.7. Equipment must be maintained in a clean condition to prevent tracking and to maintain a high value of insulation resistance (usually at least 1 MΩ).

Insulation materials are non-metallic and have very few of the generally good physical properties associated with metals. Insulation is adversely affected by many factors such as humidity, temperature, electrical and mechanical stress, vibration, chemicals, oil, dirt and, of course, old age.

Traditional insulation materials include cotton, silk, paper, etc. They may be either dry or treated with suitable varnishes or resins to exclude moisture and other harmful substances. Other

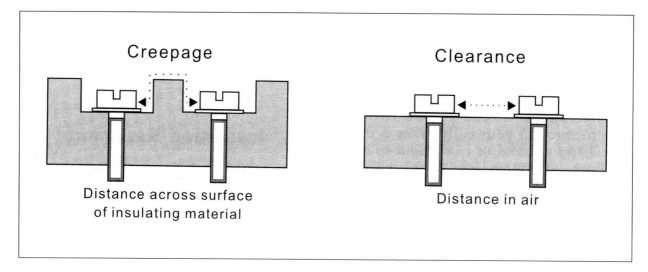

Fig. 1.7 Creepage and clearance distances.

materials include mica, glass fibre, etc., and more modern materials such as PVC and other plastics and compounds. An extensively used medium not normally considered as an insulation material is the *air* surrounding the electrical components.

The majority of insulation materials in common use cannot withstand temperatures much in excess of 100°C.

All electrical equipment heats up when carrying load current with the consequent rise in temperature. This temperature rise is above that of the ambient cooling air temperature.

All marine electrical equipment is constructed and rated to work satisfactorily in a maximum ambient air temperature of 45°C (Lloyds). Under these conditions the expected temperature rise will not exceed the permitted temperature limit set for the insulation material. It is therefore the insulation material that dictates the maximum permitted operating temperature of the electrical equipment.

For this purpose, insulation is classified according to the maximum temperature at which it is safe to operate. Various classes of insulation are listed in British Standards (BS) and classes A, E, B and F are used for marine

electrical equipment. The maximum temperature allowed for each of these classes is:

Insulation Class	A	E	B	F	H	C
Max. Temp.	55°C	70°C	80°C	105°C	130°C	>130°C

These are steady surface temperatures measured with equipment stopped and no flow of cooling air. *Hot-spot* temperatures of 105°C (Class A) and 130°C (Class B) are generally accepted as normal at the centre of coils and windings of machines with these surface temperatures. A machine operating continuously with these hot-spot temperatures would have an expected life of 15 to 20 years before the insulation failed completely. However, the life expectancy would be halved for every 10°C above these allowed hot-spot temperatures.

1.7. Circuit Testing

This section looks at the various electrical circuit testing operations you

may need to carry out, and at the instruments you will need.
The main tests are for:

Insulation Resistance (IR)	Using a (megger) tester (at 500 V d.c. for a 440 V circuit) Do not use a multimeter for this task
Continuity Resistance (Low Ω)	Typically using a multimeter
Component Resistance (Ω or kΩ)	
Voltage (a.c. or d.c.)	
Current	Using a clampmeter (or multimeter for small currents)

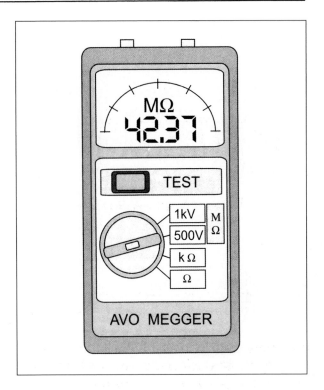

Fig. 1.8 Insulation resistance (IR) tester.

1.8. Insulation Testing

A measurement of the insulation resistance (IR) gives one of the best guides to the state of health of electrical equipment. The resistance should be measured between insulated conductors and earth, and between conductors.

An insulation tester is a high reading resistance meter using a high test voltage – usually 500 V d.c. The test voltage is produced either by an internal hand-driven generator or by a battery and electronic voltage charger. A test voltage of 500 V d.c. is suitable for testing ships' equipment rated at 440 V a.c. Test voltages of 1000 V and 5000 V are used for high voltage (HV) systems on board ship.

There are several manufacturers of insulation testers available but the Megger trade name is known worldwide.

To prove the basic operation of the tester, short the two probes together,

switch to "MΩ" and press the test button or rockerswitch. The pointer should indicate approximately "0 Ω".

Before applying the test, the equipment to be tested must be disconnected from the live power supply and locked-off according to standard safety procedures.

A *megger* type IR tester can be used to check whether the circuit to be tested is *live*. Switch the instrument to "MΩ" and connect the probes to pairs of equipment terminals. DO NOT press the button. The meter will now indicate that the circuit is *live* or not. If the circuit is *dead* it is then safe to press the test button. Confirm that a reliable earth connection is obtained by connecting the probes to two separate earth points on the equipment frame while testing for low resistance continuity.

For an IR test on a three-phase machine, measure and log the phase-to-phase insulation resistance values. Three readings should be measured as U–V, V–W, W–U as shown in Fig. 1.9.

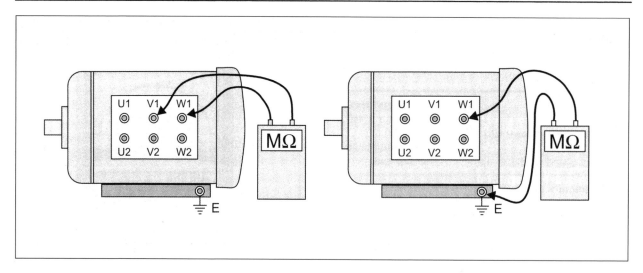

Fig. 1.9 IR test connections.

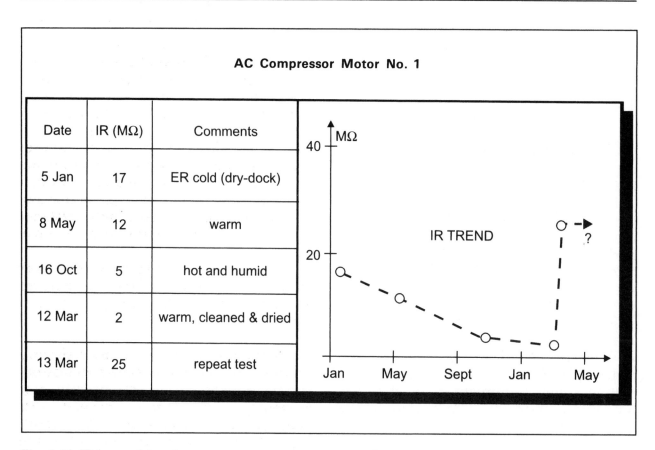

Fig. 1.10 IR log and trend.

Measure and log the phase-to-earth insulation resistance values. Three readings should be measured as U–E, V–E, W–E:

Note: Insulation resistance *decreases* with increase of temperature.

QUESTION

Why should the measurement of the insulation resistance of a machine ideally be made while the machine is hot?

ANSWER

Insulation becomes more *leaky* (its IR value falls) at high temperatures. So testing while hot shows the realistic IR value at, or near, its working temperature. Insulation resistance can vary considerably with changing atmospheric conditions. A single reading gives little information. However, the regular recording of test results may show a downward trend which indicates impending trouble which can be remedied by preventive maintenance.

An example of an IR log for a motor is shown in Fig. 1.10 together with its graphical trend.

1.9. Continuity Testing

An insulation tester normally also incorporates a low voltage continuity test facility. This is a low resistance instrument for measuring the continuity (or otherwise) of conductors. It can be used to measure the low resistance of cables, motor windings, transformer windings, earthing straps, etc. The procedure for use is similar to that for the insulation tester.

✔ PROVE the correct operation of the instrument.

✔ ISOLATE and lock off the equipment to be tested.

✔ PROVE the equipment to be dead.

✔ Switch the instrument to "Ω" or "continuity".

✔ Connect the probes to the circuit.

✔ Operate the test switch and check the indication on the "Ω" scale. Log all readings.

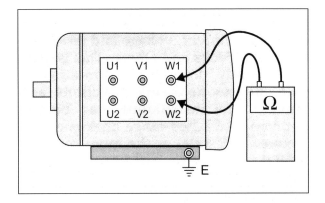

Fig. 1.11 Continuity test connections.

In the case of three-phase motors and transformers, etc. the *comparison* between readings is usually more important than the absolute value of the readings. All readings should be identical. If one reading is significantly smaller than the others this could indicate the possibility of short-circuited turns in that winding. Conversely, a high continuity resistance value indicates a high resistance fault or an open-circuit (e.g. a loose connection).

Some models of insulation/continuity testers also provide facilities to measure resistance in the "kΩ" range and "a.c. voltage" (acV).

To measure very low continuity resistance values such as those between bus-bar joints and circuit breaker contacts it is necessary to use a *micro-ohmmeter*. This type of tester drives a set d.c. current, e.g. 10 A, through the circuit while measuring the resulting volt-drop across it.

A set of four test leads are used – two to apply the current and two to measure the volt-drop directly at the current injection points.

The meter then calculates $R = V/I$ (*Ohms Law*), and displays the result as a digital readout in milli-ohms (mΩ) or micro-ohms (μΩ).

1.10. Multimeters

Routine electrical test work involves measuring current, voltage and resistance i.e. **Amps**, **Volts** and **Ohms**. This is most conveniently done using a multimeter with all the necessary functions and ranges. The instrument may be the traditional switched-range analogue type (pointer and scale) or the more common digital type with auto-ranging and numerical display.

Digital meters have a clear numeric readout which may be supported by a bar-graph display. Where distorted voltage waveforms are likely (e.g. with variable frequency motor drives) it is necessary to use a "true-rms" meter for accuracy. Digital meters are also available which *display* the test voltage waveform shape with a storage oscilloscope facility on the LCD screen.

In all instrument models an internal battery is fitted for use when measuring resistance.

Before measuring the resistance of a component it is essential that the circuit is switched off, locked off, and any capacitors discharged. The instrument is likely to be damaged otherwise.

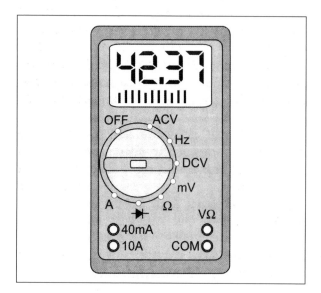

Fig. 1.12 Digital multimeter.

The multimeter should be *proved* for correct operation before use. The manufacturer's instructions should be carefully followed for this but a general procedure is as follows:

Use the *correct* probe leads and insert into the correct sockets on the meter.

If the multimeter is an *analogue* type:

Ensure the pointer indicates zero — adjust if necessary. Set selector switches to "Ω" and connect probe tips together. Pointer should deflect to indicate 0 Ω. If not at the zero point adjust trimming controls. Check each resistance range in this way.

Set selector switch to "acV" (highest range). Connect probes to a suitable known live supply (with *CARE*) such as the electrical workshop test panel. Pointer should indicate correct voltage.

Very special care is necessary when using a multimeter to check for a live voltage. If the multimeter has been accidentally set to the *current* or *resistance* range the instrument acts as a low resistance across the live supply. The resulting *short-circuit* current may easily cause the meter to explode with local fire damage and very serious consequences for the operator.

Fused probe leads are therefore highly recommended for use with a multimeter.

Instrument battery failure is checked when the instrument is set to read "Ω" with the probe tips connected together. If the pointer fails to reach "0 Ω" after adjustment of the resistance range trimmer, the battery must be replaced. The instrument should be *switched-off* when not in use to preserve battery life.

If the multimeter is a *digital* type:

Switch on and connect the two probe tips together. Set selector switches to "dcV" (highest range). Display should indicate zero (000).

Repeat for all "dcV" selector switch positions and note the *shift* of the decimal point. Separate the probe tips. Set selector switches to "Ω" (highest range).

Display should indicate "0L" (over-range) or "100" (depends upon model). Connect probe tips together – display should indicate zero (000).

Repeat for all "Ω" selector switch positions and note movement of the decimal point.

Set selector switches to "acV" (highest range). Connect probes to a suitable known live supply. Display should indicate correct voltage.

Test the d.c. voltage range also and note the polarity indication on the meter.

Instrument battery failure is usually indicated by the numeric display. The display may include "BT" or the decimal-point may *blink*, or some other display effect may be used.

The instrument should be switched off when not in use to preserve battery life.

These simple proving tests should be performed *every time* before using the instrument for *real*. It is obviously very dangerous to touch conductors believing them to be *dead* having checked them with a faulty instrument.

- To measure *resistance*:

✔ PROVE the correct operation of the instrument

✔ ISOLATE and lock off the equipment to be tested

✔ PROVE the equipment to be dead

✔ SWITCH the instrument to the appropriate resistance range, connect the probes to the equipment and note the resistance value

✔ Disconnect the probes and switch the instrument to *OFF*.

- To measure *voltage*:

✔ PROVE the correct instrument operation

✔ SWITCH the instrument to the *highest* voltage range (either acV or dcV as appropriate)

✔ CONNECT the probes to the terminals being tested. *Take great care not to touch the probe tips and remember that the equipment being tested is LIVE.*

✔ NOTE the voltage reading.

If a *lower* voltage range would give a more accurate reading, adjust the selector switches accordingly to shift the decimal point. However, most digital meters have an auto-ranging facility.

No harm will be caused to the instrument by operating the selector range switches while still connected to a live supply. But *GREAT CARE* must be taken *not* to switch into either the *current* or *resistance* mode. This would almost certainly operate the instrument overload device and may cause severe damage to the instrument and danger to yourself. Take your time to operate the selector switches during the operation and THINK about what you are doing. *Fused* probe leads are highly recommended.

✔ Disconnect the probes and switch the instrument to *OFF*.

- To measure *current*:

Most test instruments can only measure up to a few amps (usually 10 A maximum). The current measuring facility is intended only for small-current components, and in particular, for electronic circuits. The instrument will almost certainly be damaged if it is used to measure the current to motors and other power circuits.

The basic current range can be extended by using external shunts (d.c.) and current transformers (a.c.). These accessories are generally purchased separately from the instrument manufacturers.

The procedure to be used to measure current in a small-current circuit:

✔ PROVE the correct instrument operation.

✔ *SWITCH* the instrument to the *highest* current range (either acA or dcA as appropriate).

✔ *TURN OFF* the power to the circuit to be tested and discharge all capacitors.

✔ *OPEN* the circuit in which current is to be measured – removing a fuse-link often gives a convenient point for current measurement.

Securely connect the probes in *SERIES* with the load in which current is to be measured.

Turn *ON* the power to the circuit being tested. Note the current size on the meter display.

Turn *OFF* the power to the circuit being tested and discharge all capacitors.

Disconnect the test probes and switch the instrument to *OFF*. Reconnect the circuit that was being tested.

Often, the most convenient way to measure current is to use a *clamp-meter* which is simply clamped around an *insulated* conductor.

1.11. Diode Tests

Electronic diodes, and other semi-conductor devices with p-n junctions (e.g. the base-emitter of a transistor) can be tested using a digital type instrument using the following procedure:

✔ *PROVE* the correct instrument operation.

✔ *SWITCH* the instrument to diode test.
   If the diode is still in circuit, turn off the power to the circuit, *discharge* all capacitors and remove fuses.
   In this test the instrument drives a small d.c. current (a few mA)

through the diode/p-n junction while it also acts as a voltmeter to measure the volt-drop across it.

✔ *CONNECT* the two probes across the diode.

✔ *READ* the forward volt-drop across the diode. This should be between 500 mV and 900 mV (0.5–0.8 V) for a healthy silicon diode or p-n junction.

✔ *REVERSE* the probe connections and the display should indicate *over-range*.
   If the display indicates over-range in *both* directions the diode is *open-circuit* faulted. If the display indicates less than 1 V in both directions, the diode may be *short-circuit* faulted.
   The associated diode circuitry may be giving false readings so the diode must be disconnected from the circuit then re-tested.

1.12. Current Clampmeters

Power currents (a.c.) can be measured simply by means of a clampmeter which acts as a current transformer. The instrument *tongs* are clipped round a single insulated conductor – the circuit is not interrupted.

The value of current is obtained from the magnetic flux strength around the conductor and is usually displayed on a digital display. Direct current (d.c.) measurement is also available with clampmeters having a flux-voltage transducer known as a "Hall-effect" device.

Many modern clampmeters are virtually multimeters with the addition of facilities to measure voltage and resistance as well as measuring currents up to 1000 A.

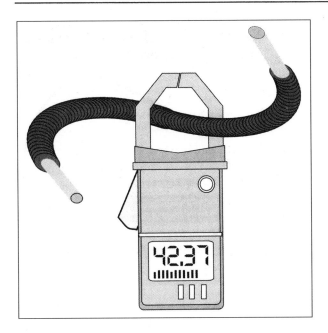

Fig. 1.13   Current clampmeter.

CARE must be taken when measuring the current in *uninsulated* conductors.

More advanced clamp-type meters can indicate power and power factor in single and three phase a.c. circuits by using additional connections to measure voltage.

QUESTION

What would a clampmeter indicate if clipped around a 3-core cable which is known to be carrying 100 A a.c. to a motor?

ANSWER

Zero.
This is because the clampmeter monitors the magnetic flux around the cable which is produced by the current. In a balanced 3-core (or 2-core for that matter) cable, the net flux is zero — hence no indication. This is why the clampmeter is only connected around a single conductor.

1.13. Live-Line Testers

When equipment is to be inspected for maintenance it is important that supplies be switched OFF and locked OFF. The equipment must then be PROVED to be dead to eliminate the danger of electric shock. A live-line (or voltage) tester is a simple device to check only whether or not a voltage exists at terminals.

Live-line testers, up to 500 V, are of various types. Some light up (e.g. screwdriver type with a neon indicator), some make a noise, others operate LED's or mechanical indicators (flags) to indicate the approximate value of voltage.
It is important that voltage testers themselves be PROVED to operate correctly before use. This can be conveniently carried out at the electrical workshop test panel.

Home-made test lamps should not be used as they can be dangerous because protective equipment, e.g. fuses and finger guards, are not fitted.

Great care is required with high voltage circuits where a special HV test probe must be used, see Chapter Eight.

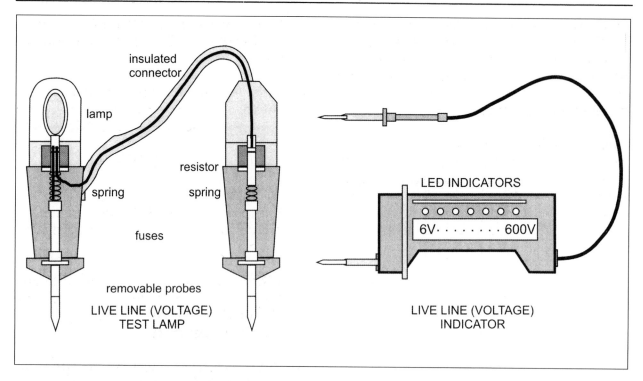

Fig. 1.14 Live-line testers.

1.14. General Electrical Maintenance

All equipment is subject to wear and tear, eventually reaching the end of its useful life when it must be replaced. As equipment nears the end of its safe working life its condition can deteriorate to such an extent as to be a danger to personnel and other plant. The purpose of maintenance, therefore, is to extend the useful life by repair and/or replacement of defective parts and to maintain it in a safe and serviceable condition.

The marine environment is particularly arduous for electrical equipment due to the damp, salt-laden atmosphere, extremes of temperature and constant vibration. Shipboard equipment is in particular need of correct maintenance.
The continuous operation of equipment on board ship demands high efficiency and optimum economy in order to help keep operational costs to a minimum to maintain financial competitiveness.

Nearly all equipment *needs* maintenance.

An efficient maintenance engineer must get to know the power system and its equipment. The ship's drawings and circuit diagrams must be checked and updated to relate them to the actual equipment. Electrical services and equipment must be kept under continuous observation so that normal healthy operating conditions become known, and abnormal operation becomes quickly apparent. Faults can then be pin-pointed and corrected before a breakdown occurs.

Maintenance can be classified as:

• Breakdown maintenance

• Planned maintenance

• Condition monitoring

Breakdown maintenance (corrective maintenance) is when equipment is left untouched until a breakdown occurs. At this time the equipment is repaired or replaced and any other specified maintenance procedure carried out.

Planned maintenance (preventive maintenance) is when equipment is regularly inspected and maintained according to a fixed timetable and set of procedures specifying the actual work to be done to prevent equipment failure.

Condition monitoring (another form of preventive maintenance) is when equipment is regularly monitored and tested. When monitoring indicates that a breakdown is imminent, the equipment is repaired or replaced and any other specified maintenance procedures are carried out. Regular *insulation testing* and *vibration testing* are two forms of condition monitoring.

There are several *disadvantages* in breakdown maintenance:

✗ A serious breakdown of equipment may cause sufficient down-time to put the ship out of commission until it is repaired.

✗ If several breakdowns occur simultaneously the available manpower on board ship may not be able to cope adequately, resulting in delays.

✗ Some items of equipment may need the specialist services of the manufacturer to carry out repairs which may cause further delays.

Planned maintenance is carried out at fixed regular intervals whether the equipment needs it or not and the aim is to prevent breakdown.

This type of maintenance has the following *advantages*:

✓ Fewer breakdowns and reduced down time produces higher levels of operating efficiency.

✓ Maintenance is carried out at times favourable to the operation of the plant.

✓ More effective labour utilisation because maintenance is carried out at times favourable to the ship's staff.

✓ Replacement equipment can be ordered in advance.

✓ Equipment is maintained in a safe condition with reduced possible dangers.

✓ Where a specialist manufacturer's services are required these can be obtained at convenient times to suit the ship operation.

✓ Replacement of short-life components at scheduled intervals.

Condition monitoring is also carried out at fixed regular intervals. The aim is to forestall breakdown by predicting probable failure from the TREND shown by the monitoring results.

The advantage of this type of maintenance is that equipment is not subjected to unnecessary maintenance.

Equipment is regularly condition-monitored according to a monitoring schedule. Measurements are taken of insulation resistance, temperature and vibration (of motors). Contacts and other parts subject to deterioration are inspected.

All findings are recorded in an historical record file. No maintenance is carried out until the trend of test results indicate that it has become necessary. The equipment is then either replaced, repaired or subjected to a major overhaul as specified on a job card.

A maintenance records system is required. The recorded measurements of insulation resistance may show a falling trend indicating a progressive degradation of insulation. The equipment should be inspected and repaired *before* the insulation resistance falls to a dangerously low value.

Hot-spot temperatures emitted from live electrical equipment can be monitored from a safe distance using an infra-red detector or camera.

The recorded measurements of the vibration of a motor may follow a rising trend indicating progressive bearing deterioration. Bearings should be replaced before failure occurs. Immediate repair or maintenance is probably not necessary but should be put in hand at the earliest convenient moment.

1.15. Fault Finding

Generally, fault finding is not an easy task.
    It is essential to have a good understanding of the operation of the particular equipment and general insight into some of the diagnostic skills used to solve the problem.

Here is a list of the general techniques used:

✔ Planning
    A good fault-finder has a mentally planned strategy. The evidence is carefully considered before deciding what action to take. In contrast, the "muddler" acts on impulse.
    A good diagnostician will use most of the following mental abilities:

❑ Memory

❑ Logical thinking

❑ Perception

❑ Spatial/mechanical ability

❑ Social skills

❑ Persistence

✔ Background (*underpinning*) knowledge
    Together with the mental abilities above, knowledge and experience are essential. This is wide ranging and includes knowledge of components, methods and systems together with their operational characteristics. The combination of knowledge and direct practical experience with the equipment is a powerful aid to fault finding.

✔ Diagnostic performance
    In addition to the necessary skills of the diagnostician, systematic use of "job aids" will improve fault finding method. Examples are:

❑ Fault charts
    A list of typical symptoms and faults for a particular equipment plus suggested remedies.
    These lists should be updated according to experience to show the most probable faults.

❑ FACERAP
    The seven letters of the mnemonic "FACERAP" are the key steps to logical fault finding:

F	(*fault*)	the name and classification of a fault;
A	(*appearance*)	the description of the fault or its related symptom;
C	(*cause*)	the operational reason for the fault;
E	(*effect*)	the consequential effect of the fault;
R	(*responsibility*)	the correct person to take remedial action;
A	(*action*)	the standard procedure adopted to rectify the fault;
P	(*prevention*)	the procedure to avoid repetition of the fault.

✓ Search strategy

Once the diagnostician can visualise the circuit or machine as a series of functions and/or use a job aid, a search strategy can be applied to locate the fault in the minimum time.

A "six step approach" is summarised as:

1. Collect evidence (stop and think).

2. Analyse evidence (check assumptions).

3. Locate fault (inspect and test).

4. Determine and remove cause.

5. Rectify fault.

6. Check system.

Conclusion?

Fault finding is not easy!

However, a *logical* approach supported by *knowledge* and *experience* will certainly help.

Chapter Two
Electrical Distribution

2.0. Introduction

This chapter examines a ship's electrical distribution network in detail. Particular attention is paid to earth faults and their detection together with a survey of the range and purpose of the various types of electrical switchgear and protection equipment. Ships' electric cables with their glanding, terminations and testing are reviewed.

2.1. Power Distribution System

The function of a ship's electrical distribution system is to safely convey the generated electrical power to every item of *consumer* equipment connected to it. Probably the most obvious element in the system is the main distribution centre, i.e. the ship's main switchboard. The main board supplies bulk power to motor group starter boards (often part of the main board), section boards and distribution boards. Protection, e.g. circuit-breakers and fuses, strategically placed throughout the system automatically disconnects a faulty circuit within the network. Transformers interconnect the high voltage and low voltage distribution sections of the system.

The operational state of a distribution system is indicated by the monitors for power, voltage, current and by protection relays for overcurrents and earth-faults at each main control centre. Study the electrical power diagrams for your own ship to see if you can relate them to the actual equipment they represent.

The vast majority of ships have an alternating current (*a.c.*) distribution system in preference to a direct current (*d.c.*) system.

The required electrical services are broadly considered as main and emergency supplies.

• Main supply

An a.c. network is cheaper to install and operate than a d.c. system. In particular, a.c. offers a higher power/weight ratio for the generation, distribution and utilisation of electricity. Simple transformers efficiently step-up or step-down a.c. voltages where required. Three-phase a.c. is effectively converted into rotary mechanical power in simple and efficient induction motors.

A ship's electrical distribution scheme generally follows shore practice. This allows normal industrial equipment to be used on board ship after being *"marinised"*, where necessary, to withstand the rigours of a sea-life (e.g. it must withstand the vibration, humidity, high temperature, ozone, sea-water, etc. encountered in various parts of the ship).

The majority of ships have a 3-phase a.c., 3-wire, 440 V insulated-neutral system. This means that the neutral point of star-connected generators is *not earthed* to the ship's hull. For continental European vessels, a 380 V, 3-phase system is common.

Ships with very large electrical loads have generators operating at high voltages (HV) of 3.3 kV, 6.6 kV and even 11 kV. Such high voltages are economically necessary in high power systems to reduce the size of current, and hence reduce the size of conductors and equipment required. Operating at such high voltages is becoming more common as ship size and complexity increase, e.g. for large cruise liners. Offshore oil and gas production platforms operate at up to 13.8 kV, where equipment weight saving is important. Distribution systems at these high voltages usually have their neutral points earthed through a resistor or earthing transformer to the ship's hull.

The frequency of an a.c. power system can be 50 Hz or 60 Hz. In Europe and most of the world the national frequency is 50 Hz but is 60 Hz in North America and in a few other countries. The most common power frequency adopted for use on board ships and offshore platforms is 60 Hz. This higher frequency means that motors and generators run at higher speeds with a consequent reduction in size for a given power rating.

Lighting and low power single-phase supplies usually operate at the lower voltage of 220 V a.c. although 110 V a.c. is also used. These voltages are derived from step-down transformers connected to the 440 V system.

The distribution system is the means by which the electrical power produced by the generators is delivered to the various motors, lighting, galley services, navigation aids, etc. which comprise the ship's electrical load.

The electrical energy is routed through the main switchboard, then distributed via cables to section and distribution boards then ultimately to the final load consumers.

The circuit-breakers and switches are the means of interrupting the flow of electric current, and the fuses and relays protect the distribution system from the damaging effects of large fault currents.

Fig. 2.1 shows an HV/LV layout of a ship's distribution system. The system is called a *radial* or *branching* system. This distribution system has a simple and logical structure. Each item of load is supplied at its rated voltage via the correct size of cable and is protected by the correctly rated protection device.

The main electrical load is divided into *essential* and *non-essential* services.

Essential services are those required for the safety of personnel and for the safe navigation and propulsion of the ship. They include certain supplies to navigational aids, communications, machinery spaces, control stations and

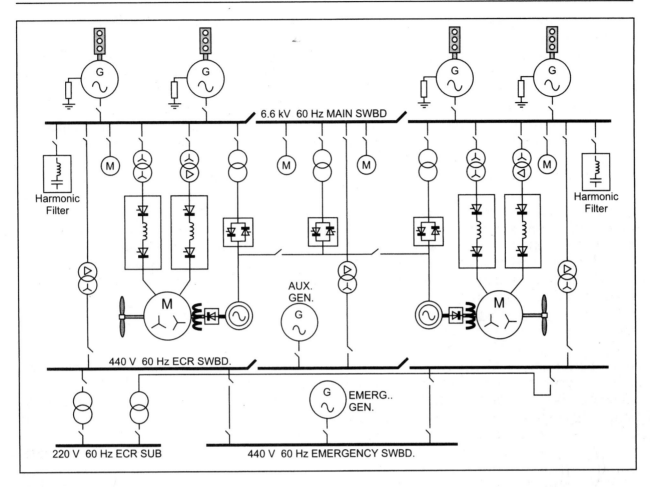

Fig. 2.1 HV/LV power system.

steering gear. The essential services may be supplied directly from the main switchboard or via section boards or distribution boards.

Emergency supplies are necessary for loads which are required to handle a potentially dangerous situation.

To maintain generator operation during an overload, a preferential load shedding arrangement is employed. This is achieved by a special overload relay, called a *preference trip relay*.

If a generator overload develops, the preference trip relay sets an alarm and acts to trip selected *non-essential* loads.

This reduces the generator load so that it may continue to supply essential circuits.

Each generator has its own normal overcurrent relay to trip its own circuit-breaker which is typically *high* set at 150% with a 20 seconds delay.

In addition, each generator has its own *preference* overload trip, this being *low* set generally at 110% current, instantaneous operation.

If a generator overload condition develops, its preference overload trip will operate to energise the timing relay. The timing relay then operates to disconnect non-essential services in a definite order at set time intervals, e.g.

- 1st trip – air conditioning and ventilation – 5 seconds

- 2nd trip – refrigerated cargo plant – 10 seconds

- 3rd trip – deck equipment – 15 seconds

This order of tripping obviously varies with the ship type. When sufficient *non-essential* load has been disconnected, the preference overload trip resets and no further load is disconnected.

The generator preference trip system can also be initiated by low generator frequency or by low speed at the generator prime-mover.

In many cases the preference trip protection is incorporated in a combined electronic relay which also monitors generator overcurrent and reverse power.

To maintain the preference relay trip settings as originally specified they must be periodically tested by calibrated current injection.

Preferential load shedding, generator scheduling and load sharing is usually part of an overall *power management system (PMS)* under computer control.

• Emergency supply

An emergency electrical power service must be provided on board in the event of a main power failure. Such a supply is required for emergency lighting, alarms, communications, watertight doors and other services necessary to maintain safety and to permit safe evacuation of the ship.

Regulations require that the emergency power source be a generator, or batteries, or both. The emergency power source must be self-contained and not dependent upon any other engine room power supply. A battery when fully charged is obviously self-contained. An emergency generator must have an internal combustion engine as prime mover and have its own fuel supply tank, starting equipment and switchboard in the near vicinity.

The emergency power source must come into action following a total mains failure. Emergency batteries can be arranged to be switched into service immediately following a main power

failure. Emergency generators can be hand cranked, but are usually automatically started by compressed air or a battery to ensure immediate run-up following a main power failure.

Although regulations may permit a battery to be the sole source of emergency power, in practice a suitable battery may be physically very large and hence a diesel driven generator is usually installed with its own small starting battery or air-start supply. Other small batteries may also be installed to locally supply control and communication equipment.

On passenger ships, regulations require that the primary emergency power supply be provided by a diesel driven generator for up to 36 hours (18 hours for non-passenger vessels). In addition, an emergency *transitional battery* must also be installed to maintain vital services (mainly lighting) for a short period — typically a minimum of 3 hours. This emergency battery is to ensure that a total blackout cannot occur in the transitional period between loss of main power and the connection of the emergency generator.

A typical ship's distribution system is shown in Fig. 2.2. The system incorporates emergency power supplies.

There is no *standard* electrical supply arrangement, all ships differing in some respect. It will be seen that both the *main* and the *emergency* consumers are supplied by the main service generators during normal operating conditions. In the event of an emergency, only the emergency services are supplied by the emergency generator.

The emergency power system must be ready and available at all times. Such reliability requires special care and maintenance. At regular intervals it must be tested to confirm that it does operate correctly. The testing is normally carried out during the weekly emergency fire and boat drill practice sessions. The main generators are not shut down but the emergency power sources are energised and connected to supply the

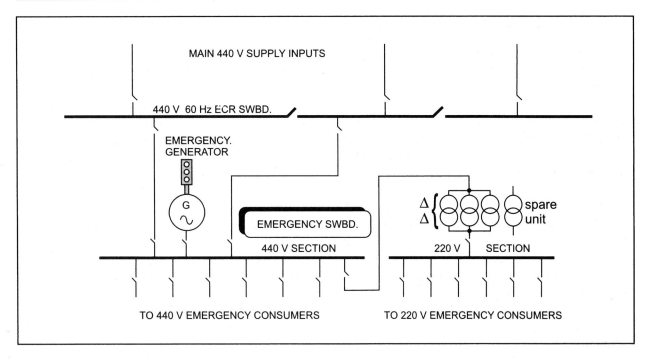

Fig. 2.2 Emergency power supplies.

emergency services for the period of the practice session.

The regulations governing the emergency source of power are detailed in International Conventions, e.g. SOLAS (Safety of Life at Sea), National regulations, e.g. IEE Regulations for the Electrical and Electronic Equipment of Ships (UK) and in the regulations of the Classification Societies such as Lloyds, Det Norske Veritas, etc.

2.2. Insulated and Earthed Neutral Systems

An *insulated* system is one that is totally electrically insulated from earth (ship's hull).

An *earthed* system has the supply neutral point connected to earth.

Shipboard main LV systems at 440 V a.c. are normally *insulated* from earth (ship's

hull). Similar systems ashore are normally *earthed* to the ground. HV systems ($\geqslant 1000$ V) are usually *earthed* to the ship's hull via a neutral earthing resistor (NER) or through a high impedance transformer to limit earth fault current.

The priority requirement on board ship is to *maintain* continuity of the electrical supply to essential equipment in the event of a single earth-fault occurring.

The priority requirement ashore is the immediate *isolation* of earth-faulted equipment which is automatically achieved by an *earthed* system.

A circuit consists essentially of two parts:

- *Conductor*, the part which carries current through the circuit;

- *Insulation*, the part which keeps the current inside the conductor.

Three basic circuit faults can occur:

- An *open-circuit fault* is due to a break in the conductor, as at A, so that current cannot flow.

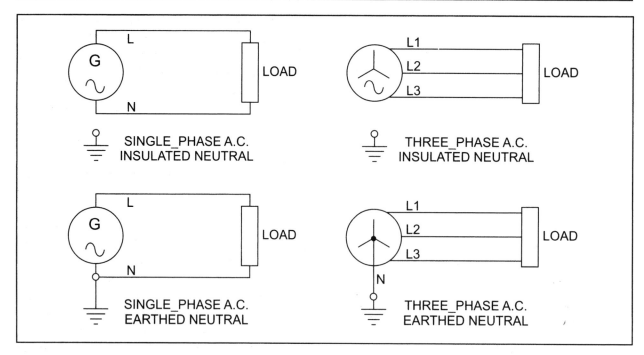

Fig. 2.3 Insulated and earthed neutral systems.

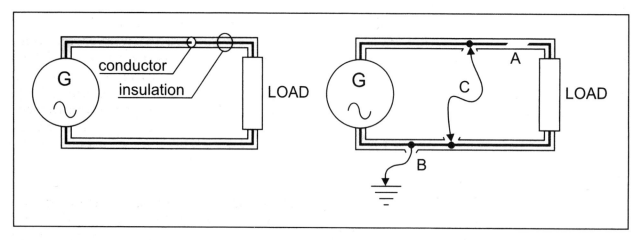

Fig. 2.4 Circuit faults.

- An *earth fault* is due to a break in the insulation, as at B, allowing the conductor to touch the hull or an earthed metal enclosure.

- A *short-circuit fault* is due to a double break in the insulation, as at C, allowing both conductors to be connected so that a very large current by-passes or "short-circuits" the load.

The *size* of fault current that will occur depends on the overall impedance left in the circuit under fault conditions.

QUESTION

A 10 A motor operates from a 220 V *insulated* system. The supply cables have a total impedance of 0.01 Ω.
If:

(a) an open-circuit fault,

(b) an earth fault and

(c) a short-circuit fault occurred, what circuit current would flow in each case?

ANSWER

(a) the open-circuit fault has infinite impedance, so:

$$I = \frac{V}{Z} = \frac{220\,V}{\infty\,\Omega} = ZERO$$

(b) the earth fault has *NO* effect on the circuit current,
so I remains at 10 A. (because this is an *INSULATED* system)

(c) the short-circuit fault impedance is limited only by the 0.01 Ω of the cables, so:

$$I_{SC} = \frac{V}{Z} = \frac{220\,V}{0.01\,\Omega} = 22{,}000\,A \ or \ 22\,kA!!$$

The majority of earth faults occur within electrical equipment due to an insulation failure or a loose wire, which allows a live conductor to come into contact with its earthed metal enclosure.

To protect against the dangers of electric shock and fire that may result from earth faults, the metal enclosures and other non-current carrying metal parts of electrical equipment must be *earthed*. The *earthing* conductor connects the metal enclosure to earth (the ship's hull) to prevent it from attaining a dangerous voltage with respect to earth. Such *earth bonding* of equipment ensures that it always remains at zero volts.

2.3. Significance of Earth Faults

If a single earth fault occurs on the live line of an *earthed* distribution system it would be equivalent to a *short-circuit* fault across the generator through the ship's hull. The resulting large earth fault current would immediately cause the line protective device (fuse or circuit breaker) to trip out the faulty circuit. The faulted electrical equipment would be immediately isolated from the supply and so rendered *safe*. However, the loss of power supply could create a hazardous situation, especially if the equipment was classed *essential*, e.g. steering gear. The large fault current could also cause arcing damage at the fault location.

In contrast, a single earth fault "A" occurring on one line of an *insulated* distribution system will not cause any protective trip to operate and the system would continue to function normally. See Fig. 2.5. This is the important point: equipment continues to operate with a *single* earth fault as it does not provide a complete circuit so no earth fault current will flow.

If a second earth fault at "B" occurred on another line in the *insulated* system, the two earth faults together would be equivalent to a short-circuit fault (via the ship's hull) and the resulting large current would operate protection devices and cause disconnection of perhaps essential services creating a risk to the safety of the ship.

An insulated distribution system therefore requires *two* earth faults on *two* different lines to cause an earth fault current to flow.

In contrast, an earthed distribution system requires only *one* earth fault on the line conductor to create an earth fault current which will trip out the faulty circuit.

An *insulated* system is, therefore, more effective than an earthed system in maintaining *continuity* of supply to essential services. Hence its adoption for most marine electrical systems.

Note: *Double-pole* switches with fuses in both lines are necessary in an *insulated* single-phase circuit.

High voltage systems (3.3 kV and above) on board ship are normally *earthed*.

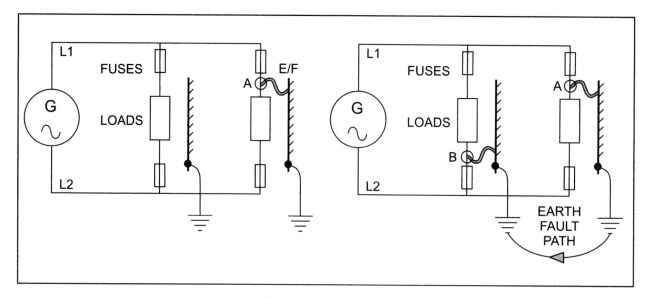

Fig. 2.5 Double earth faults in an insulated system.

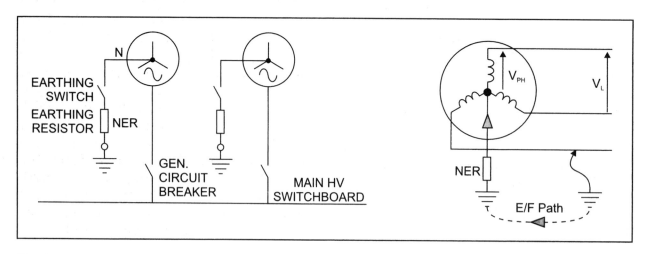

Fig. 2.6 Neutral earthing in HV system.

Such systems are usually earthed via a resistor connecting the generator neutrals to earth as shown in Fig. 2.6.

The ohmic value of each earthing resistor is usually chosen so as to limit the maximum earth fault current to not more than the generator full load current. Such a Neutral Earthing Resistor (NER) is usually assembled from metallic plates. The use of such an earthed HV system means that a single earth fault will cause current to flow in the neutral connection wire. This is monitored by an earth fault (E/F) relay to create alarm and trip functions.

QUESTION

What would be the ohmic value of an NER to limit the earth fault current to the full load rating of a 2 MW, 0.8 pf, 3.3 kV, 3-phase a.c. generator?

ANSWER

In a 3-phase system; $P = \sqrt{3}.V_L.I_L.\cos\phi$ where V_L is line voltage (3.3 kV), I_L is the line current and $\cos\phi$ is the power factor.

The generator full load current is:

$$I_L = \frac{2,000,000}{\sqrt{3} \cdot 3,300 \cdot 0.8} = 437 \, A$$

Under E/F conditions a phase voltage of:

$$V_{PH} = \frac{3,300}{\sqrt{3}} = 1905 \, V \text{ drives the fault current}$$

through the NER. So its ohmic value

has to be: $\dfrac{1905 \, V}{437 \, A} = 4.4 \, \Omega$

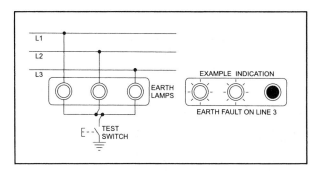

Fig. 2.7 Earth fault monitoring with lamps.

Certain essential loads (e.g. steering gear) can be supplied via a transformer with its secondary unearthed to maintain security of supply in the event of a single-earth fault.

Regulations insist that tankers have only insulated distribution syslems. This is intended to reduce danger from earth fault currents circulating in the hull within hazardous zones which may cause an explosion of the flammable cargo.

An exception allowed by regulating bodies occurs where a tanker has a 3.3 kV earthed system. Such a system is permitted providing that the earthed system does not extend forward of the engine room bulkhead and into the hazardous area.

Electrical supplies forward of the engine room bulkhead are usually 3-phase 440 V *insulated* and obtained from a 3-phase 3.3 kV/440 V transformer.

Regulations require that an earth fault monitor is fitted to the main switchboard to indicate the presence of an earth fault on each *isolated* section of a distribution system, e.g. on the 440 V *and* 220 V sections. An earth fault monitor can be either a set of indicator lamps or an instrument (calibrated in kΩ or MΩ) to show the system IR value to earth.

Earth indication lamps in a 3-phase a.c. system are arranged as shown in Fig. 2.7. When the system is healthy (no earth faults) then the lamps glow with equal *half* brilliance. If an earth fault occurs on one line, the lamp connected to that line goes *dim* or extinguished. The other lamps experience an increased voltage so will glow brighter than before. Earth indication lamps have been the most common method used for many years, being an inexpensive installation which is easy to understand. Their major disadvantage is that they are not very sensitive and will fail to indicate the presence of a high impedance earth fault. This has led to the development of *instrument type* earth fault indicators which are being increasingly used.

One common type of earth fault instrument-type monitor connects a small *d.c. voltage* to the distribution system. Any resulting *d.c. current* is a measure of the insulation resistance of the system.

The injection-type instrument limits the maximum earth fault monitoring current to only 1 mA (compared with about 60 mA for earth lamps), and the meter indicates insulation resistance directly in kΩ or MΩ. The monitor triggers an alarm when its set value is reached.

This type of arrangement has been developed to meet regulations which demand that on tankers, for circuits in or passing through hazardous zones, there must be continuous monitoring of the system insulation resistance. Visual and

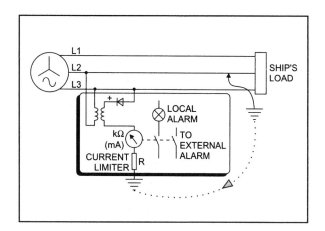

Fig. 2.8 Earth fault monitoring by d.c. injection.

audible alarms are given if the insulation resistance falls below a pre-set value.

An HV system (1 kV − 11 kV) is usually earthed at the generator neutral point via a *neutral earthing resistor* (NER). This arrangement allows the neutral (and hence earth fault) current to be monitored for alarm/trip by a current transformer (CT) and E/F relay.

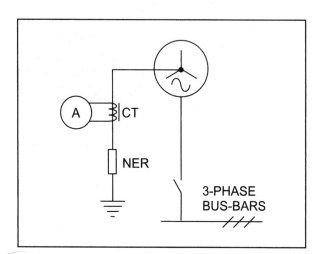

Fig. 2.9 NER circuit.

Alternatively, a special three-phase *earthing transformer* is connected to the HV system bus-bars. This high impedance earthing transformer is arranged to limit the maximum permitted E/F current and initiate an alarm/trip voltage signal to a connected protection relay.

Measurement of the earth fault current in an *earthed* system can be provided by various means; one method is shown in Fig. 2.10.

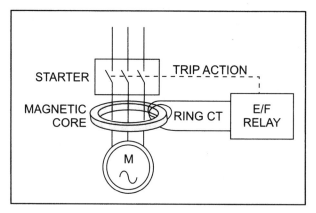

Fig. 2.10 Core-balance CT.

Here the current transformer (CT) measures the phasor sum of the 3 line currents supplied to the motor. If the motor is healthy (no earth faults) the phasor sum of the currents measured by the CT is zero.

If an earth fault (E/F) occurs in the motor, an earth fault current flows and the phasor sum of the currents is now not zero. The current monitored by the E/F relay is used to trip the contactor in the starter to isolate the faulty motor circuit.

The earth fault monitor on the switch-board shows the presence of an earth fault on the distribution system. It is up to the maintenance staff to *trace* (search for) the exact location of the fault and then to *clear* it as quickly as possible.

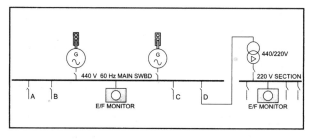

Fig. 2.11 Earth fault monitors in a distribution system.

An apparently simple method would be to open the circuit-breakers feeding loads A, B, C, etc. one at a time and by watching the earth fault monitor while observing which circuit-breaker, when tripped, clears the earth fault. The earth fault must then be on that particular circuit.

In practice, circuits cannot be disconnected at random in this way. Some vital service may be interrupted causing the main engines to stop ... perhaps in dangerous narrow waters.

Tracing the earth fault must be co-ordinated with the operational requirements of the ship's electrical services. The method of earth fault *clearance* will be described fully for a lighting distribution circuit shown in Fig. 2.12.

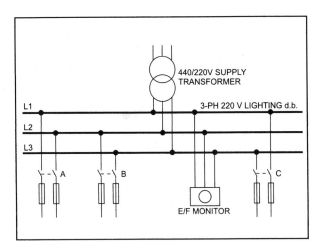

Fig. 2.12 Three phase to single phase distribution.

Suppose the earth fault monitor on the 220 V lighting distribution board (d.b.) indicates the presence of an earth fault. Switches A, B, C, are sequentially opened and closed in turn until the earth fault monitor indicates the earth faulted circuit. Suppose this is switch B.

Circuit B supplies a distribution fuse-board (d.f.b.) located near its lighting circuits. Here there is no earth fault monitor so an IR (megger) tester must be used.

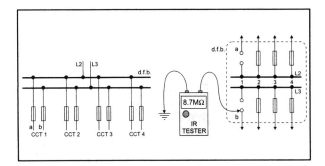

Fig. 2.13 TR testing at distribution fuse board.

At this d.f.b. fuse-pair No. 1 is removed to isolate the supply to the load. (Fig. 2.13)

The IR tester (megger) is now connected with one lead to earth (hull) and the other lead to "b" (*the outgoing terminal* as shown), and a test applied. If healthy (IR > 1 MΩ), connect the test lead to "a" and repeat the test. If both "a" and "b" are healthy, circuit 1 is healthy and fuse-pair 1 can be replaced.

Fuse-pair 2 is now removed and tested at "a" and "b". If an earth fault is indicated (IR = low) then the faulted circuit has been located

All fuse-pairs are checked in turn to confirm whether healthy or faulted.

At the faulted circuit, the fuses should be removed, all switches should be opened, and all lamps taken out as shown in Fig. 2.14.

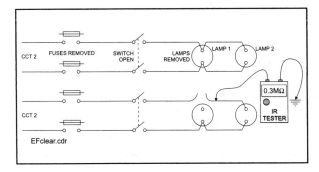

Fig. 2.14 IR test on a lighting circuit.

This breaks the circuit into several isolated conductor sections.

At the supply distribution board, test at "a" and then at "b". If both have an IR>1 MΩ then the conductors connected to "a" and "b" are clear and healthy.

Close the switch and re-test at "a". If the IR is low then the earth fault lies on the conductors beyond the switch.

At lamp 1 remove the fitting and disconnect the conductors as shown to further break down the circuit. Use the IR tester on each of these disconnected leads. If one conductor is indicated as having an earth fault (suppose it is the conductor between L_1 and L_2) then the earth fault lies at lamp 1 *or* lamp 2 *or* on the conductor.

Both lamp fittings must now be opened and visually inspected to trace the exact location of earth fault.

The method of tracing the earth fault is essentially that of continually breaking down the circuit into smaller and smaller sections until it is finally located.

When located, the damaged insulation must be repaired. The method of repairing the earth fault depends upon the cause of the earth fault and this is determined by visual examination.

A lamp fitting that is damaged must be replaced. Dampness in insulation must be dried out by gentle heat and then some precaution must be taken to prevent the future ingress of moisture.

Insulation that has been mechanically damaged or weakened by overheating must be made good again. If surface dirt is the cause, a thorough cleaning will probably cure the fault.

2.4. Distribution Circuit Breakers

Details of *main* circuit-breakers for main generators and main feeder circuits are included in Chapter 3.

The function of any circuit-breaker is to safely *make* onto and *break* open the *prospective short-circuit fault current*

expected at that point in the circuit. The main contacts must open rapidly while the resulting arc is transferred to special arcing contacts above the main contacts. Arc chutes with *arc-splitters* quickly stretch and cool the arc until it *snaps*. The CB is *open* when the arc is quenched.

Feeder and distribution circuits are usually protected by the moulded-case (MCCB) type or the miniature (MCB) type of circuit-breakers.

• MCCBs

These are small, compact air circuit-breakers fitted in a moulded plastic case. They have a *lower normal* current rating (50–1500 A) than main breakers and a *lower breaking* capacity. See Fig. 2.15.

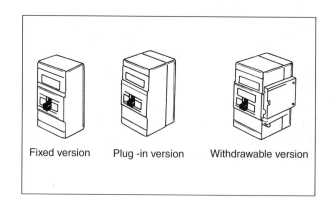

Fixed version   Plug -in version   Withdrawable version

Fig. 2.15 MCCB outline construction.

They usually have an adjustable thermal overcurrent setting and an adjustable or fixed magnetic overcurrent trip for short-circuit protection built into the case. An undervoltage trip coil may also be included within the case.

Operation to close is usually by a hand operated lever but motor-charged spring closing can also be fitted. MCCBs are reliable, trouble free and require negligible maintenance. If the breaker operates in the *ON* position for long periods it should be tripped and closed a few times to free the mechanism and clean the contacts. Terminals should be checked for tightness otherwise overheating damage will develop.

The front cover of larger MCCBs (around 1000 A rating) can usually be removed for visual inspection and cleaning. Following tripping under a short-circuit fault, the breaker should be inspected for damage, checked for correct operation, and its insulation resistance measured. A test result of at least 5 MΩ is usually required. Any other faulty operation usually requires replacement or overhaul by the manufacturer.

MCCBs can be used for every application on board ship from generator breakers to small distribution breakers. The limited breaking capacity may demand that *back-up* fuses be fitted for very high prospective short-circuit fault levels.

- **MCBs**

These are very small air circuit-breakers fitted in moulded plastic cases. See Fig. 2.16. They have current ratings of 5–100 A and generally thermal over-current and magnetic short-circuit protection. They have a very limited breaking capacity (about 3000 A) and are commonly used in final distribution boards instead of fuses. The d.b. is supplied via a fuse or MCCB with the required breaking capacity.

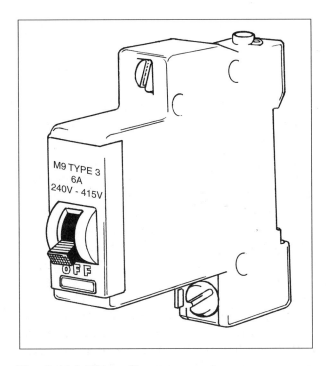

Fig. 2.16 MCB outline construction.

MCBs must be replaced if faults develop – no maintenance is possible.

2.5. Transformers

Electrical generation on board ship is typically at 3-phase a.c., 440 V, 60 Hz, while fixed lighting and other low power loads are supplied with 220 V a.c. single-phase from very efficient (typically > 90 %) static transformer units. Ships with HV generation require 3-phase transformers to supply the LV engine-room and accommodation sub-switchboards e.g. using 6600/440 V units. See Fig. 2.17.

The principle of operation of a single-phase transformer is simple. An applied a.c. voltage V_1 to the *primary* winding sets up an alternating magnetic flux in the laminated steel core.

The flux *induces* an emf in the *secondary* whose size is fixed by the ratio of primary and secondary turns in the pair of phase windings (N_1 and N_2) to give: $\dfrac{V_1}{V_2} = \dfrac{N_1}{N_2}$

The secondary voltage V_2 is available to drive current through a load.

It is the load connected to the secondary that sets the size and power factor angle of the load current I_2. This is matched on the primary side from:

$$\frac{V_1}{V_2} = \frac{I_2}{I_1}$$

Transformers are rated in apparent power (VA or kVA) units.

QUESTION

A 440/110 V single phase transformer supplies a load of 5 kW at 0.8 power factor load.

Calculate secondary and primary currents (ignoring transformer power losses).

ANSWER

From: $P_2 = V_2.I_2.\cos\phi$, $I_2 = \dfrac{P_2}{V_2.\cos\phi}$

$$= \frac{5000}{110 \times 0.8} = \underline{\underline{56.82\ A}}$$

$$I_1 = I_2 \times \frac{V_2}{V_1} = 56.82 \times \left(\frac{110}{440}\right) = \underline{\underline{14.2\ A}}$$

or, check from $P_1 = V_1.I_1.\cos\phi$

The transformers are generally air cooled, being mounted in sheet steel enclosures which are often located adjacent to the main switchboard. Alternatively, they may be fitted *within* the switchboard so transformer enclosures are not required.

Three-phase 440/220 V lighting transformers. are usually composed of three separate single-phase units inter-connected to form a 3-phase arrangement. This enables easy replacement of a single-phase unit if it develops a fault. The alternative is to use a single 3-phase unit with all windings mounted on a common magnetic core. This type has to be completely isolated in the event of a fault on one phase only.

Transformers for use on 3-phase *insulated* systems are generally interconnected in a *delta-delta* circuit configuration using copper links between the phase windings. See Fig. 2.18.

If a fault develops on one phase of such an arrangement, the faulty unit can be disconnected (via the links) creating an *open-delta* or "*V*" connection and a 3-phase supply will still be available, although at a reduced power capacity. This is obviously a useful safeguard.

In some cases, a spare 4th transformer is available to replace the faulty unit.

Transformers for use on 3-phase HV/LV *earthed* systems ashore are generally connected delta-star to provide a 3-phase,

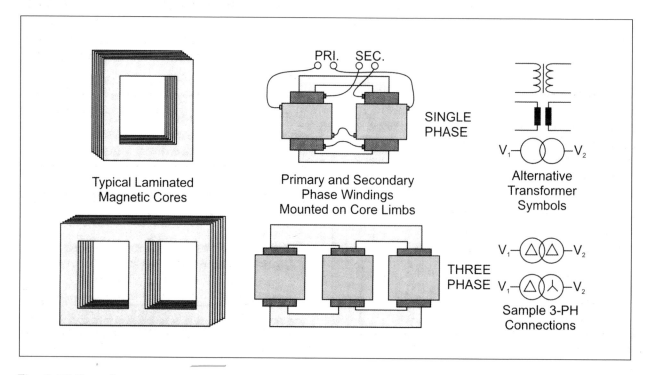

Fig. 2.17 Transformer arrangements.

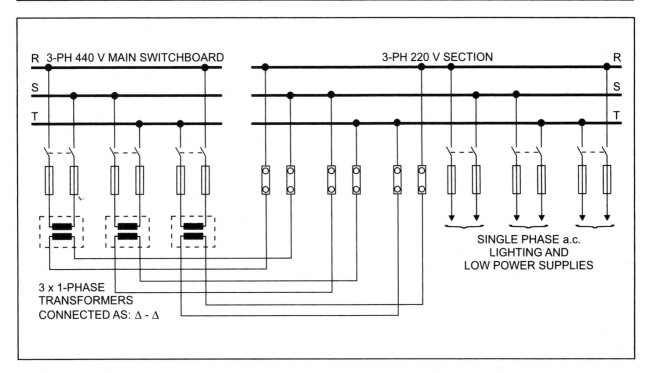

Fig. 2.18 Delta-delta transformer connection.

4-wire LV supply, e.g. a 6600/400 V ratio gives a secondary *line* voltage of 400 V plus a line-neutral *phase* voltage of $400/\sqrt{3} = 230$ V. An earth fault occurring on a such neutral-earthed system will immediately operate the protective fuse or circuit-breaker. This interruption of supply leads to rapid identification of the faulty circuit.

Transformers are static items of equipment which are usually very reliable and trouble-free. However, like all electrical equipment, transformers must be subjected to the usual maintenance checks.

At regular specified intervals, transformers must be disconnected, covers removed and all accumulated dust and deposits removed by a vacuum cleaner and suitable brushes. Windings must be inspected for any signs of damage or over-heating. Winding continuity resistance values are measured, recorded and compared with each other for balance. Any differences in continuity readings will indicate winding faults such

as short-circuited turns. The insulation resistance of all windings must be measured both with respect to earth and to the other phase windings. The cause of any low insulation resistance reading must be investigated and rectified. Cable connections must be checked for tightness. Covers must be securely replaced and the transformers re-commissioned.

All test results and observations should then be recorded for future reference.

2.6. Instrument Transformers

Transformers are used to supply instruments and protection relays with proportionally *small* currents and voltages derived from the large currents and voltages in a high power network. See Fig. 2.19.

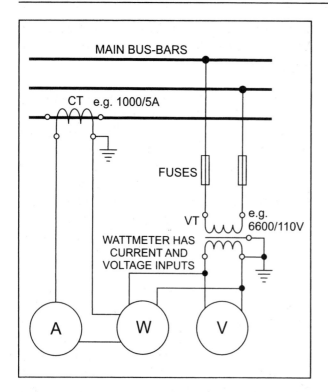

Fig. 2.19 Instrument connections with CT and VT.

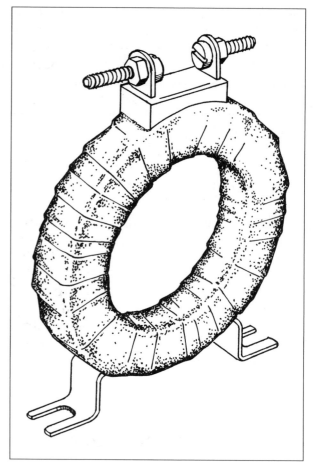

Fig. 2.20 Bar primary CT.

Voltage transformers (VTs) supply volt-meters and the voltage operated coils of instruments and relays. A standard secondary voltage of 110V is used. Current transformers (CTs) supply ammeters and the current operated coils of instruments and relays with a standardised 5 A or 1 A.

The use of VTs and CTs allows standardised instruments and relays to be used. They also improve safety by providing low voltage and low current isolated supplies for monitoring instruments and protection relays.

VTs are built like small power transformers. They are not normally used at voltages less than 3 kV. CTs can be of the wound primary or bar primary type.

The bar primary type CT is used with very high primary current ratings the wound primary type being used for small step-down ratios, e.g. 1000/5 A bar primary; 50/5 A wound primary. The ratio specified on a VT details its input and output voltages, e.g. 3.3 kV/110 V is used on a 3.3 kV mains circuit

and steps the voltage down to 110 V. The associated instrument will have its scale calibrated 0–3.3 kV and will be marked "3.3 kV/110 V VT ratio".

The ratio specified on a CT similarly details its input and output currents, e.g. 150/5 A CT is used on a 150 A mains circuit and steps the current down to 5 A. The associated instrument will have its scale calibrated "0–150 A" and will be marked "150/5 A CT ratio".

The use of instrument transformers does not eliminate danger to operators. The 110 V output from a VT will apply a severe, possibly lethal shock to unsuspecting fingers! The secondary circuit of a CT must *never* be opened while mains primary load current is flowing. Excessive heating will be developed in an *open-circuited* CT with an extremely high voltage arising at the open secondary terminals. If an ammeter is to be removed from circuit, the CT secondary output terminal must be first *short-circuited*, with the primary circuit switched off. The secondary short circuit will not damage the CT when the primary current is switched on. For further safety, one end of the secondary winding of a CT or VT is connected to earth.

Status indicator lamps on switchboards are commonly of the transformer type, having a small transformer built into the lamp fitting. The transformer provides a 6 V or 12 V output. The lamp is of low wattage with small bayonet cap fitting. Although not an accurate instrument transformer, the lamp transformer is similar in function to a VT.

2.7. Shore Supply Connection

A shore-supply is required so that the ship's generators and their prime-movers can be shut down for major overhaul during a dry-docking period.

There must be a suitable connection box conveniently located to accept the shore supply cable. The connection box is often located at the entrance to the accommodation or in the emergency generator room.
  The connection box must have suitable terminals to accept the shore supply cable, including an earthing terminal to earth the ship's hull to the shore earth.

The connection box must have a circuit-breaker or an isolator switch and fuses to protect the cable linking the connection box to the main switchboard, with a data plate giving details of the ship's electrical system (voltage and frequency) and showing the method for connecting the shore supply cable. A voltmeter is fitted to indicate *polarity* of a *d.c.* shore supply.

For an a.c. shore supply a *phase-sequence indicator* is fitted to indicate correct supply phase sequence. This indicator may be arranged as two lamps connected as an unbalanced load across the three phases via resistors and capacitors. The sequence is *"right"* (*or correct*) when the *right* side lamp is bright and the other is dark. An alternative P.S.I. indicator is a rotary pointer driven by a small 3-phase induction motor.
  At the main switchboard an indicator is provided, usually a lamp, to indicate that the shore supply is available for connection to the bus-bars via a connecting switch or circuit-breaker. It is not normally possible to parallel the shore supply with the ship's generators. The ship's generators must, therefore, be disconnected before the shore supply can be connected to the main switchboard. Normally, the shore supply switch on the main switchboard is interlocked with the generator circuit-breakers so that it cannot be closed if the generators are still connected.

QUESTION

Why is it essential to know if the phase sequence of the incoming shore supply is *"correct"*?

ANSWER

By *"correct"* we mean that it is the *same* sequence as the ship's supply (red-yellow-blue). A reversed phase sequence (red-blue-yellow) will produce a *reversed* shaft rotation in all 3-phase motors because the direction of their rotating magnetic fields will be reversed with disastrous results.
  This fault is remedied by interchanging any two conductors of the shore supply cable at the connection box.

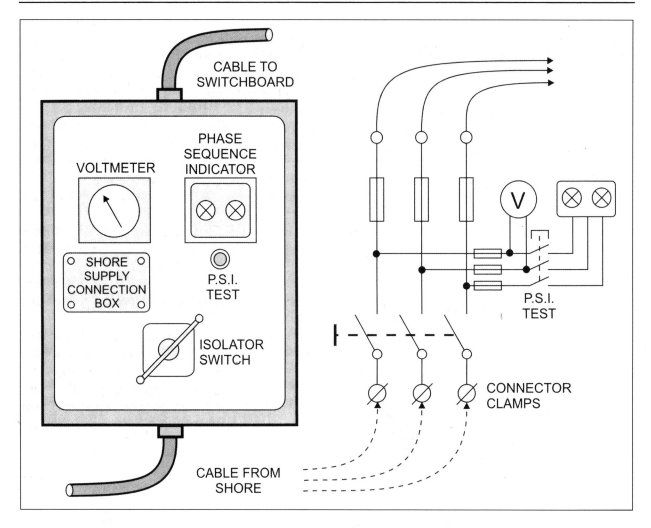

Fig. 2.21 Shore connection box and indicators.

Fig. 2.21 shows a typical shore connection arrangement but some variations occur. For example, the shore supply may be connected directly to the emergency board which then *back-feeds* to the main switchboard.

The shore supply may have a different frequency and/or voltage to that of the ship's system.

A higher *frequency* will cause motors to run faster, be overloaded and overheat.

A higher *voltage* will generally cause equipment to take excess current and overheat. It will also cause motors to accelerate more rapidly and this may overstress the driven loads.

A lower voltage is generally not so serious but may cause motors to run slower and overheat, and may cause motors to stall.

If the shore supply frequency differs from the ship's normal frequency then, ideally, the shore supply voltage should differ in the same proportion.

QUESTION

If your ship is designed for 60 Hz at 440 V – what value should the shore supply voltage be if operating at 50 Hz?

ANSWER

Supply voltage should be reduced to about 380 V.

2.8. Circuit Protection

Many forms of electrical protection are available which are designed to protect the distribution system when a fault occurs. Protection relays are used to monitor overcurrent, over/under voltage, over/under frequency, earth leakage, unbalanced loading, over-temperature, reverse power (for generators) etc. The HV power system shown in Fig. 2.22 lists typical protective relay functions.

As most protection relays monitor current and/or voltage, we will limit our examination to *overcurrent* and *undervoltage* protection together with an appreciation of *protective discrimination*. (Reverse power protection is included with generator protection in Chapter Three)

No matter how well designed and operated, there is always the possibility of faults developing on electrical equipment. Faults can develop due to natural wear and tear, incorrect operation, accidental damage and by neglect.

The breakdown of essential equipment may endanger the ship, but probably the most serious hazard is *FIRE*. Overcurrent (I^2R resistive heating effect) in cables and equipment will cause overheating and possibly fire.

The size of conductor used in cables and equipment is such that with rated full load current flowing, the heat developed does not raise the temperature beyond about 80°C (i.e. 35°C rise above an ambient of 45°C).

A copper conductor can withstand very high temperatures (melts at 1083°C), but its insulation (generally organic materials such as cotton or plastic compounds) cannot withstand temperatures much in excess of 100°C. At higher

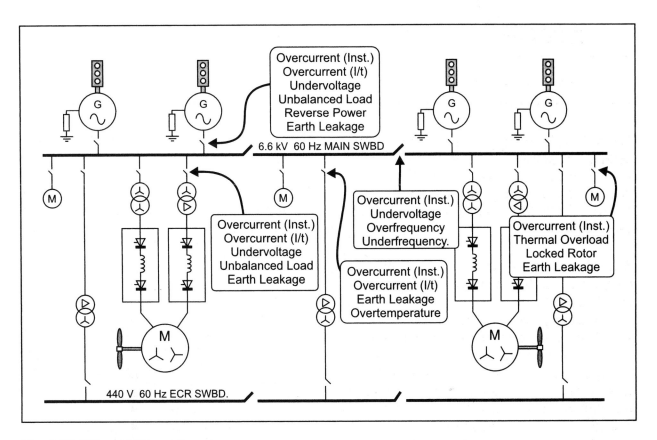

Fig. 2.22 HV protection scheme.

temperatures the insulation suffers irreversible chemical changes, loses its insulation properties and becomes burnt out. Short-circuit and overload currents must, therefore, be detected and rapidly cleared before damage occurs.

QUESTION

Suggest *three* reasons why protection equipment is essential in an electrical distribution system.

ANSWER

✔ To disconnect and isolate faulty equipment in order to maintain the power supply to the remaining healthy circuits in the system

✔ To prevent damage to equipment from the thermal and magnetic forces that occur during short circuit and overload faults

✔ To protect personnel from electric shock

The protection scheme consists of circuit-breakers, fuses, contactors, overcurrent and undervoltage relays. A circuit-breaker, fuse or contactor interrupts the fault current. An overcurrent relay detects the fault current and initiates the *trip* action.

The circuit-breaker or fuse must be capable of safely and rapidly interrupting a short-circuit current. They must be mechanically strong enough to withstand the thermal and magnetic forces produced by the fault current. The size (strength) of the circuit-breaker or fuse is specified by its *breaking capacity* which is the maximum fault current it can safely interrupt.

For example, an MCCB may be continuously rated at 440 V with a rated current of 600 A. Its breaking capacity may be 12.5 MVA which means it can safely interrupt a fault current of 16,400 A (from $12.5 \times 10^6/\sqrt{3}.440 = 16,400$ A).

The *prospective fault current* level at a point in a circuit is the current that arises due to a short-circuit at that point. See Fig. 2.23.

The size of this short-circuit fault current is determined by the total impedance of generators, cables and transformers in the circuit between the generator and the fault. See Fig. 2.24. This total impedance is generally very small so the maximum fault current (called the *prospective fault current*) can be very large.

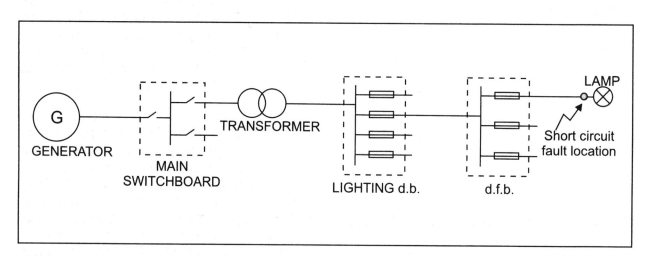

Fig. 2.23 Short-circuit fault location.

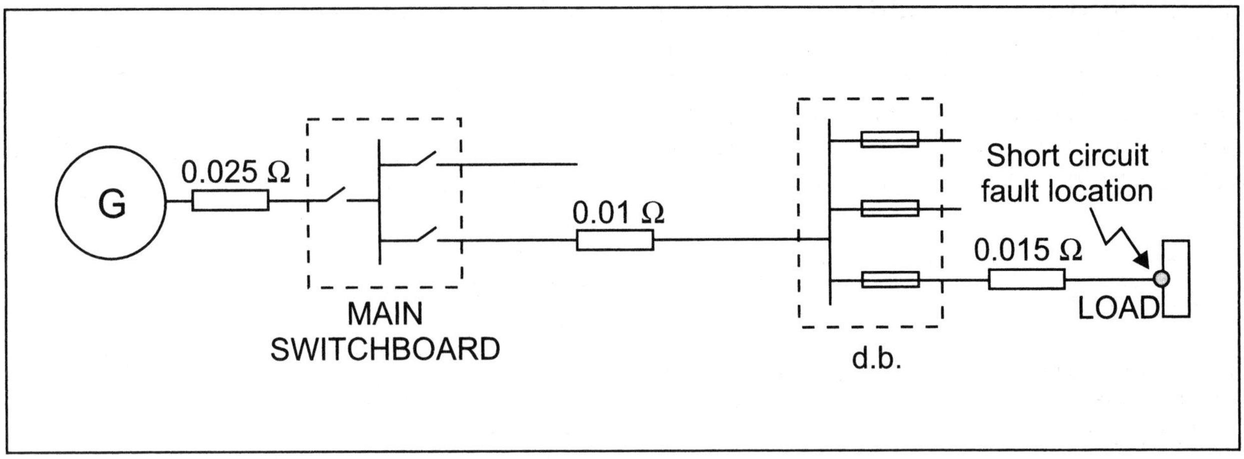

Fig. 2.24 Fault circuit.

Example

A 440 V, 5 kW, 0.8 pf 3-phase load is supplied as shown in Fig. 2.24.

The normal full load POWER is

$P = \sqrt{3}.V_L.I_L.\cos\phi \; watts$

So the load full load current is

$I_L = \dfrac{P}{\sqrt{3}.V_L.\cos\phi} = \dfrac{5,000}{\sqrt{3}.440.0.8} = \underline{8.2 \; A}$

Suppose now a *short-circuit fault* occurs at the load terminals

The total impedance is

$Z_F = 0.025 + 0.01 + 0.015 = 0.05 \; \Omega$

and the prospective short-circuit fault

current is $I_F = \dfrac{V}{Z_F} = \dfrac{440 \; V}{0.05 \; \Omega} = \underline{8,800 \; A}$

So the prospective fault current level at the load is $\underline{8800 \; A}$

and, for a short-circuit at the d.b. the

fault level is: $\dfrac{440 \; V}{(0.025 + 0.01)\Omega} = \underline{12,571 \; A}$

for a short-circuit at the main switchboard

the fault level is: $\dfrac{440 \; V}{0.025 \; \Omega} = \underline{17,600 \; A}$

Note that the fault level increases, the nearer the fault occurs to the generator.

The circuit-breaker or fuse must have a *breaking-current capacity* in excess of the *prospective fault current* level expected at the point at which it is fitted.

If less, the circuit breaker (or fuse) is liable to explode and cause fire.

The ability of a protection system to disconnect only the faulted circuits and to maintain the electrical supplies to healthy circuits is called *protective discrimination*.

Discrimination is achieved by *co-ordinating* the current ratings and time settings of the fuses and overcurrent relays used between the generator and the load as shown in Fig. 2.25. The protective devices nearest the load having the lowest current rating and shortest operating time. Those nearest the generator having the highest current rating and longest operating time.

If a short-circuit fault occurs in the lampholder in Fig. 2.25, the fault current will be large enough to operate all protection devices from the generators to the fault. However, the 5 A fuse protecting the lamp circuit has the lowest current rating and shortest operating time in the system so will be the quickest to operate. This action will *clear* the fault and leave all other healthy circuits still connected.

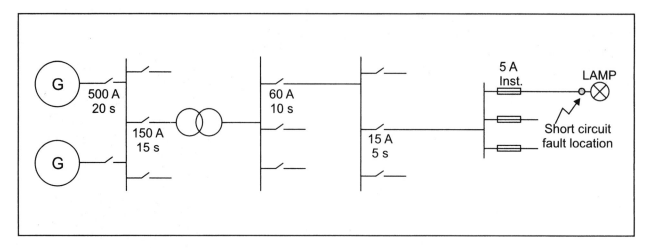

Fig. 2.25 Protective discrimination scheme.

In the case of fuses, it is generally accepted that discrimination will be achieved if consecutive fuses have a ratio of about 2:1. The shipbuilder specifies the current ratings of fuses, together with the current and time settings of relays, in the protection scheme.

It is important that the original settings are maintained to achieve correct discrimination.

❑ Overcurrent Protection

The general term "overcurrent" applies to a relatively small increase over the full load current (FLC) rating (e.g. due to mechanical overloading of a motor) rather than the massive current increase caused by a *short-circuit* fault.

Generally, an overcurrent, supplied from a CT, is detected by a *relay* with an appropriate time-delay to match the protected circuit.

Short-circuit faults in LV distribution circuits are mainly detected and cleared almost *instantaneously* by fuses, MCCBs or MCBs.

Main supply feeders are usually protected against short-circuits by circuit breakers with instantaneous magnetic trip action.

Overcurrent relay types:

- *Magnetic*
- *Thermal*
- *Electronic*

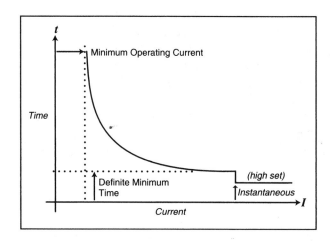

Fig. 2.26 Inverse current/time (I/t) curve.

All relay types have an inverse current-time characteristic called OCIT (overcurrent inverse time), i.e. the bigger the current the faster it will operate. See Fig. 2.26. The basic *inverse* I/t curve would tend towards zero time for the highest currents. To make the relay action more precise at very high fault currents the action is arranged to operate at a *definite* minimum time which is fixed by the design. This type is called an OCIDMT (overcurrent inverse and definite minimum time) relay action. The OCIDMT can also be combined with an *instantaneous* (high set) trip to give the fastest action against extremely high currents due to a short circuit fault.

A *magnetic* relay, as shown in Fig. 2.27, directly converts the current into an electromagnetic force to operate a *trip* switch. One type is the attracted armature action similar in construction to a simple signalling relay but with an adjustment for the current setting. The time of operation is *fixed* at a definite *minimum* time which is usually less than 0.2 seconds. This is regarded as *instantaneous* i.e. with no deliberate time-delay.

To obtain a magnetic inverse-time action, e.g. for motor overload protection, an induction disc movement is usually employed. This construction is similar to a kWh energy meter used in a house but the disc movement is constrained by a spring so is not allowed to actually rotate. The disc travel is very small but sufficient to operate a set of trip switch contacts. Both current and time settings are adjustable. A combined relay including an attracted armature element

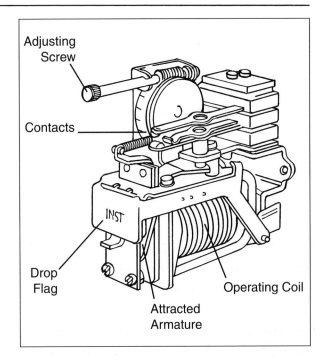

Fig. 2.27 Magnetic overcurrent relay (instantaneous action).

and induction disc element will give an instantaneous action (high set current) and an inverse/time characteristic.

Fig. 2.28 shows a *thermal* relay which utilises the bending action of a bimetallic bar (one per phase) to open a normally-closed (NC) contact which then trips a

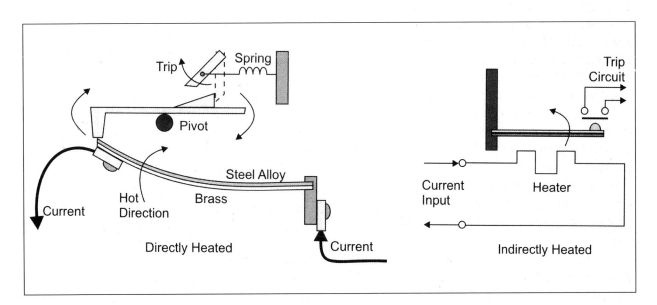

Fig. 2.28 Bimetallic thermal relay action.

contactor or circuit-breaker. A small circuit current will be allowed to flow directly through the bimetallic strip but larger currents will be directed through a heater coil surrounding the strip. The three bimetal strips in a three phase relay, all bend in the same direction with balanced overcurrents to cause a trip. A mechanical bell-crank trip arrangement can also operate with unbalanced (*differential*) currents. This is particularly effective with a single-phasing motor fault. In this case, two of the bimetal strips bend further in the normal direction with increased line current, while the other cools down allowing this strip to move relatively backwards (*differential* action).

The time taken to heat the bimetal strip to cause sufficient bending fixes the required time to trip. Resetting the relay can only be achieved after the strip has cooled down back to the ambient temperature. The *inverse* I/t overcurrent characteristic of a thermal relay is very useful for the indirect temperature protection of motors. Its thermal time delay is, however, far too long for a short-circuit fault so back-up *instantaneous* protection must also be used in the form of fuses or a circuit breaker.

An *electronic* overcurrent relay usually converts the measured current into a proportional voltage. This is then compared with a set voltage level within the monitoring unit which may be digital or analogue. In an analogue unit (as shown in Fig. 2.29) the time delay is obtained by the time taken to charge up a capacitor. This type of relay has separate adjustments for overcurrent and time settings together with an instantaneous trip. The electronic amplifiers within the relay require a low voltage d.c. power supply, e.g. 24 V d.c. derived from a 110 V a.c. auxiliary supply.

Here, the input from a line current transformer (CT) is rectified to produce a d.c. voltage which is proportional to the line current. This voltage charges capacitor C2 at a rate set in conjunction with potentiometer R5 which determines the inverse-time characteristic for the relay. When this capacitor voltage exceeds the predetermined level (set by R2) the detector circuit drives power transistor T2 to operate the output electromagnetic relay RLA which switches trip and alarm contacts in the external circuits.

An instantaneous trip operation is obtained by applying the output of the bridge rectifier directly to the input of the amplifier with a voltage set by R4. Hence, for higher values of fault current, the inverse-time delay circuit is by-passed.

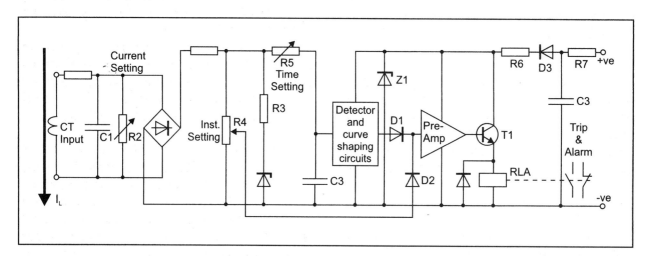

Fig. 2.29 Electronic overcurrent relay circuit.

Both the magnetic and electronic relays can be designed to give an almost instantaneous trip (typically less than 0.05 seconds or 50 ms) to clear a short-circuit fault.

Thermal relays are commonly fitted in *moulded case circuit breakers* (MCCBs) and in miniature circuit-breakers (MCBs) to give a *"long time" thermal overcurrent* trip in addition to a *magnetic* action for an *instantaneous* trip with a *short-circuit* fault.

Overcurrent protection relays in large power circuits are generally driven by current transformers (CTs).

The CT secondary usually has a 5 A or 1 A rating for full load current in its primary winding.

All overcurrent relays can be tested by injecting calibrated test currents into them to check their current trip levels and time delay settings.

Primary injection is where a calibrated test current is fed through the normal load circuit. This requires a large current injection test set. The test set is essentially a transformer and controller rather like a welding set, i.e. it gives a low voltage – high current output.

Small secondary injection currents (5–50 A) are fed current directly into the overcurrent relay usually via a special test plug/socket wired into the relay. Secondary injection does *not* prove the CT performance (as it is disconnected during the test) but is the usual method for testing an overcurrent relay.

The setting up of an overcurrent relay is obviously critical to its protective duty so is carried out in strict accordance with the manufacturer's instructions. Such setting up is done during *new ship* trials and at subsequent periodic surveys.

• Fuse Protection

A fuse is the most common type of protection against a *short-circuit* fault in LV distribution circuits, motor circuits and for portable appliances. It is relatively simple, inexpensive and reliable. As re-wireable fuses tend to be less reliable than the cartridge type and are open to abuse (fitting the wrong size of fuse wire), they are not recommended for marine practice. HRC (*high rupturing capacity* – e.g. 80 kA) cartridge-type fuse links are normally used. A typical construction is shown in Fig. 2.30.

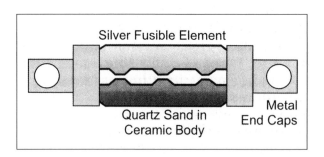

Fig. 2.30 HRC fuse construction.

A disadvantage of a fuse is its insensitivity to *small* overcurrents. An HRC fuse will *blow* at currents as low as 25% overload, but only after about 4 hours.

The advantage of a fuse is its very high speed of operation (a few milliseconds) at high short-circuit fault current – faster than a circuit-breaker.

Fuses are fitted in circuits to give protection against *short-circuits*. Protection against relatively small overcurrents (e.g. due to shaft overloading on a motor) is provided where necessary by an *overcurrent relay* (OCR).

A starter overcurrent relay protects the motor against relatively small overcurrents. The fuse links provide *back-up* protection for the supply cables and generators against a *short-circuit* fault.

Motor fuses are typically rated at 2–3 times the motor full load current in order to withstand the large starting current surge (up to 6 times full load) of the motor. The motor manufacturer will specify the correct rating of fuse link for a particular motor rating. Hence a typical fuse designation for a motor circuit could be "32M63" which indicates a continuous rating of 32 A but a rating of 63 A for the brief starting period.

Important points to note concerning fuses are:

- In the event of a fuse blowing, the cause of the fault must be located and repaired *before* the fuse link is replaced.

- The replacement fuse link must be of the correct current rating, grade and type. Usually this means the replacement fuse link is identical to the blown fuse link.

- Replace all three fuses in a 3-phase supply even if only one is found blown after a fault. The others may be seriously weakened which makes them unreliable for future use.

The reference symbols used on an HRC fuse link are devised by the particular manufacturer. They include the current rating, voltage, application (e.g. motor, transformer, diode, general use), physical size, and type of fixing arrangement.

❏ Undervoltage Protection

An undervoltage (U/V) release mechanism is fitted to all generator breakers and some main feeder circuit-breakers. Its main function is to trip the breaker when a severe voltage dip (around 50%) occurs. This is achieved by lifting the mechanical latch (which keeps the contacts closed) to allow the trip spring to function which opens the breaker contacts. The U/V release on a generator circuit-breaker also prevents it being closed when the generator voltage is very low or absent.

As shown in Fig. 2.31, an undervoltage relay, which may be magnetic or electronic, also provides *back-up* protection to short-circuit protection. As an example, suppose during generator paralleling procedures, an attempt was made to

close the wrong circuit-breaker e.g. the breaker of a stopped and dead generator. If this circuit-breaker was closed, the dead generator would be the equivalent of a short-circuit fault on the bus-bars and cause a blackout. The undervoltage relay prevents the closure of the circuit-breaker of the dead generator.

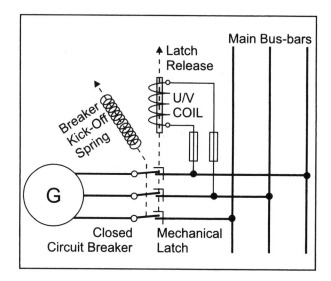

Fig. 2.31 Under-voltage protection.

QUESTION

A 3-phase short-circuit occurs on the main bus-bars and the short-circuit trip of the running generator breaker fails to operate. Explain how the undervoltage relay provides a *back-up* trip.

ANSWER

The short-circuit reduces the bus-bar voltage to zero which causes the U/V release to trip the breaker.

Undervoltage protection is also required for motor starters. The starter contactor normally provides this protection as it drops out when the supply voltage is lost or is drastically reduced. The starter circuit will not normally allow the motor to re-start when the voltage supply is restored except when special automatic re-starting facilities are provided.

Undervoltage protection can be electro-magnetic or electronic.

Checking and calibration of generator undervoltage relays can only be done accurately by calibrated *voltage injection*. A known variable voltage is directly applied to the undervoltage relay to check:

- The voltage at which the relay *pulls-in*

- The voltage at which the relay *drops-out*

Generator U/V relays are usually *slugged* to allow a time-delay which prevents spurious tripping during transient voltage dips (typically 15%) caused by large motor starting currents.

2.9. Electric Cables

Ship wiring cables have to withstand a wide variety of environmental conditions, e.g. extremes of ambient temperature, humidity and salinity. Improved materials have led to ship wiring cables of a fairly standard design that are safe, durable and efficient under all conditions.

The normal distribution voltage on ships is 440 V and cables for use at this voltage are designated 600/1000 V, i.e. 600 V to earth or 1000 V between conductors.

Higher voltage systems require cables with appropriate ratings, e.g. for a 3.3 kV 3-phase *earthed* neutral system the required cable rating is 1900/3300 V. For 3-phase *insulated* systems the cable rating would be 3300/3300 V.

Cables are constructed of several basic parts:

Conductors are of annealed stranded copper which may be circular or shaped. Cables with shaped conductors and cores are usually smaller and lighter than cables with circular cores.

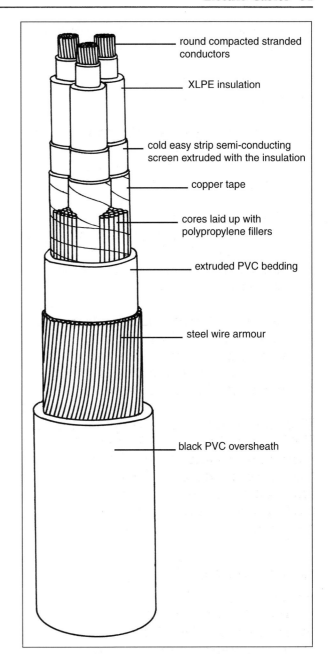

round compacted stranded conductors

XLPE insulation

cold easy strip semi-conducting screen extruded with the insulation

copper tape

cores laid up with polypropylene fillers

extruded PVC bedding

steel wire armour

black PVC oversheath

Fig. 2.32 XLPE cable construction.

Cable insulation has a thickness appropriate to the system voltage rating. Insulation materials are generally organic plastic compounds. Butyl rubber, which is tough and resilient, has good heat, ozone and moisture resistance. These excellent properties enable butyl rubber to replace natural rubber as an insulant. Even so, butyl rubber has now been largely superseded by ethylene propylene rubber (EPR) insulation. EPR has similar electrical and physical properties to butyl rubber but with better resistance to moisture and ozone. It should not, however, be exposed to oils and greases.

Cross-linked polyethylene (XLPE) as shown in Fig. 2.32, is also used as an insulant but has inferior mechanical and thermal properties when compared with EPR. Polyvinyl chloride (PVC) is not generally used for ships' cables, even though it is very common ashore. PVC tends to soften and flow at high temperatures (melts at 150°C), and hardens and cracks at low temperatures (−8°C). Even at normal temperatures PVC tends to flow and become distorted under mechanical stress − for example *necking* occurs at cable glands causing the gland to lose its watertight properties.

Multicore shipwiring cables have the cores identified by either colour, printed numerals on untaped cores or numbered tapes on taped cores.

QUESTION

What is the purpose of the *sheath* on a cable?

ANSWER

The *sheath* of a cable protects the insulation from damage and injury − it is not classed as an insulant. Sheath materials are required to be heat, oil and chemical resistant and flame retardant (HOFR). The sheath must also be tough and flexible.

Polychloroprene (PCP or neoprene) is a common sheath material but has been largely superseded by chlorosulphonated polyethylene (CSP or hypalon). CSP-HOFR sheathing compound is well suited to shipboard conditions. It offers good resistance to cuts and abrasions, resists weather and ozone, acid fumes and alkalis, and is flexible.

Extra mechanical protection is provided by armouring with basket-woven wire braid of *either* galvanised steel or tinned phosphor bronze. The non-magnetic properties of phosphor bronze are preferred for single-core cables. A protective outer sheath of CSP compound covers the wire braid. The wire braiding also acts as a screen to reduce interference (caused by magnetic fields) in adjacent communication and instrumentation circuits.

QUESTION

Will cable materials burn?

ANSWER

Yes, all organic materials will eventually burn in a severe fire. Cable sheath materials commonly in use are organic plastic compounds that are classed as flame retardant, i.e. will not *sustain* a fire. Most cable materials now achieve this property by developing chlorine gas and acid fumes to smother the flame. PVC is notorious for its release of deadly acid fumes, but PCP and CSP do the same. EPR and XLPE do not. Some new materials do not produce acid fumes when burning − an important feature for fire-fighting personnel. However, burning cable materials still tend to produce dense black smoke.

- MIMS cables:

Mineral Insulated, Metal Sheathed cables are very useful in high temperature, fire-risk areas. These cables have a magnesium oxide powder as insulation with a metal sheath − usually copper (MICC − Mineral Insulated, Copper Covered) which is further covered with PVC for weatherproofing where necessary. A special termination is used with MIMS cables to provide a moisture-proof seal for the hygroscopic insulation powder. For an MICC cable this is achieved by

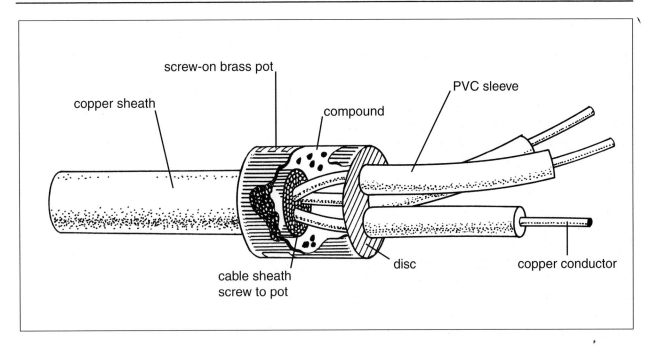

Fig. 2.33 MICC cable termination.

a compound filled brass pot screwed directly on to the copper sheath as shown in Fig. 2.33.

The current rating of a cable is the current the cable can carry continuously without the conductor exceeding 80°C with an ambient air temperature of 45°C (i.e. a 35°C rise). This rating must be reduced (de-rated) if the ambient exceeds 45°C, or when cables are bunched together or enclosed in a pipe or trunking which reduces the effective cooling.

MICC cable current ratings are based upon a copper *sheath* temperature of 150 °C maximum.

For all types of cable the size of conductors required for a particular installation is estimated from current rating tables issued by suppliers. These tables show current ratings for a range of cable types, conductor area and volt-drop/amp/metre.

The volt drop in cables from the main switchboard to the appliance must not exceed 6% (in practice it is about 2%). The cables installed must comply with both the current rating and the volt-drop limitation. Cable volt drop only becomes a problem in very long cables.

QUESTION

What is the purpose of a cable gland?

ANSWER

Cables are insulated, mechanically protected and watertight. They may be armoured and suitable for installation in a hazardous explosive area. A cable gland maintains these properties where the cable is terminated at an appliance, e.g. at a motor terminal box.

The cable gland is screwed into the appliance terminal box. Nuts on the gland compress sealing rings to maintain watertight seals on the inner and outer sheaths and to clamp the armour braiding. The gland must be matched to the size and type of cable. A typical Ex-protected gland construction (which

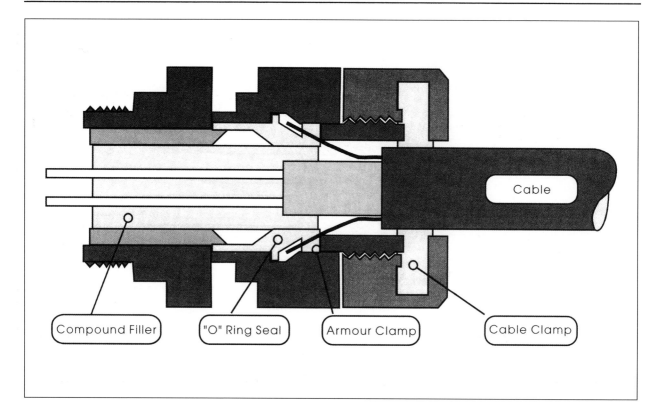

Fig. 2.34 Exd cable gland.

is more complicated than an equivalent industrial type) is shown in Fig. 2.34.

In most cases earthing of the cable armouring is done by the cable gland. Where cables pass through watertight bulkheads and fire-stop barriers they must be specially glanded to maintain the integrity of such bulkheads.

Conductor termination sockets can be *soldered* to the conductors but are more frequently *crimped* onto each wire by a compression tool.

Cable sockets must be securely attached to the appliance terminal screw by nuts and *shakeproof* washers A loose terminal will invariably become a source of localised overheating. Periodic maintenance should always include checking the tightness of terminal connections.

Small cables are terminated in terminal blocks of various designs.

Cables should be periodically inspected and tested, ideally when checking their connected appliances. Cable insulation resistance should be measured and the value recorded. Cables in exposed and damp situations, e.g. for deck lighting, may develop a low insulation resistance. Usually this is a result of mechanical damage or a faulty gland permitting the ingress of water. Cables can be dried out by injecting a heating current from a current injection set or a welding transformer as shown in Fig. 2.35.

The procedure requires care not to overheat the cables which could cause further damage. The cable should be disconnected at both ends from equipment, and connected as shown. The injection cables must have good connections at each end. Current flow and cable temperature should be carefully monitored. When satisfactory insulation values have been restored, a final check should be made with the cable at normal ambient temperature.

The injected heating current must *never* exceed the rated current for the cable — it is advisable to use an ammeter

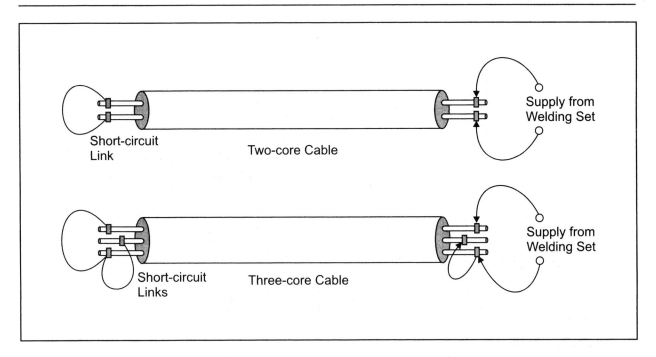

Fig. 2.35 Cable dry-out connections.

and to start at the lowest available setting on the injection set. The voltage should be in the region of 30 to 55 V depending upon the current setting. The cable temperature can be measured with a contact thermometer secured to the cable or with an infra-red sensor and should not be allowed to exceed a temperature rise of 30°C.

Temperature and insulation resistance should be measured and recorded every hour.

When the insulation resistance becomes steady the heating should be carried out for a further four hours before switching off.

Final readings of at least 20 MΩ to earth and 100 MΩ between cores should be expected.

Mechanical damage to cables must be made good either by repairing the damage or replacing that section of cable. Unprotected metal armouring and insulation material are vulnerable to attack by moisture, chemicals and corrosive gases, while exposed live conductors are obviously dangerous. A temporary repair may be effected by preparing and binding the damaged section with a suitable adhesive plastic electrical insulating tape.

Such a repair will *not* be acceptable in a hazardous zone on a tanker. Permanent cable repairs must be made as soon as possible.

Chapter Three
Generators and
Main Circuit Breakers

3.0. Introduction

The electrical power demand aboard ship will vary according to the ship type (tanker, bulk carrier, ro-ro, container, ferry, cruise liner, offshore support etc.) and its day-to-day operational needs (at sea or in port). To meet the power demand, two or more main generators are used which are backed up by an emergency generator and an emergency battery service.

The construction, operation, protection and maintenance of generators is described together with a review of main circuit breakers and the main switchboard.

3.1. AC Generator Operation

Main generator power ratings range from, typically, 100 kW to 2 MW at 440 V, 60 Hz a.c. or 380 V, 50 Hz a.c. driven by diesel, steam turbine, gas turbine or propulsion shaft-driven prime movers. As the demand for increased electrical power installations arise (e.g. for specialist offshore vessels and cruise liners) it is necessary to generate at high voltage (HV) with voltages typically at 6.6 kV, 60 Hz but 3.3 kV and 11 kV are also used.

An emergency generator, typically 20 kW to 200 kW at 440 V or 220 V,

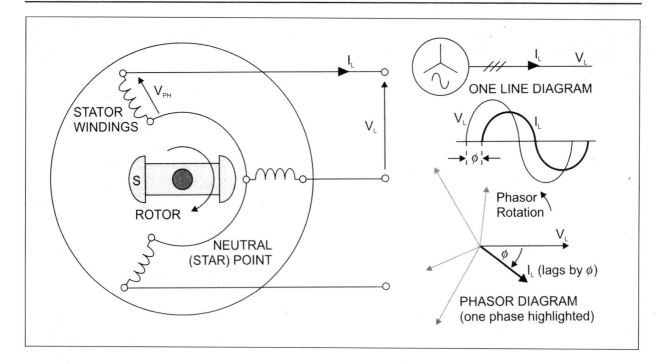

Fig. 3.1 Principle of generator operation.

will be diesel driven and fitted with an automatic start facility.

Battery supplies from lead-acid or alkaline cells, usually rated at 24 V d.c., provide sufficient power for the emergency alarm and communication systems together with some lighting and power essential for safety during a main power failure.

As the vast majority of ships use alternating current (a.c.) generators (sometimes called alternators), the principles and operational features will cover this type only, and ignore the direct current (d.c.) type.

The basic principle of an a.c. generator is very simple. Pairs of electromagnetic poles are driven (by the prime mover) past fixed coils of wire on the stator as shown in Fig. 3.1.

An alternating electromotive force (*emf*) which, ideally, has a *sinusoidal* waveform, is *induced* into each stator phase winding.

The useful emf level (*E*) is called the *root mean square* (*rms*) value and all equipment is rated in rms terms. A peak, or maximum, level is *1.414* (√2) times larger than the *rms* level. e.g. if *E* is *440 V*, then $E_{MAX} = 1.414 \times 440 = 622$ *volts*.

The size of emf generated depends on the strength of magnetic flux (Φ) *and* the rate at which this flux cuts the coils, so

$$E \propto n.\Phi$$ where *n* is the rotational

speed of the rotor poles in rev/s. The voltage available at the generator terminals is $V = E - (I.Z)$ [*phasor calculation*] where *I* is the load current flowing in the stator phase windings. An internal phase volt-drop of (*I.Z*) occurs due to the impedance *Z* of a phase winding which is made up from its resistance and reactance.

The *frequency f* (measured in Hertz) of the emf is the number of waveform cycles per second. This obviously depends on the rotational speed and the number of poles, so $$f = n.p$$ or $f = (N/60).p$

where *n = speed in rev/s*, *N = rev/min* and *p = pairs of poles*. Related speeds and frequencies with the number of pole-pairs are given in the table below:

pole-pairs (p)	for 60 Hz rev/min (N)	for 50 Hz rev/min (N)
1	3600	3000
2	1800	1500
3	1200	1000
4	900	750

These two basic relationships for emf and frequency dictate how to control the voltage and frequency output of a generator. In practice the speed is maintained practically constant by the generator's prime-mover which fixes the output frequency. The constant speed then allows the size of generated emf to be directly controlled by the size of pole flux (*excitation*).

A practical a.c. generator has three sets of coils, called phase windings, located in slots in the stator surrounding the rotating magnetic poles. The emf induced in each phase is 120° out of phase with the other two phases. Three-phase windings are labelled as U-V-W with colour coding of red, yellow and blue used on terminals and bus-bars. One end of each of the three phase windings are joined together to form the *neutral point* of a *star* connection.

The other ends of the phase windings are connected to outgoing conductors called *lines*.

The three output *line* voltages (represented by V_L) and the 3 output *line* currents (represented by I_L) combine to create the three-phase electrical power output of:

$$P = \sqrt{3}.V_L.I_L.\cos\phi \ watts$$

In a *star* connection, any line voltage V_L, is made up from two phase voltages, where $V_L = \sqrt{3}.V_{PH}$. The √3 factor is due to the 120° displacement between phase voltages. e.g. if $V_L = 440\ V$, then $V_{PH} = 254\ V$.

The *rated* values of a machine always refer to *line* conditions (as stated on rating plate).

Angle ϕ is the phase angle between V_{PH} and I_{PH} which is determined by the types of electrical load on the generator (e.g. lighting, motors, galley equipment etc.).

$\cos\phi$ is the *power factor* of the electrical load and is typically about 0.8 lagging which means that the current waveform *lags* about 37° behind the voltage.

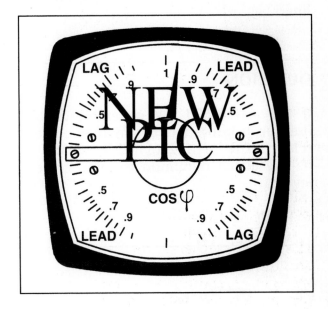

Fig. 3.2 Power factor meter.

QUESTION

The power factor meter shown in Fig. 3.2 has its scale divided into *four* segments – each calibrated 0–1.0. What is the significance of each segment?

ANSWER

An indication in the top half of the scale shows that the machine is generating. The bottom half of the scale indicates that the generator is *motoring*. Both top and bottom halves are further split into lagging and leading power factor sections.

A three-phase a.c. generator rated at 500 kW, 440 V at 0.83 lag will deliver a full load line current of:

$$I_L = \frac{P}{\sqrt{3}\,.\,V_L\,.\,\cos\phi} = \frac{500{,}000}{\sqrt{3}\,.\,440\,.\,0.83} = \underline{\underline{790.5\ A}}$$

This means that the phase windings, cable conductors and generator circuit breaker must be capable of carrying this full load current (FLC) continuously without exceeding their temperature limits.

QUESTION

If the above 500 kW generator circuit-breaker is protected by an over-current relay (OCR) setting of 125% what will be the actual minimum tripping current level?

ANSWER

The full load line current is 790.5 A so the generator overcurrent relay will trip at: *125% × 790.5 = 988 A*

The speed of an auxiliary diesel driven generator (DG) is accurately managed by an electronic fuel governor which maintains an almost constant output frequency over its load range.

A propulsion-shaft driven (SG) generator can be an efficient method for extracting electric power from the ship's main engine as the power is derived from lower cost fuel than that used for an auxiliary DG unit. The SG may be fitted directly in-line with the slow speed propulsion shaft or, more commonly, be gear-driven up to a higher speed.

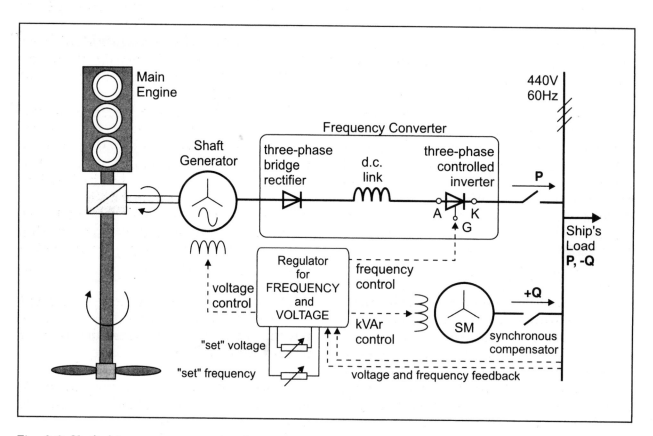

Fig. 3.3 Shaft-driven generator control.

Also, by using a shaft generator as the main source of electric power during long sea passages, the DG units operate for short periods only with a reduced maintenance requirement.

An apparent disadvantage of a shaft generator is that it has no direct *frequency* control as this is determined by the main engine which is set for the ship's full-away speed range (e.g. 70–100%). This means that the frequency must be separately regulated at the *output* of the shaft generator to maintain a constant 60 Hz to the ship's electric power consumers. Such a frequency regulator utilises an electric a.c.-d.c.-a.c. converter as shown in Fig. 3.3.

At the three-phase rectifier stage the a.c. generator frequency is converted to a d.c. voltage. The three-phase controlled inverter converts the d.c. back to a *fixed* output frequency by sequenced thyristor switching. A d.c. link inductor coil is interposed between the rectifier and inverter to *smooth* the normal current flow and act as a current-limiter in the event of a short circuit fault.

An inverter thyristor switch is turned-on by a positive current pulse to its gate when its anode is positive with respect to its cathode. The thyristor is only turned-off when its current is reduced to (approximately) zero. This is a problem for the inverter thyristors when driving into the ship's inductive load (typically about 0.8 power factor lagging). In this case the current continues to flow in a thyristor *after* its voltage has gone through a zero point causing disruption of the inverter switching sequence.

To overcome this problem it is necessary to have the thyristor current *in-phase* with its voltage so that turn-off is automatically achieved (line commutation) at the end of each a.c. half-cycle. The addition of *leading kVAr* compensation to the power system to create an overall unity power factor solves the problem. Hence, the SG/converter must only supply true power P (kW). At every instant the leading kVAr (+ Q) must exactly match the

lagging kVAr (– Q) of the ship's load so the compensation must be automatically controlled. The practical solution is to include a synchronous motor, operating as a synchronous compensator, whose operating power factor is controlled by regulating its d.c. field current.

Overall, the bus-bar voltage is fixed by the field flux in the shaft generator and the bus-bar frequency is regulated by the controlled inverter.

3.2. Generator Construction and Cooling

• Construction

The two main parts of any rotating a.c. machine are its *stator* and *rotor*.

The fabricated steel stator frame supports the stator core and its three phase windings as shown in Fig. 3.4.

The stator core is assembled from laminated steel with the windings housed in slots around the inner periphery of the cylindrical core.

The stator coils are interconnected (in the end-winding regions) to form three separate phase windings with six *ends*. These phase ends are found in the stator terminal box as shown in Fig. 3.5.

In some cases only three terminals are available in the terminal box. In this case, the neutral or star point connection is an internal part of the stator winding arrangement.

The main outgoing cables connected to these terminals conduct the generator's electric power to its circuit-breaker at the main switchboard.

The rotor of a main a.c. generator provides the field excitation from its electromagnetic poles.

Two constructional forms of rotor are available as shown in Fig. 3.6.

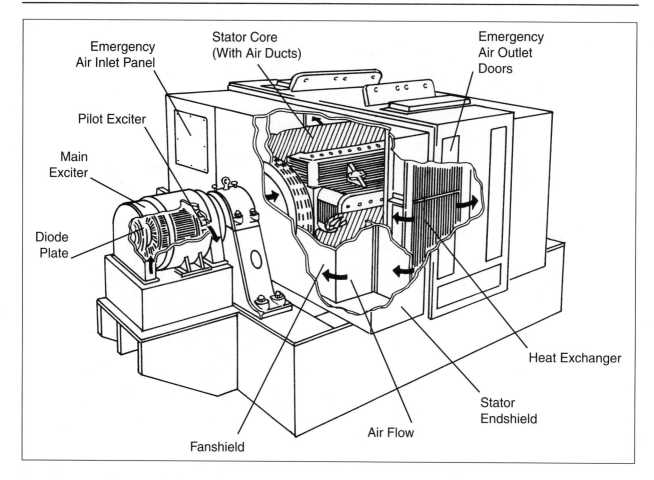

Fig. 3.4 Generator construction.

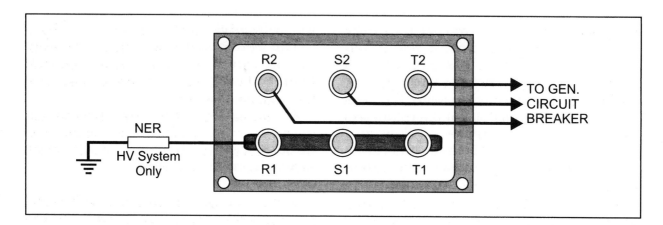

Fig. 3.5 Generator terminal box.

- *salient pole type*

- *cylindrical type*

The salient pole type has projecting poles bolted or keyed onto the shaft hub. Field excitation windings are fitted around each pole. This type of rotor is used with medium and slow shaft speeds (1800 rpm and below) and is the most common arrangement for marine generators.

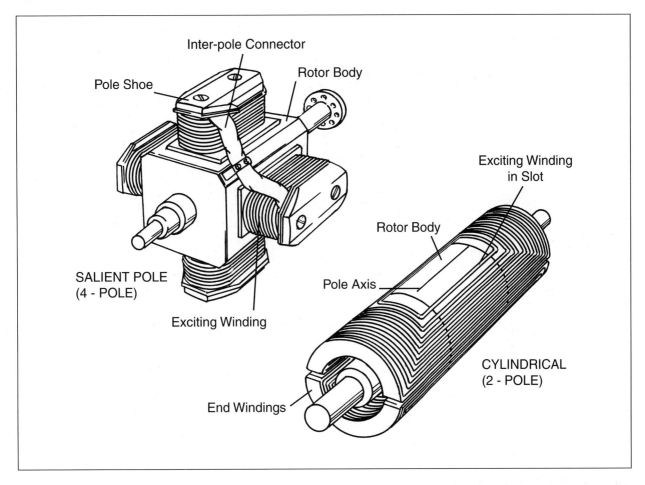

Fig. 3.6 Generator rotors, salient and cylindrical construction.

Cylindrical type rotors are generally used with large power, high speed (1500–3600 rpm) steam/gas turbine drives. The excitation windings are wedged into axial slots around the steel rotor. Unwound sections of the rotor form the pole faces between the winding slots.

The shaft bearings of *large* generators (and motors) are usually insulated to prevent stray currents from circulating through. Unbalanced (stray) end-winding magnetic flux induces an emf *along* the steel shaft. This will cause a current to circulate through the shaft, bearings and bedplate to produce arcing across the bearing surfaces and degradation of the oil layer. Under generator unbalanced fault conditions the bearing problem may be severe.

To prevent the flow of shaft current, one bearing (usually the non-drive end) is electrically isolated from earth by a thin layer of insulating material beneath the bearing pedestal. The pedestal holding-down bolts must also be insulated by suitable sleeving.

In normal operation the effectiveness of the pedestal insulation can be checked by measuring its voltage to earth which may show as a few volts.

The rotor poles are supplied with direct current (d.c.) from an *exciter*. If the exciter equipment is a conventional d.c. generator or is *static* (see section on excitation methods), the d.c. excitation current is fed into the field windings via carbon brushes on a pair of shaft-mounted slip-rings.

To eliminate the maintenance problems associated with rotating contacts, a *brushless* arrangement is usual for marine generators. All brush gear, commutators

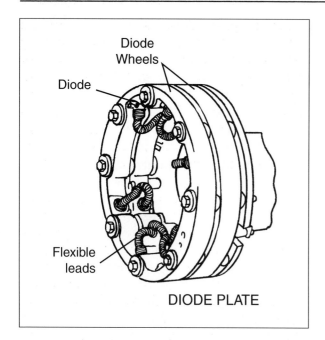

Fig. 3.7 Rotor diode plate.

and slip rings are eliminated by using an *a.c.* exciter with its output being rectified by shaft-mounted silicon diodes as shown in Fig. 3.7. The diodes are connected as a three phase a.c./d.c. bridge circuit.

The six diodes, mounted on the shaft, convert the a.c. exciter output to d.c. which is then fed directly into the main generator rotor field windings.

Note, the a.c. exciter has its own d.c. field poles fitted on its stator while the rotor carries its three-phase a.c. exciter output windings. This construction layout is inverted compared with that of the main generator.

• Cooling

Power losses, typically 10% of the generator rating, cause internal heating in the windings and magnetic cores of both rotor and stator. This heat must be continuously transferred out of the generator to prevent excessive temperature rise causing breakdown of winding insulation.

Forced air circulation in a closed circuit (to prevent ingress of dirt) via an air cooler is pressurised by a fan on the rotor shaft:

Cooling air is forced through ventilation ducts in the stator core, between rotor poles and through the air gap (a few millimetres) between stator and rotor.

Water cooling of the circulating air may also be used for generators with a large power rating. Temperature detectors (resistance type, thermistors or thermocouples) are used to monitor the temperature of stator windings, bearings and the cooling air/water of the generator. Single or grouped temperature alarms are activated at the main watchkeeping position.

While the generator is stopped during standby or maintenance periods, low power electric heaters within the machine prevent internal condensation forming on the winding insulation. These heaters may be switched on manually or automatically from auxiliary contacts on the generator circuit-breaker. Heater power supplies are normally 220 V a.c. single-phase supplied from a distribution box local to the generator.

QUESTION

The water cooling system on a large generator is out of service due to a faulty inlet valve. How will this affect the generator operation?

ANSWER

The generator can only be used to supply a much reduced electrical power output to keep the machine temperatures below their maximum permitted levels. External emergency doors in the generator's air cooling ducts may be opened in such cases. The penalty is that the normally closed air circuit of the generator is now open to the engine room atmosphere.

3.3. Excitation Methods

The two factors essential for the production of a generated emf in an a.c. generator are <u>rotational</u> speed (*n*) and <u>magnetic flux</u> (*Φ*). Field windings on the rotor create strong magnetic field poles when direct current is passed through them.[Various methods have been devised to supply the correct d.c. field (excitation) current to produce the required a.c. output voltage from the stator terminals.]The excitation must be continually regulated to maintain the generator output voltage as the load power demand fluctuates.

Broadly, the excitation methods are either *rotary* or *static*. A rotary method utilises an a.c. or d.c. exciter which is shaft-mounted and rotates with the main generator rotor. Traditionally, rotary exciters were d.c. generators with stationary field poles, rotating armature, commutator and brushgear. Now the most common arrangement is to use a shaft mounted a.c. exciter.

In some applications, a small additional rotary *pilot* exciter may be used to supply current to the main exciter field. A pilot exciter is a small *permanent* magnet a.c. generator which is driven from the generator shaft. Its output voltage is generally at a high frequency (e.g. 1000 Hz) but this is rectified to d.c. before being fed into the main exciter field.

A "brushless" excitation scheme is shown in Fig. 3.8. The absence of brushes, brushgear and carbon dust improves reliability and considerably reduces generator maintenance. Rectification of the a.c. exciter voltage is achieved by six shaft-mounted silicon diodes. The suppression resistor connected across the main generator field protects the diodes against voltage surges arising from sudden changes in excitation current.

QUESTION

What is likely to happen if one of the rotating diodes fails and becomes:

(a) an open circuit? and

(b) a short-circuit?

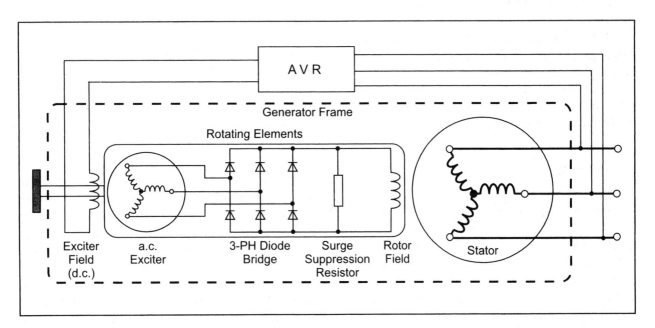

Fig. 3.8 Brushless excitation scheme.

ANSWER

(a)   the remaining healthy diodes would continue to supply the main field. In *manual (hand)* control the total field current, and hence generator voltage, will be slightly reduced. Under AVR control, the exciter field current would be automatically boosted to maintain the correct generator voltage while the diode failure would probably be un-detected. The exciter will gradually overheat.

(b)   a short-circuited diode is more serious as it leads to a short-circuited exciter. Rapid overheating of the exciter will occur.

Although diode failures are rare, some generator field systems are fitted with an electronic detector relay to give an alarm and/or trip signal should such a fault occur. Usually, the detector monitors the exciter field current whose size and shape are noticeably affected by a diode failure.

Generators with rotary exciters, con-ventional or brushless, have a relatively sluggish response to sudden load changes. For example, it may take typically up to one second to correct a 15% *voltage dip* caused by the start-up of a large pump motor.

QUESTION

What factors govern the overall voltage response of a generator to sudden (transient) load changes?

ANSWER

The main opposition to changes in the field current required to correct the generator output voltage are:

- Inductance of main rotor field winding

- Inductance of exciter field winding

- Regulator (manual or automatic) response

The transient voltage response of a generator can be improved by eliminat-ing the rotary exciter in favour of a *static* excitation method. In this arrangement, the generator field draws its d.c. current via a static excitation transformer/rectifier unit fed directly from the generator voltage *and* current output. This arrangement is known as *compounding* as it is controlled by voltage (shunt effect) and current (series effect) feedback.

Response times as low as 0.1 second to correct a 15% voltage dip are common with static excited *compound* generators. This fast response is most desirable on general/bulk cargo ships where heavy and frequent load surges arise from deck cranes and winch gear.

Such static excitation equipment may be located within the generator casing or inside the main switchboard. This type of generator has two shaft slip-rings and brushgear to connect the static excitation equipment to the rotor field winding.

The basic scheme of a self-excited *compounded* generator is shown in Fig. 3.9 (single-phase operation is shown for simplicity).

Note, *compounded* means that the excitation is derived from the generator output voltage *and* its current.

On no-load, the generator excitation is provided by the PRI.1 winding of the excitation transformer. On load, the generator current injects an additional excitation current via PRI.2 of the transformer to maintain a constant output voltage. If the excitation components are carefully designed, the generator voltage of a compounded generator can

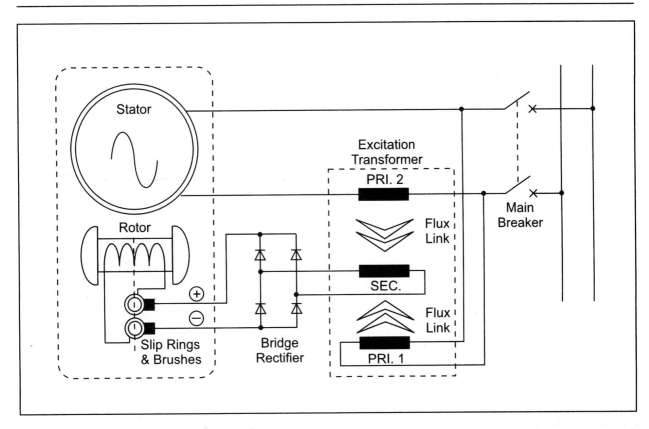

Fig. 3.9 Single-phase compound excitation circuit.

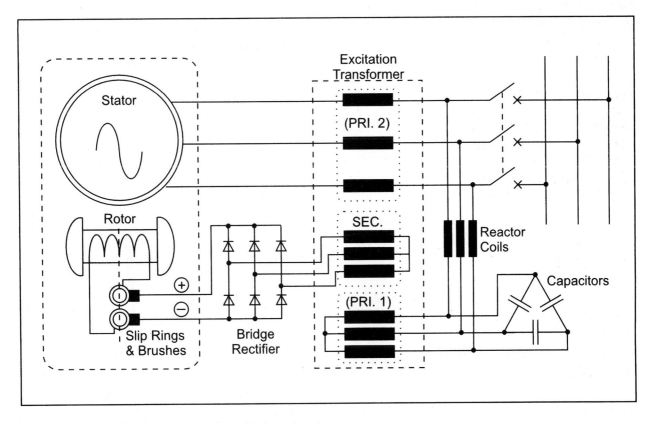

Fig. 3.10 Three-phase compound excitation circuit.

be closely maintained at all loads without the use of an AVR or manual voltage *trimmer*. However, some generator manufacturers do include an AVR and a manual trimmer rheostat in such a compounded static excitation scheme. This addition may provide closer voltage regulation over the load range and allow manual control of the generator voltage, e.g. for synchronising and kVAr load balancing between generators.

A practical 3-phase static excitation scheme has additional components such as reactors and capacitors. The circuit in Fig. 3.10 has no AVR or manual trimmer regulator. A load current surge will automatically feed back an adjustment to the field excitation to correct the resulting voltage surge so quickly that the output voltage remains practically constant.
   Compound excitation systems require the static components to be designed to closely match its associated generator.

3.4. Automatic Voltage Regulation

Sudden load current surges (e.g. due to motor starting) on a generator cause a corresponding change in its output voltage. This is due to an internal voltage drop in the generator windings and the effect is usually called *voltage dip*. Similarly, load shedding will produce an *overvoltage* at the bus-bars. An un-regulated or non-compounded generator excitation system would not be realistic on board ship due to the varying voltage caused by the fluctuating load demand. Automatic voltage regulation (AVR) equipment is necessary to rapidly correct such voltage changes. See Fig. 3.11.

An AVR will control the generator's voltage to ±2.5% (or better) of its set value over the full load range. This is its *steady-state* voltage *regulation*. Transient voltage dip is usually limited to 15% for a specified sudden load change with recovery back to rated voltage within 1.5 seconds. In special cases where unusually large surges are expected (e.g. from heavy-duty cargo cranes) the generator/AVR performance limits may be extended.

The AVR senses the generator output voltage and acts to alter the field current to maintain the voltage at its set value. A manual *trimmer* regulator may be fitted on the generator control panel to set the voltage level e.g. 440 V. More usually, the voltage trimmer potentiometer is

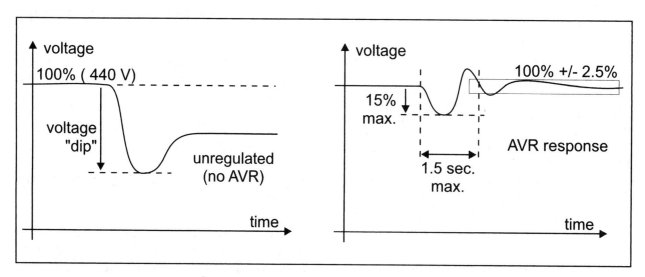

Fig. 3.11 Generator/AVR voltage response.

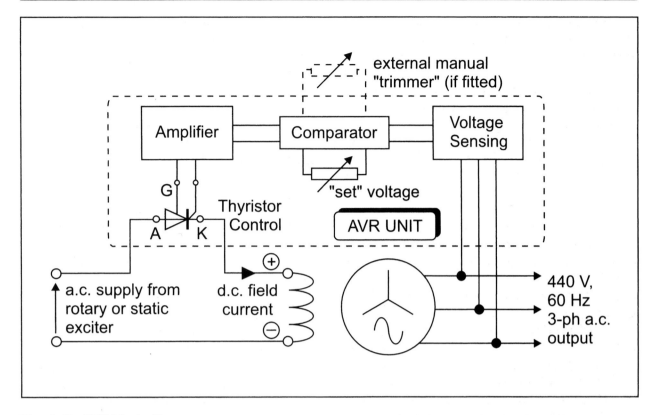

Fig. 3.12 AVR block diagram.

on the control card of the AVR so is not accessible to an operator.

The control circuit for a modern AVR consists of transformers, rectifiers, zener diodes, transistors and thyristors. These are mounted on one or more circuit cards fitted either within the switchboard or local to the generator.

Although the AVR control circuit design varies with the manufacturer the basic scheme contains the following elements shown in Fig. 3.12.

The voltage sensing unit transforms down, rectifies and smooths the generator output voltage. This produces a low voltage d.c. signal that is proportional to the a.c. generator voltage. This *actual* d.c. signal is compared with a set d.c. value produced by a reference circuit of zener diodes and resistors. An *error* signal output from the comparator is then amplified and made suitable for driving the field circuit regulating thyristor(s).

A thyristor is a fast-acting electronic switch controlled by a voltage signal at its gate terminal. This device rectifies and regulates the generator field current.

Additional components and sub-circuits are included in the AVR to ensure:

• Rapid response time with voltage stability

• Fair current (and kVAr) sharing when generators are to be operated in parallel

• Quick voltage build-up during generator run-up

• Overvoltage/undervoltage alarm/trip protection

The complete AVR circuit is fairly complex and includes a few pre-set variable resistors for the control of sensitivity, offset-error and stability (proportional, integral and differential control). These are adjusted and set during generator trials to achieve an optimum and stable performance. It is recommended that you resist the temptation to *fiddle* with such pre-set controls unless fully competent with such a feedback control system.

AVR running checks, as guided by the manufacturer, consist of a.c. and d.c. voltage measurements at installed test points. These are compared with values found acceptable during previous generator trials. The test voltmeter type and its range are usually specified for each test.

Most ships will carry a spare AVR unit or spare *cards* which may be interchanged after a suspected failure. An AVR changeover should only be attempted when its generator is stopped and locked off. Checks at the test points on the new AVR excitation field current level and the manual regulator operation (if fitted) should be proven with the generator running on no-load before attempting to synchronise on to the bus-bars.

When generators are load sharing in parallel, check for approximately equal current (or kVAr) sharing between the machines. This will indicate correct operation of their AVRs.

QUESTION

What precaution must be taken when testing the insulation of generator cables and wiring connected to an AVR unit?

ANSWER

Electronic components such as transistors, integrated circuit chips, thyristors, etc. are likely to be damaged during a high voltage (500 V) megger test. To test the generator and its cables to earth and protect the electronic parts, either:

- Short-circuit all outgoing cable terminals during the IR test

- Remove electronic card(s)

- Disconnect all cables at both ends and test separately

3.5. Generators in Parallel

Main generator units (gas-turbine, steam turbine or diesel drives) have to be run in parallel to share a total load that exceeds the capacity of a single machine. Changeover of main and standby generator units requires a brief parallel running period to achieve a smooth transition without *blackout*. For simplicity and security it is not normally possible to run a main generator in parallel with either the emergency generator or a shore supply. Circuit breaker interlocks are used to prevent such an arrangement.

Essentially, parallel running is achieved in the two stages of:

- *Synchronising then Load Sharing*

Both operations are, of course, usually carried out automatically but manual control is still in common use and is generally provided as a *back-up* to the auto control.

The generator already *on-the-bars* is called the *running* machine and the generator to be brought into service is the *incoming* machine.

To smoothly parallel the *incoming* generator, it must be *synchronised* with the live bus-bars.

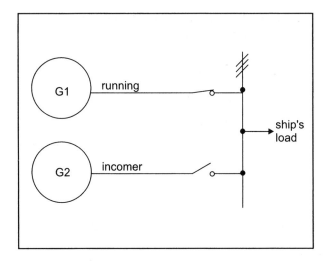

Fig. 3.13 Two generators to be synchronised.

QUESTION

What are the likely consequences of attempting to close the incomer's circuit breaker when the generator voltages are *not* in synchronism?

ANSWER

At the instant of closing the breaker, the voltage phase difference causes a large circulating current between the machines which produces a large magnetic force to *pull* the generator voltages (and field poles) into synchronism. This means rapid acceleration of one rotor and deceleration of the other. The large forces may physically damage the generators and their prime-movers and the large circulating current may trip each generator breaker.

Result?
Blackout, danger and embarrassment!

To achieve *smooth* manual synchronising, the incomer must be brought up to speed to obtain approximately the same frequency as shown on the bus-bar frequency meter e.g. 60 Hz.

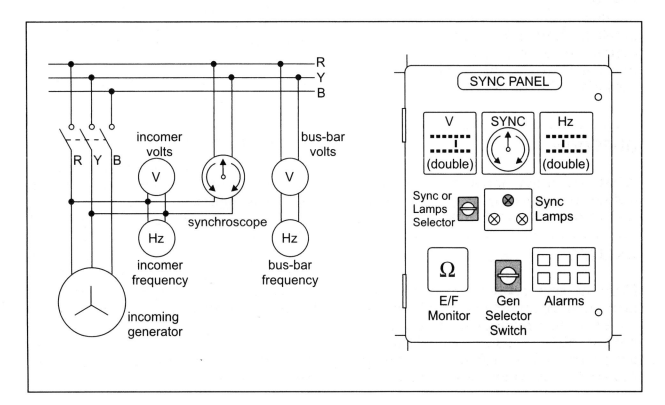

Fig. 3.14 Synchronising instruments.

The incoming generator voltage is set by its AVR or manually *trimmed* (if available) to be equal to the bus-bar voltage.

Fine tuning of the speed can now be observed on the *synchroscope* or *synchronising lamps*. The incomer is adjusted so that the synchroscope indicator rotates slowly clockwise (fast direction) at about 4 seconds per indicator revolution.

The circuit-breaker should be closed as the indicator approaches the *12 o'clock* (in-phase) position. Breaker closing between *5-to and 5-past* the 12 o'clock synchroscope position is satisfactory as long as the pointer rotation is fairly slow.

QUESTION

What indication is available to show the optimum synchronised condition?

ANSWER

The incoming generator ammeter pointer will show very little *kick* when correctly synchronised.

A traditional pointer-type synchroscope is usually short-time rated (e.g. up to 20 minutes) to avoid overheating – do not forget to switch it off after a paralleling procedure.

Modern synchroscope indicators use a circular set of LED's (light emitting diodes) which sequentially light up to show the phase difference between the generator voltages.

As a back-up, or alternative, to the synchroscope a set of lamps may be used. The correct synchronised position may be shown by either of the following methods:

• Lamps *dark* method (2 lamps)

• Lamps *bright* method (2 lamps)

• *Sequence* method (3 lamps)

In each case the lamps are connected between the incoming generator and the bus-bars. The *sequence method*, as shown in Fig. 3.15, is preferred as it displays a *rotation* of lamp brightness which indicates whether the incoming machine is running fast (clockwise) or slow (anti-clockwise). As with the synchroscope, the lamp sequence must appear to rotate slowly clockwise. Correct synchronisation occurs when the top or key lamp is dark and the two bottom lamps are *equally* bright.

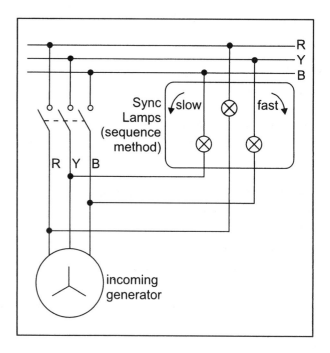

Fig. 3.15 Synchronising with three lamps.

QUESTION

How could you monitor the correct instant for synchronising without the aid of a synchroscope or synchronising lamps?

ANSWER

Connect a voltmeter as shown in Fig. 3.16, (expect up to 500 V on a 440 V system)

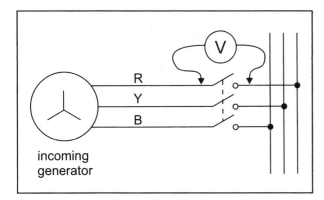

Fig. 3.16 Synchronising with a voltmeter.

across one pole of the *open* incoming generator circuit breaker. This procedure is more easily (and *safely*) performed at the synchroscope terminals behind the door of the synchronising panel at the *front* of the main switchboard. Check the circuit diagrams before such testing.

Adjust the generator speed until the voltmeter *very slowly* fluctuates from zero to maximum.

Close the breaker when the voltmeter indication passes through zero. Note, for this operation, an analogue (*pointer and scale*) meter is easier to follow than a digital type.

A *check-synchronising* unit has an electronic circuit to monitor the voltage, phase angle and frequency of the incoming generator with respect to the bus-bars. Circuit breaker operation is initiated by the watchkeeper but the check-synchronising monitor only allows a *permit-to-close* signal when all the synchronising conditions are within acceptable limits. This method provides a useful safeguard against operator error but retains overall watchkeeper control for adjusting the voltage and frequency.

Auto-synchronising of an incoming generator does everything an operator would do – senses and controls the voltage and frequency then initiates a circuit-breaker *close* signal at the correct instant. The auto-synchronising equipment uses electronic circuits to monitor the size of voltage, frequency and phase angle difference, then acts to regulate them until they are equal to the existing bus-bar conditions.

Usually, the *check* or *auto synchroniser* units are switched between a set of generators as and when required.

When an incoming generator has been successfully synchronised the synchronising equipment should be switched off.

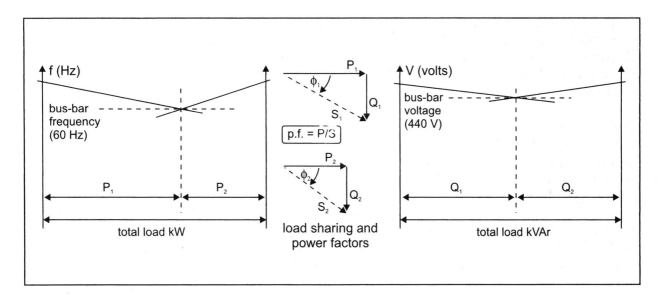

Fig. 3.17 Generator load-sharing.

The total bus-bar load can now be shared between generators or totally transferred to the new machine. In parallel operation, a generator governor directly controls *Power* (kW) while its AVR trimmer or manual voltage regulator controls *Reactive Volt Amps* (kVAr) or *power factor*.

Manual kW load sharing is achieved by raising the governor setting of the *incoming* machine while lowering the setting on the *running* machine. The *balance* of power sharing is dictated by the *governor (speed) droop* of each generator prime mover. Current (or kVAr) sharing is set by the *voltage droop* of each generator AVR. See Fig. 3.17.

For equal load sharing of kW and kVAr, each machine must have similar *droop* characteristics which are typically 2–4% between no-load and full-load values.

An overall balance of load sharing for kW and kVAr can be seen by comparing the *power factor (cosφ)* meters of each generator.

QUESTION

Two generators are load sharing in parallel:

Generator 1 delivers 500 kW at 0.8 power factor lag, and

Generator 2 delivers 400 kW and 350 kVAr lag.

Calculate:
(a) the kVAr loading of Generator 1
(b) the p.f. of Generator 2
(c) the total bus-bar loading in kW, kVAr and power factor

ANSWER

(a) $\cos\phi_1 = 0.8$ so $\phi_1 = 36.9°$
   now (from PQS power triangle):
   $Q = P.\tan\phi_1 = 500.\tan36.9° = \underline{\underline{375 \ kVAr}}$

(b) $\tan\phi_2 = \dfrac{Q_2}{P_2} = \dfrac{350}{400} = 0.875$

   so $\phi_2 = 41.2°$

   then, $p.f_2 = \cos\phi_2 = \cos41.2°$
   $= \underline{\underline{0.75 \ Lagging}}$

   Total $P = 500 + 400 = \underline{\underline{900 \ kW}}$

   and Total $Q = 375 + 350 = \underline{\underline{725 \ kVAr}}$

(c) *Overall* $\tan\phi = \dfrac{Q}{P} = \dfrac{725}{900} = 0.81$

   and $\phi = 38.9°$
   so, overall load p.f. $= \cos38.9°$
   $= \underline{\underline{0.78 \ Lagging}}$

Auto-load sharing equipment is yet again more *black-box* electronics. The circuits *compare* the kW loading of each generator (via CTs and VTs) and any difference is used to provide an error signal to raise/lower the governor setting of each prime mover as necessary. Such equipment is usually trouble-free, requiring little maintenance other than an occasional visual inspection, cleaning and checking the tightness of connections. Manual load sharing is the obvious fallback if the auto-control equipment fails.

QUESTION

Two generators are load sharing equally in parallel when a total loss of excitation occurs in No. 2 machine. What is the likely outcome?

ANSWER

Generator No. 2 will run as an *induction generator* drawing its excitation kVAr from No. 1. Both generator currents will rise rapidly with No. 1 becoming more lagging while No. 2 runs with a leading p.f. (indicated on *cosφ* meter). A *loss* of excitation trip (if fitted) or the over-current relay should trip No. 2 generator probably causing an overload on No. 1. Alternatively, No. 1 trips on overcurrent which deprives No. 2 of excitation and its breaker trips out on undervoltage.

Result — total power failure!

3.6. Emergency Generators

The power rating of an emergency generator is determined by the size and role of the ship. On some small vessels a few kW will suffice for emergency lighting only. Larger and more complicated vessels, e.g. LPG carriers, passenger liners, etc., may require hundreds of kW for emergency lighting, re-starting of the main engine auxiliaries and to supply fire-fighting pumps.

The construction and operation of an emergency generator is similar to that of a main generator. Excitation supplies, either static or rotary, will usually be governed by an automatic voltage regulator. In some cases where a static compounded exciter provides a reasonably constant generator voltage, the AVR may be omitted.

Generally, the emergency generator output voltage is at the same level as that of the main generators, e.g. 440 V, 60 Hz, 3-phase a.c.. In an HV/LV system e.g. 6.6 kV/440 V, the emergency generator will usually operate at 440 V and the emergency switchboard will be interconnected with the Engine Room 440 V switchboard in normal operation.

However, smaller emergency generator sets may deliver power at 220 V 3-phase a.c. or even single-phase a.c. for lighting and essential navigation aids only. An emergency generator is connected to its own emergency switchboard and they are located together in a compartment above the water-line, e.g. on the boat deck. In normal operation the emergency board is supplied from the main board by a cable called the *interconnector*.

It is not normally possible to synchronise the emergency and main generators. Special interlocks in the control circuits of the circuit-breakers, at each end of the *interconnector*, prevent parallel running.

Starting of the emergency generator prime mover is generally *automatic*. The run-up is initiated by an electrical relay which monitors the normal voltage supply (e.g. 440 V).

Falling mains frequency or voltage causes the *start-up* relay to operate the engine starting equipment. The prime mover may be electrically cranked from its own 24 V battery and starter motor or air started from its own air reservoir fitted local to the generator engine.

A *manual* start-up may be initiated by push buttons in the main control room and in the emergency generator room. Small generator prime movers can usually be manually cranked with a starting handle.

Correct functioning of the auto-start equipment is obviously vital to the production of emergency power. Weekly testing of the emergency generator should include simulation of the loss of normal power. The start-up equipment may provide a push button to interrupt the normal voltage supply to the control panel which then triggers the start-up sequence. Loss of main power supply can easily be simulated by pulling a fuse in the auto start panel which supplies the under-voltage or under-frequency relay.

Emergency generators should be regularly checked and run up to speed for short test runs to comply with safety regulations. These no-load running checks should, when practicable, be supplemented occasionally by an actual *load* test. This requires the disconnection of normal mains power from the emergency board while the emergency generator is loaded up to near its rated value. Only a proper load test will prove the performance of the emergency generator, its prime-mover, and the circuit-breaker operation.

3.7. Generator Protection

Apart from direct temperature measurement of the stator windings and the internal air, the protection of a generator is largely based on the sensing of current and voltage from CTs and VTs. The number and type of protective relay functions increases with the generator kVA rating and voltage level. Protective

relays are electromagnetic (traditional) or electronic (increasingly more common) which are mounted on the generator front panel of the main switchhoard. Some protective functions may be grouped together within a single relay case. Settings for level and time-delay must be periodically checked by injecting currents and/or voltages directly into the relay (usually via a special multi-pole socket adjacent to the relay and internally wired to it). Also see Chapter Two for general circuit protection methods. Some typical relay types employed for generator protection are outlined in Fig. 3.18.

❑ OCIT

The Over Current Inverse Time relay function monitors general balanced overloading and has current/time settings determined by the overall protective discrimination scheme.

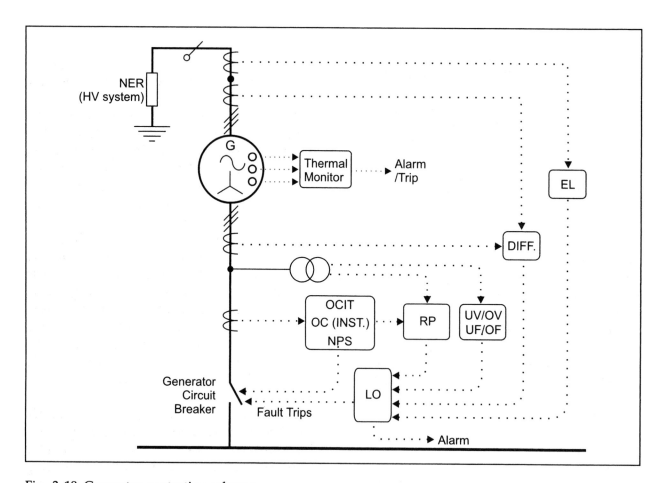

Fig. 3.18 Generator protection scheme.

Typical setting *ranges* for current (I) and time (t) are:

I >: 0.7–2.In, (In = *normal* or *rated* generator current) and t: 1–10s

❏ OC(INST.)

"Instantaneous" trip to protect against extremely high overcurrent caused by a short-circuit fault. Typical setting ranges are:

I ≫ : 2–10.In, and t: 0.1–1s

❏ NPS

A Negative Phase Sequence relay determines the amount of *unbalance* in the stator currents which is an indirect measure of the generator stator and rotor temperature. A relatively small degree of unbalance causes a significantly increased temperature rise so the NPS current setting is low at around 0.2.In.

❏ DIFF

This is a *differential* measurement of current at *each end* of a stator phase winding. This comparison of current is to detect an *internal* fault in the stator windings which may be caused by partially short-circuited coil turns and/or earth faults.

Current settings for this very serious fault are very low e.g. about 0.1.In.

❏ EL

An Earth Leakage relay (sometimes called Zero Phase Sequence) detects an earth fault current returning back through the earthed neutral connection. In a ship's HV generator system the earth fault current is limited by a high impedance NER (neutral earthing resistor) or earthing transformer so the pick-up current setting is very low, e.g. 1–5A with a time delay of 0.1–0.5 s.

❏ UV/OV

Under Voltage and Over Voltage functions are monitored by these relays with settings of around 0.8.Un and 1.2.Un respectively (Un = rated voltage) with time delays of about 2s. An overvoltage function may not be required in many protection schemes.

❏ UF/OF

Under and Over Frequency settings are typically 58 Hz and 62 Hz for a 60 Hz system.

❏ LO

This is the master Lock Out or trip/hand-reset relay responsible for tripping the generator circuit breaker. Its action is instantaneous when triggered by a protective relay. It can also be used to trip the generator prime-mover and initiate generator field suppression together with the signalling of an alarm.

❏ RP

Generators intended to operate in parallel must have *reverse power protection* (RP).

A reverse power relay monitors the *direction of power* flowing between the generator and the load. If a prime-mover failure occurred the generator would act as a *motor*. The reverse power relay detects this fault and acts to trip the generator circuit-breaker.

The *pick-up* power level setting and time-delay setting are adjustable and are pre-set to suit the prime-mover. If the prime mover is a turbine, very little power is absorbed when motoring and a reverse-power pick-up setting of 2–3% is usual. If the prime mover is a diesel then a setting range of 5–15% is usually adopted. A time delay range of about 0.5–3 s is usual.

The RP relay operation is easily checked during a generator changeover. The outgoing generator is gradually throttled down so that it *motors* causing the reverse power relay to trip its generator circuit-breaker.

3.8. Generator Maintenance

Regular inspection and the correct maintenance of generators and their associated control gear is essential to prevent failure and inefficient operation.

CAUTION: Always ensure that the generator prime-mover is shut down and locked off before you begin any maintenance. Also ensure that the generator circuit breaker is locked off, auto-start circuits are disabled and electric heaters are switched off and isolated.

All wiring to the generator should be inspected for damage or frayed insulation and tightness of terminal connections. Particularly check for signs of oil and water contamination of cable insulation within terminal boxes.

Check that the cooling air intake and exhaust openings are not blocked and are free of dirt and dust.

Inspect and clean the generator rotor and stator windings by removing dust with a dry lint-free cloth. Low pressure, dry compressed air may be used to dislodge heavier dirt but be careful not to drive the dirt deeper into the windings. An industrial type vacuum cleaner is very effective for removing dirt from the windings. Use a rubber or plastic coated nozzle on the vacuum cleaner tube to prevent abrasive damage to the sensitive winding insulation. Oil on the surface of winding insulation will reduce the insulation resistance and shorten its life. The oily deposits can be removed by washing the windings with special degreasant liquids. Minor abrasions to winding insulation can be repaired, after cleaning, by the application of a suitable air-drying varnish.

Rotor sliprings must be checked for uniform (even) wear and that the carbon brushes have free movement in their boxes. Correct brush pressure can be checked using a pull-type spring balance and compared with the manufacturer's instructions. A *pull* of around 1–1.5 kg is usual. If the brushes become too short (below about 2 cm) the reduced spring pressure will cause sparking at the slipring contact. Replace brushes with the correct type and *bed* them to the curvature of the slip rings. This can be done by placing a thin strip of glass paper (not emery paper) over the slip ring with its cutting surface under the carbon brush. Pull the glass paper around the slip ring until the brush surface has the same contour as the ring. The last few passes of the glass paper should be made in the same direction as the normal rotor direction. Remove all traces of carbon dust with a vacuum cleaner.

Generator excitation transformers, AVR components and rotating diodes must be kept free of dirt, oil and dampness. A special contact grease is used between the diode connections to prevent electrolytic action occurring between dissimilar metals. Check such contacts for tightness but do not disturb them unnecessarily.

Measure the insulation of the stator and rotor windings to earth and between stator phases (assuming that the neutral point is available for disconnection at the terminal box).

Remember to disconnect or short-circuit any electronic circuit components which are likely to be damaged by a high voltage insulation test. Consult the wiring diagrams and the manufacturer's instructions before testing. Record the IR values and note the prevailing temperature and humidity. Compare with previous test results. A *minimum* IR value is usually taken to be 1 MΩ but a lower value may be acceptable to a surveyor based on 1 kΩ/volt, e.g. 450 kΩ or 0.45 MΩ for a 450 V generator. However, it is the historical *trend* of the machine IR values which will give a better picture of the insulation condition.

Generators with very low IR values (less than 0.5 MΩ) should be given a thorough cleaning then dried out. If the IR has recovered to a reasonable value which has become steady during the drying period, its windings should be covered with high-quality air-drying insulating varnish. Should the IR value remain low during a dry-out, the machine insulation needs to be completely re-impregnated or rewound (generally by a specialist contractor).

After maintenance, no-load running checks should precede synchronising and loading. On load, particularly check for excess temperature rise and load-sharing stability when running in parallel.

Finally, if a generator is to be left idle or a long time, make sure that its windings are suitably heated to prevent internal condensation forming on its insulation. As with all electrical equipment — dirt, overheating and dampness are the enemy!

3.9. Main Switchboard

A typical layout of a ship's main switchboard is shown in Fig. 3.19.

The central section of the main switchboard is used for the control of the main generators. The switchgear cubicles on either side of the generator panels are used for essential services and flanking these are the grouped motor starter panels.

Handles for opening the doors on switchboard cubicles are usually linked (or interlocked) to an isolating switch. This ensures that supplies to components in the cubicle are switched off before the door can be opened.

Fused isolators are isolating switches that incorporate fuses. The action of opening the switch isolates the fuses so that they can be replaced safely.

Fused isolators can also be interlocked with the cubicle door handle. Motor starters frequently incorporate this arrangement.

One type of interlocked fused isolator can be completely withdrawn and removed to ensure complete safety when carrying out maintenance on equipment.

Maintenance on fused isolators consists of periodically checking the operating mechanism. Contacts must be inspected for damage and lightly greased with an electrical lubricant. The interlock mechanism (if fitted) should also be examined for correct and safe operation.

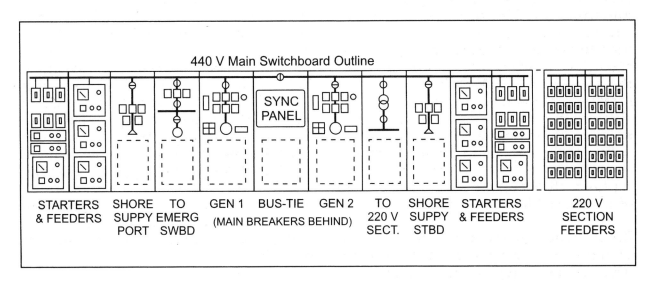

Fig. 3.19 Main switchboard layout.

A separate section switches the three phase 220 V a.c. low power and lighting services. Check your own switchboard and particularly note the controls and instruments on the generator panels; the link to the emergency switchboard; steering gear supplies (duplicated); other essential services to the engine-room; navigation equipment supplies and section board feeders.

Note the alarms and insulation resistance (earth fault) monitors on both the 440 V and the 220 V sections.

The 440/220 V lighting transformers may be located inside the main switchboard or, more likely, will be separately mounted nearby.

The main generator supply cables are connected directly to their respective circuit-breakers. Short copper bars from each generator circuit breaker connect it to the three bus-bars which run through the length of the switchboard. The bus-bars may be seen if the rear doors of the switchboard cubicle are opened, but they may be in a special enclosed bus-bar duct acting as an internal fire barrier.

Take care when opening doors on switchboards, live parts are exposed – you are in danger.

The ship's electrical diagrams will include drawings of the front, and perhaps the rear, of the main switchboard showing the *as-fitted* equipment.

The electrical distribution diagrams will follow the physical arrangement of the main switchboard layout.

You should study the electrical circuit and layout diagrams for your ship to identify, locate and appreciate the role of each key component in the scheme. Efficient fault-finding on a distribution network can only be achieved by a thorough understanding of the scheme and its *normal* operation.

Switchboard instruments and controls for particular functions are grouped together.

For example, the generator synchronising panel has all the instruments, relays and switches necessary for generator paralleling.

Each generator panel has all the instruments, relays, switches, controls and status lamps necessary for control of the generators.

The instruments on panels of *outgoing* circuits are usually limited to an ammeter, status lamps, function switches (e.g. manual/off/auto) and push buttons.

Low power control and instrument wiring is of relatively small cross-section, with multicoloured plastic insulation which is clearly identified against the larger main power cables.

The instrumentation and control wiring is supplied from fuses which are located behind the appropriate panel. Green and yellow striped earth wiring from instruments and panel doors etc., is connected to a common copper earth-bonding bar running the length of the switchboard at its rear. This earth bar is electrically bonded to the ship's steel hull.

3.10. Main Circuit Breakers

LV generator circuit-breakers and other large distribution circuit-breakers (600–6000 A) on board ship are traditionally of the air break type called ACB (*air circuit breaker*). This means that the circuit-breaker contacts separate in *air*. An ACB outline is shown in Fig. 3.20.

High voltage (HV) installations e.g. at 6.6 kV and 11 kV generally use the vacuum interrupter type or gas-filled (sulphur hexafluoride – SF6) breakers. Outlines shown in Fig. 3.21.

In a vacuum interrupter the contacts only need to be separated by a few millimetres as the insulation level of a vacuum is extremely high. The quality of the vacuum in the sealed interrupter

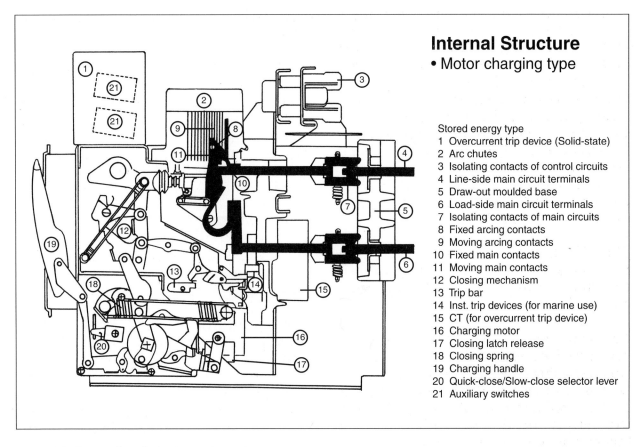

Internal Structure
• Motor charging type

Stored energy type
1 Overcurrent trip device (Solid-state)
2 Arc chutes
3 Isolating contacts of control circuits
4 Line-side main circuit terminals
5 Draw-out moulded base
6 Load-side main circuit terminals
7 Isolating contacts of main circuits
8 Fixed arcing contacts
9 Moving arcing contacts
10 Fixed main contacts
11 Moving main contacts
12 Closing mechanism
13 Trip bar
14 Inst. trip devices (for marine use)
15 CT (for overcurrent trip device)
16 Charging motor
17 Closing latch release
18 Closing spring
19 Charging handle
20 Quick-close/Slow-close selector lever
21 Auxiliary switches

Fig. 3.20 Circuit breaker components.

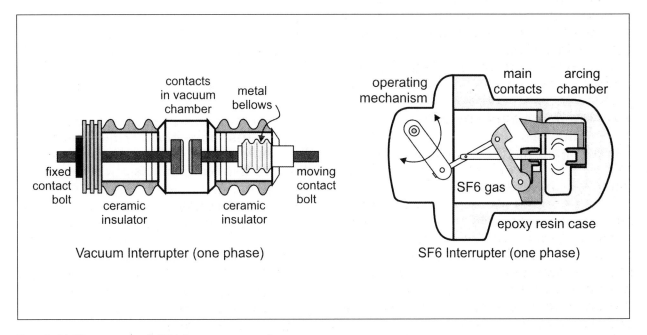

Fig. 3.21 Vacuum and SF6 interrupter units.

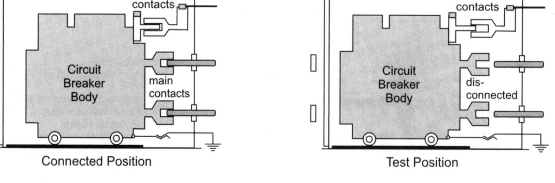

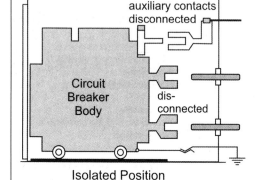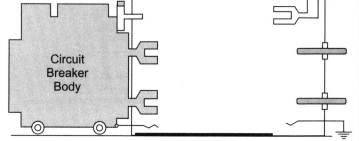

Fig. 3.22 Circuit breaker positions.

chamber is checked by applying a short duration HV pulse (e.g. 10 kV for a 6.6 kV breaker) across the open contacts.

In the gas breaker the contacts separate in a special interrupter chamber containing SF6 gas typically at 500 kPa (5 bar) at 20°C.

The operating mechanism for vacuum and SF6 breakers is similar to that employed for an ACB.

Fig. 3.22 shows how each main circuit breaker is mounted on guide rails inside a main switchboard cubicle from which it must be withdrawn and isolated from the bus-bars for maintenance and testing.

The breaker and its guide rails are usually mounted in a special cassette bolted into the switchboard cubicle and electrically connected to the bus-bars. If repair work demands that the breaker is to be completely removed from its cassette then usually a special hoist or *fork-lift* is required for large, heavy-duty units.

The action of withdrawing the circuit breaker causes a safety shutter to cover the live bus-bar contacts at the rear of its cubicle.

The mechanical linkage in a circuit-breaker is quite complex and should not be interfered with except for maintenance and lubrication as specified by the manufacturer.

The main fixed and moving contacts are of copper (sometimes of special arc-resistant alloy or silver tipped) and usually silver-alloy coated. Main contacts should not be scraped or filed. If the main contacts suffer severe burning they will probably require realignment as specified by the manufacturer.

Arcing contacts *normally* suffer burning and may be dressed by a smooth file as recommended by the manufacturer. Carborundum and emery should not be used — the hard particles can embed themselves in the soft contacts and cause future trouble.

The arc chutes or arc splitter boxes confine and control the inevitable arc to rapidly accelerate its extinction. These must be removed and inspected for broken parts and erosion of the splitter plates.

Various types of circuit breaker closing mechanism may be fitted:

• Independent Manual Spring

The spring charge is directly applied by manual depression of the closing handle. The last few centimetres of handle movement releases the spring to close the breaker. Closing speed is independent of the operator.

• Motor Driven Stored Charge Spring (most common type for marine applications)

Closing springs are charged by a motor-gearbox unit. Spring recharging is automatic following closure of the breaker which is initiated by a push-button. This may be a direct mechanical release of the charged spring, or more usually, it will be released electrically via a solenoid latch.

• Manual Wound Stored Charge Spring

This is similar to above method but with manually charged closing springs.

• Solenoid

The breaker is closed by a d.c. solenoid energised from the generator or bus-bars via a transformer/rectifier unit, contactor, push button and, sometimes, a timing relay.

WARNING: Circuit breakers store energy in their springs for:

• Store-charge mechanisms in the closing springs.

• Contact and kick-off springs.

Extreme care must be exercised when handling circuit breakers with the closing springs charged, or when the circuit breaker is in the *ON* position.

Isolated circuit-breakers racked out for maintenance should be left with the closing springs *discharged* and in the *OFF* position.

Circuit-breakers are held in the *closed* or *ON* position by a mechanical latch. The breaker is tripped by releasing this latch allowing the kick-off springs and contact pressure to force the contacts open.

Tripping can be initiated:

• Manually — a push button with mechanical linkage trips the latch.

• Undervoltage trip coil or relay (trips when de-energised).

• Overcurrent/short-circuit trip device or relay (trips when energised).

• Solenoid trip coil — when energised by a remote push-button or relay (such as an electronic overcurrent relay).

Mechanical interlocks are fitted to main circuit breakers to prevent racking-out if still in the *ON* position.

Care must be taken not to exert *undue force* if the breaker will not move, otherwise damage may be caused to the interlocks and other mechanical parts.

Electrical interlock switches are connected into circuit-breaker control circuits to prevent incorrect sequence operation, e.g. when a shore-supply breaker is closed onto a switchboard.

The ship's generator breakers are usually interlocked *OFF* to prevent parallel running of a ship's generator and the shore supply.

Chapter Four
Motors and Starters

4.0. Introduction

The drive power for compressors, pumps and fans aboard ship comes from electric motors. By far the most common type of motor is the 3-phase a.c. *cage-rotor* induction motor. It is popular because it is simple, tough and requires very little attention. Another advantage is that starting and stopping these motors can be done with simple and reliable direct-on-line contactor starters. Three phase induction motors are usually supplied at 440 V, 60 Hz, but 3.3 kV and 6.6 kV, 60 Hz are sometimes used for very large drives such as bow thrusters, cargo pumps, air compressors and gas compressors.

Special types of motor can also be found on board ships. DC commutator motors are sometimes used for driving deck machinery where speed control is important. Single-phase a.c. motors are used in low power drives such as galley equipment and domestic tools.

High power synchronous a.c. motors are frequently used for electric propulsion drives, see Chapter Eight.

This Chapter will deal principally with the three-phase a.c. cage rotor induction motor, together with its control and protection. Additionally, the more common types of motor speed control methods are outlined, followed by maintenance procedures for motors and starters.

4.1. Motor Construction

The induction motor has two main components, the *stator* and the *rotor*. The *stator* carries three separate insulated phase windings which are spaced 120° (electrical) apart and lying in slots cut into a laminated steel magnetic core. This type of stator winding is similar to the construction used for an a.c. generator. The ends of the stator windings are terminated in the stator terminal box where they are connected to the incoming cable from the three-phase a.c. power supply.

The *rotor* consists of copper or aluminium conductor bars which are connected together at their ends by short-circuiting rings to form a *cage* winding. The conductor bars are set in a laminated steel magnetic core. The essential reliability of the induction motor comes from having this type of simple, robust rotor which usually has no insulation on the conductor bars and does not have any troublesome rotary contacts like brushes, commutator or sliprings. The diagram in Fig. 4.1 and the following component list identifies the main items used in the construction of a typical totally enclosed, fan ventilated (TEFV) induction motor.

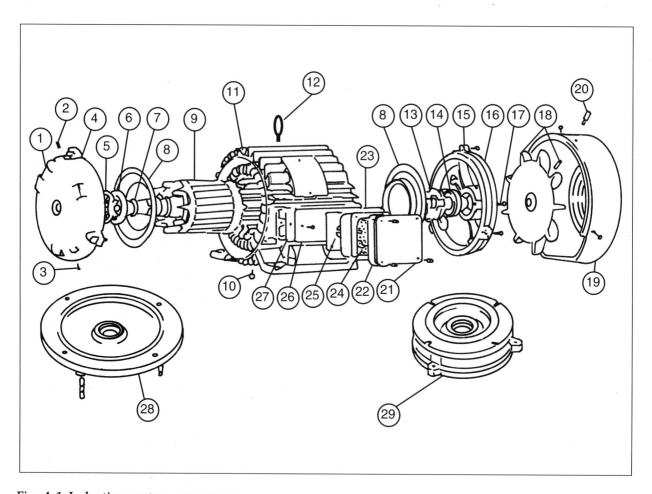

Fig. 4.1 Induction motor components.

No.	Component	No.	Component	No.	Component
1	endshield, driving end	11	stator frame	21	terminal box cover
2	grease nipple	12	eyebolt	22	terminal box gasket
3	grease relief screw	13	inside cap	23	terminal board
4	end securing bolt	14	ball bearing	24	terminal box
5	anti-bump nuts	15	circlip	25	terminal box gasket
6	ball bearing, drive end	16	endshield	26	raceway plate
7	false bearing shoulder	17	inside cap screws	27	raceway gasket
8	flume	18	fan	28	"D" flange
9	cage rotor	19	fan cover	29	"C" face flange
10	drain plug	20	lubricator extension pipe		

4.2. Enclosures and Ratings

❑ Motor Enclosures

Enclosure protection for electrical equipment is defined in terms of its opposition to the ingress of solid particles and liquids. The enclosure protection is defined by the *Ingress Protection* (IP) Code where a two-figure number is used to indicate the degree of protection against the ingress of solids and liquids as shown below.

Drip-proof open ventilated motors are used where the risk of liquids leaking from overhead pipes and valves may be a problem. Air is drawn into the machine by an internal fan to provide cooling. The ventilation ducts are fitted with mesh screens to prevent any objects from entering the motor and causing damage. These screens must always be kept clean and free from dust otherwise the motor will overheat due to inadequate ventilation.

When a greater degree of protection is required the enclosure is made *Totally Enclosed Fan Ventilated* (TEFV) and *jet-proof*. No *external* air is allowed inside the motor. To improve heat transfer the

motor casing is finned to increase the surface area, and airflow across the fins is achieved by means of an external fan and cowl arrangement.

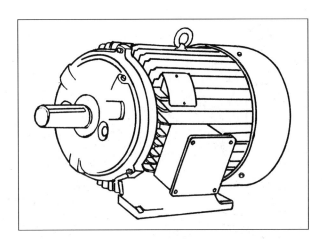

Fig. 4.2 TEFV motor enclosure.

Motors located outside on weatherdecks have deck watertight enclosures but the external fan is omitted because of the possibility of ice formation.

Deck watertight motors (IP56) have sealed bearings and a watertight terminal box. They can be completely immersed in shallow water for short periods. Sealing washers are fitted under all screws and a coat of special corrosion resisting paint is generally applied to all external and internal surfaces.

1st numeral	**Degree of Protection** of persons against contact with live or moving parts inside the enclosure and protection of equipment against ingress of *solid bodies*	2nd numeral	**Degree of Protection** against ingress of *liquids*
0	No protection of persons against contact with live or moving parts inside the enclosure. No protection of equipment against ingress of solid foreign bodies.	0	No protection
1	Protection against accidental or inadvertent contact with live or moving parts inside the enclosure by a large surface of the human body, for example, a hand but not protection against deliberate access to such parts. Protection against ingress of large solid foreign bodies.	1	Protection against drops of condensed water: Drops of condensed water falling on the enclosure shall have no harmful effect.
2	Protection against contact with live or moving parts inside the enclosure by fingers. Protection against ingress of medium size solid foreign bodies.	2	Protection against drops of liquid: Drops of falling liquid shall have no harmful effect when the enclosure is tilted at any angle up to 15 ° from the vertical.
3	Protection against contact with live or moving parts inside the enclosure by tools, wires or such objects of thickness greater than 2.5 mm. Protection against ingress of small solid foreign bodies.	3	Protection against rain: Water falling in rain at an angle up to 60° with respect to the vertical shall have no harmful effect.
4	Protection against contact with live or moving parts inside the enclosure by tools, wires or such objects of thickness greater than 1 mm. Protection against Ingress of small solid foreign bodies.	4	Protection against splashing: Liquid splashed from any direction shall have no harmful effect.
5	Complete protection against contact with live or moving parts inside the enclosure. Protection against harmful deposits of dust. The ingress of dust is not totally prevented, but dust cannot enter in an amount sufficient to interfere with satisfactory operation of the equipment enclosed.	5	Protection again water-jets: Water projected by a nozzle from any direction under stated conditions shall have no harmful effect.
6	Complete protection against contact with live or moving parts inside the enclosure. Protection against ingress of dust.	6	Protection against conditions on ships' decks (deck watertight equipment): Water from heavy seas shall not enter the enclosure under prescribed conditions.
Note that the higher the numeral of the 1st and 2nd characteristic, the greater degree of protection the enclosure offers:		7	Protection against immersion in water: It must not be possible for water to enter the enclosure under stated conditions of pressure and time.
e.g. Jet-proof IP55 meets all the less onerous degrees such as IP22, IP23, IP34 and IP54.		8	Protection against indefinite immersion in water under specified pressure. It must not be possible for water to enter the enclosure.

Insulation Class	Maximum Temp. (°C)	Typical Materials
A	105	Cotton, natural silk, synthetic silk, presspan
E	120	Wire enamels with a base of polyvinyl acetyl, epoxy or polyamide resins
B	130	Mica products, wire enamels with a base of polyterephthalate, laminated glass-fibre materials
F	155	Mica products, glass fibre, wire enamels with a base of imide-polyester and esterimide
H	180	Mica products, glass fibre, wire enamels with a base of pure polyimide

Deck motors for tankers must have a flameproof (Exd) enclosure if they are within 3m (4.5m for some ships) of an oil tank outlet.

❏ Motor Ratings

The motor converts electrical energy taken from the electric power supply into rotational mechanical energy at the motor shaft. Power *losses* occur during the energy conversion which results in the production of heat in the motor. These losses increase when the load on the motor increases because the motor takes more current from the supply.

The life of the insulating materials used on motor windings depends on the temperature at which it is operated. Insulating materials are selected for marine practice based on an ambient temperature of 45°C. An adequate life-span for the insulation is based on the assumption that the maximum temperature limit is not exceeded.

Motor nameplate definitions:

• *Rated Full Load Current (FLC)*

This is the maximum value of current that the motor can continuously take from the supply without exceeding the temperature limit for the insulating materials used.

• *Rated Voltage*

The motor has been designed to operate successfully when connected to this value of supply voltage. If the rated voltage is not applied, overheating, stalling and burn-out can result.

• *Rated Frequency*

The motor speed is directly affected by the supply frequency; so are the motor losses. If the motor is operated at other than rated frequency overheating can occur.

• *Power Rating*

This is the shaft power output of the motor when it is connected to rated voltage and frequency when drawing its rated current from the supply.

• *Rated Speed*

This is the full load speed of the motor when connected to rated voltage and frequency.

• *IP Number*

Indicates the degree of protection given by the motor enclosure.

The motor rating details are shown on the motor nameplate as in the example in Fig. 4.3.

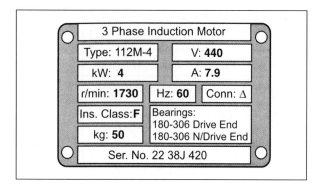

Fig. 4.3 Motor rating label.

Standard three-phase a.c. induction motors are manufactured in about 60 frame sizes with power ratings from about 0.37 kW to 500 kW. A sample selection of output power ratings and their average full load current (FLC) for 4-pole, 440 V motors are listed below:

kW	0.55	1.5	4.0	11	22	37	55	75	100	200	500
A	1.4	3.1	7.9	20.1	39	64	90	125	162	321	780

4.3. Induction Motor Operation

When the 3-phase a.c. supply voltages are connected to the three stator phase windings, the resulting phase currents produce a multi-pole magnetic flux (Φ). This flux is physically *rotated* around the stator core by the switched sequence of the R-Y-B currents at a speed called *synchronous speed* (n_s). The value of synchronous speed depends on how many magnetic pole-pairs (p) fixed by the stator winding arrangement *and* by the frequency (f) of the voltage supply connected to the stator winding.

$$n_s = \frac{f}{p} \ rev/s \quad or \quad N_s = \frac{f.60}{p} \ rev/min$$

QUESTION

What is the synchronous speed of a 6-pole motor supplied at 60 Hz?

ANSWER

20 rev/s or 1200 rev/min

The stator rotating magnetic flux cuts through the rotor conductors to induce an alternating emf into them. Since the rotor conductors are connected together at the ends, the induced emf's set up rotor currents.

The rotor currents also produce a magnetic flux which interacts with the stator rotating flux which produces a *torque (T)* on the rotor conductor bars as shown in Fig. 4.4.

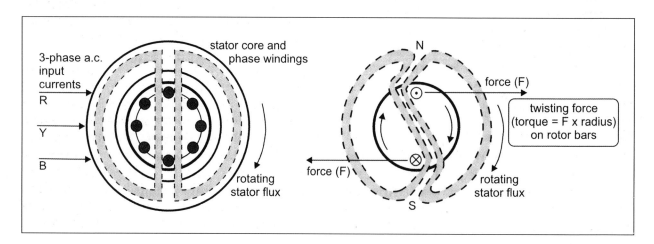

Fig. 4.4 Induction motor action.

Rotor torque size is determined as:
$T \propto \Phi.I_R.cos\phi$ where Φ is the stator flux, I_R is the rotor current and ϕ is the angle between Φ and I_R. The rotor reactance varies with the *rate* of cutting flux which depends on the rotor speed. Hence $cos\phi$ (power factor) will vary during motor start-up as it accelerates up to its rated speed. If $cos\phi$ is ignored (for simplicity) then the shaft torque is approximately given by: $T \propto V^2$ (as $\Phi \propto V$ and $I_R \propto \Phi$).

The *direction* of the rotor torque causes the rotor to rotate in the same direction as the rotating magnetic field.

QUESTION

How is the rotor direction reversed?

ANSWER

Simply by swapping over any two supply line connections at the stator terminal box. This reverses the direction of the rotating magnetic field.

An induction motor *cannot* run normally at synchronous speed. This is because the rotor conductors would then be stationary with respect to the rotating magnetic field. No emf would be induced in the rotor and there would be no rotor current and no torque developed. Even when the motor is on no-load the rotor speed has to be slightly less than the synchronous speed n_S *so that current can be induced* into the rotor conductors to produce the torque to overcome the mechanical rotational losses of friction and windage.

Slip speed is the *difference* between the synchronous speed (n_s) of the rotating magnetic flux and actual rotor speed (n_R).

Slip is usually expressed as a percentage of the synchronous speed:

$$s = \left(\frac{n_s - n_R}{n_s} \right).100\%$$

QUESTION

If a 6-pole motor is supplied at 60 Hz and runs with a slip of 5%, what is the actual rotor speed?

ANSWER

The synchronous speed is 1200 rpm, and the rotor slips by 5% of 1200, i.e. by 60 rpm so the rotor runs at 1140 rpm.

If the load torque on the motor shaft is increased, the rotor will tend to slow down (increasing the slip) which allows the rotor conductors to cut the flux at an increased rate. This causes more current to flow in the rotor which is matched by more stator supply current to meet the increased shaft torque demand. The motor will now run at this new, slightly reduced, speed. The fall of motor speed between no-load and full-load is very small (between 1% and 5%) so induction motors are considered to be *almost* constant speed machines.

The characteristic in Fig. 4.5 shows the variation of torque with slip for a standard cage-type induction motor. Also shown is a typical load characteristic which indicates the torque necessary to drive the load at different speeds.

At start-up the motor develops more torque than is necessary to turn the load so the motor and load accelerate. The speed increases until, at the intersection of the two characteristics, the torque developed by the motor is the same as the torque required by the load at that speed. The motor and load will then run at this steady speed as the torque supplied exactly matches the demand.

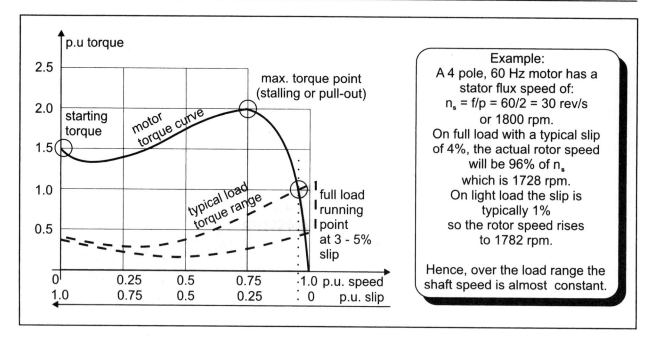

Fig. 4.5 Motor torque/speed curve and shaft loading.

4.4. Control Equipment

When an induction motor is connected directly to its three-phase a.c. supply voltage, a very large stator current of 5–8 × full-load current (FLC) is taken. This is due to the *maximum* rate of flux cutting (s = 100%) in the rotor, creating large *induced* rotor currents.

The corresponding supply power factor at start-up is very low, typically about 0.2 lagging, which rises to about 0.5 lagging on no-load then to about 0.85 lagging on full-load.

This starting surge current reduces as the motor accelerates up to its running speed.

Operating on light loads at low power factor is inefficient as the supply current is relatively high causing significant I^2R resistive (copper) losses. The only way to improve the power factor of the motor on light loads is to reduce the supply voltage. This can be achieved with an electronic voltage controller called a *soft-starter* and/or *energy manager* which can match the supply voltage to the start-up and load conditions. Such a controller aims to maintain the operating power factor as high as possible to minimise supply current and power losses. Note, this type of *voltage* controller does not control shaft speed (which is controlled by *frequency*).

Most induction motors are *Direct-on-Line* (DOL) switch-started because such starters are inexpensive and simple to operate and maintain. The high starting current surge will not cause serious heating damage to the motor unless the motor is repeatedly started and stopped in a short time period.

When very large motors are started DOL they cause a significant disturbance of voltage (*voltage dip*) on the supply lines due to the large starting current surge.

This voltage disturbance may result in the malfunction of other electrical equipment connected to the supply e.g. lighting *dip* and flickering effects.

To limit the starting current some large induction motors are started at reduced voltage and then have the full supply

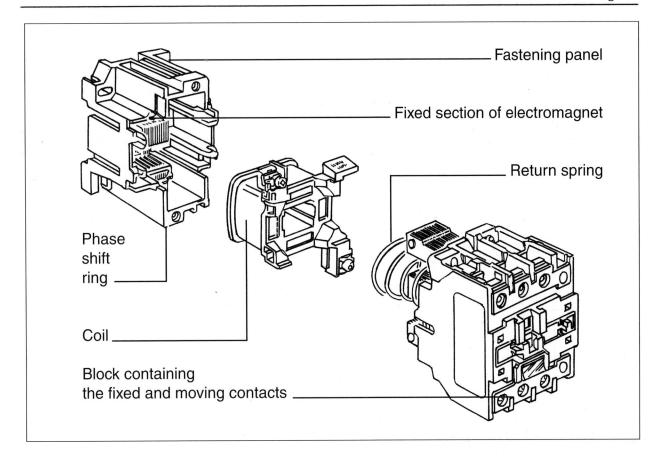

Fastening panel

Fixed section of electromagnet

Return spring

Phase
shift
ring

Coil

Block containing
the fixed and moving contacts

Fig. 4.6 Contactor construction.

voltage reconnected when they have accelerated close to their rated speeds.

Reduced voltage starting is used for large motors driving loads like cargo pumps and bow thrusters.

Two methods of reduced voltage starting by *switching* are called *star-delta starting* and *autotransformer starting* but an electronic *"soft" starting* option is also used.

Contactors, as shown in Fig. 4.6, perform the switching action in starters to connect and disconnect the power supply to the motor.

The contactor is an electromagnetically operated 3-pole switch initiated from local and/or remote stop/start push buttons. If the current goes above the rated current for the motor, its contactor will be tripped out automatically by an overcurrent relay (OCR) to disconnect the motor from the supply (see motor protection).

4.5. Direct-on-Line Starting

In the example circuit shown in Fig. 4.7, the induction motor is *directly switched* onto the three-phase a.c. power supply lines. This is a very simple starting arrangement which is used for the majority of induction motor drives.

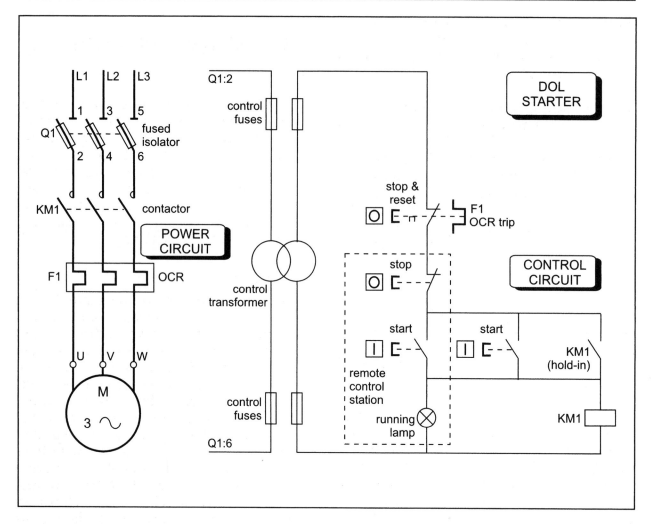

Fig. 4.7 DOL starter circuit.

The switching sequence for this starter circuit is as follows:

power circuit operation	control circuit operation
manual closing of fused-isolator Q1	control circuit voltage available (e.g. 110V from control transformer)
closing of line contactor KM1 KM1 contactor "holds-in"	press start button "I" (local or remote) auxiliary contact on KM1 "latches" contactor remote indicator lamp "on"
KM1 contactor drops out, motor stops	press stop button "O" (local or remote) on overload the OCR trips out the stop button OCR must be manually reset (after thermal time delay)

Further circuit additions can be made for remote control (e.g. by liquid level switch) and motor reversing (with an extra contactor).

DOL switching demands a short duration (a few seconds) but large starting current, typically 5 × FLC fixed by the motor impedance. This is generally acceptable to the supply generator as long as the corresponding *voltage dip* is not greater than 10–15% within the run-up period. For large motor drives this starting surge will cause an unacceptable *voltage dip* at the supply bus-bars with likely malfunctions of other consumers e.g. lighting flicker and possible drop-out of supply contactors. The voltage dip is further compounded as all the other connected motors compensate by demanding an increased current to maintain their original power output. If prolonged, this sudden current loading may cause supply line and generator protection to trip. Hence large motors (e.g. bow and stern thrusters) require a more complicated starting method to limit the size of starting current and so protect the generator supply and other consumers. This means applying a reduced voltage at start-up.

4.6. Reduced Voltage Starting

During the run-up period the size of motor starting current can be limited by applying a reduced supply voltage or inserting some additional circuit impedance. The most common arrangement is to apply reduced voltage which is sub-divided into the methods of *star-delta* switching, *auto-transformer* starting and *"soft" starting*.

❑ Star-Delta Starting

If a motor is direct-on-line started with the stator winding *star* connected, it will only take *one-third* of the starting current that it would take if the windings were *delta* connected. The starting current of a motor which is designed to run *delta* connected can be reduced in this way.

Star-delta starters for small motors may be operated by a manual changeover switch. For large power motors, the phase windings are automatically switched using contactors controlled by a timing relay as shown in Fig. 4.8. A choice of time delay relays are available whose action is governed by thermal, pneumatic, mechanical or electronic control devices.

The switching sequence for this starter circuit is as follows:

power circuit operation	control circuit operation
manual closing of fused-isolator Q1	control circuit voltage available (e.g. 110V from control transformer)
closing of contactor KM1: star connection closing of KM2: motor supply opening of KM1: star connection opens closing of KM3: delta connection	press start button S2 to close KM1 KM1 closes KM2 "hold-in" of KM1 – KM2 by KM2 auxiliary opening of KM1 by KM2 auxiliary closing of KM3 by KM1 auxiliary
KM2 & KM3 contactors drops out, motor stops	Stop by S1 button or OCR trip F1
Note: KM2 has a pair of auxiliary contacts with a time delay action (typically 40 ms) between the opening of the N/C and the closing of the N/O contacts	

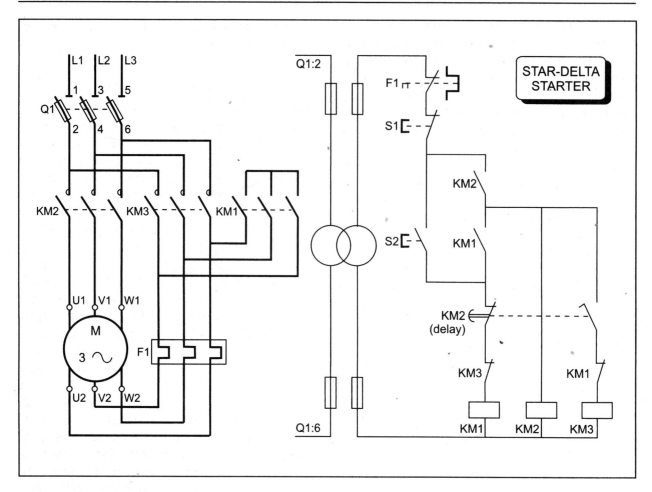

Fig. 4.8 Star-delta starter circuit.

QUESTION

Why is the time delay necessary between the KM2 auxiliary contacts?

ANSWER

To provide an electrical interlock between contactors KM1 and KM3. This is to prevent a full *short-circuit* fault across the supply lines during the changeover from *star* to *delta*.

At the instant of starting when the supply has just been switched on and the motor has not yet started to rotate, there is no mechanical output from the motor. The only factors which determine the current taken by the motor are the supply voltage (V) and the *impedance* of the motor phase windings (Z_{PH}).

Compare the starting current when *star* connected to the starting current when *delta* connected as in Fig. 4.9.

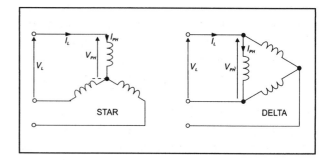

Fig. 4.9 Star-delta connections.

ratio of:
$$\frac{I_{L(Y)}}{I_{L(\triangle)}} = \frac{V_L/\sqrt{3}.Z}{\sqrt{3}.V_L/Z} = \frac{1}{3}$$

This shows that the starting current of a *delta* connected motor can be reduced to one third if the motor is *star* connected for starting. The shaft torque is also reduced to one-third which reduces the shaft acceleration and increases the run-up time for the drive but this is not usually a problem.

When an induction motor is running on load it is converting electrical energy input to mechanical energy output. The input current is now determined by the load on the motor shaft.

An induction motor will run at the same speed when it is *star* connected as when it is *delta* connected because the flux speed is the same in both cases being set by the supply frequency.

This means that the power output from the motor is the same when the motor is *star* connected as when the motor is *delta* connected, so the power inputs and *line* currents must be the same when running in either connection.

If the motor is designed to run in *delta* but is run as *star* connected, and on full load, then each stator phase winding will be carrying an *overcurrent* of $\sqrt{3} \times$ rated phase current. This is because phase and line currents are equal in a *star* connection.

This will cause overheating and eventual burnout unless tripped by the overcurrent relay. Remember that the motor copper losses are produced by the I^2R heating effect so the motor will run $(\sqrt{3})^2 = 3$ times hotter if left to run in the *star* connection when designed for *delta* running. This malfunction may occur if the control timing sequence is not completed or the *star* contactor remains closed while a mechanical interlock prevents the *delta* contactor from closing.

For correct overcurrent protection, the overcurrent relays must be fitted in the *phase* connections and not in the line connections. Check the position of the overcurrent devices in the previous schematic diagram, Fig. 4.8, for an automatic *star-delta* starter.

❏ Autotransformer Starting

Starting a large motor with a long run-up period will demand a very high current surge from the supply generator for a few seconds. This causes a severe voltage dip which affects every load on the system. Reduced voltage starting will limit the starting surge current. One way to reduce the initial voltage supplied to the motor is to step it down using a transformer. Then, when the motor has accelerated up to almost full speed, the reduced voltage is replaced by the full mains voltage. The transformer used in this starter is not the usual type with separate primary and secondary windings. It is an *autotransformer* which uses only one winding for both input and output. This arrangement is cheaper, smaller and lighter than an equivalent double-wound transformer and it is only in operation during the short starting period. For induction motor starting, the autotransformer is a 3-phase unit, and, because of expense, this method is only used with large motor drives, e.g. electric cargo pumps.

Fig. 4.10 shows the supply voltage is connected across the complete winding and the motor is connected to the reduced voltage tapping. A number of tappings are usually available on the transformer winding, giving voltage outputs ranging from about 50% to 80% of the mains supply voltage. e.g. a 60% tap on an autotransformer supplied at 440 V would provide a voltage output of 60% of 440 = 264 V.

The autotransformer usually has a few tapping points to give a set of reduced voltages (e.g. 40%, 50% and 65%) which help to match the motor current demand to the supply capability.

As with the *star-delta* starter, the auto-transformer may use what is called an *open-transition* switching sequence or a *closed-transition* switching sequence

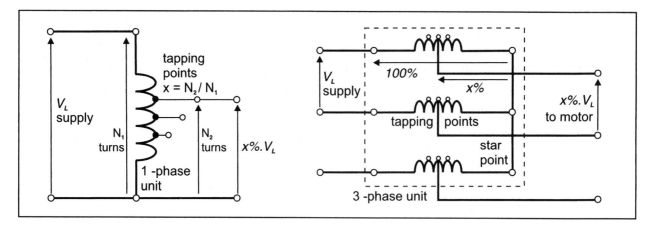

Fig. 4.10 Autotransformer connections.

between the start and run conditions. In the former, the reduced voltage is supplied to the motor at start then disconnected and the full supply voltage rapidly reconnected to the motor.

The problem with *open-transition* is that a very large surge current can flow after the transition from reduced to full voltage.

QUESTION

What causes the large current surge in open transition starters when going from the start to the run condition?

ANSWER

All motors generate a back emf against the supply voltage when they are running. When the supply is removed from a running induction motor the magnetic field does not immediately collapse. The motor begins to slow down but still generates an emf. When reconnected in open transition, the supply voltage and motor emf are not necessarily in phase (the condition is similar to synchronising a generator onto the bus-bars). An additional current surge is therefore likely at the changeover stage, causing further voltage dip and so affect other consumers. *Closed transition* starters overcome this because the motor is never actually disconnected from the supply during the starting cycle. Most autotransformer starters used the closed transition method.

A typical circuit *closed transition* starter circuit is shown in Fig. 4.11.

The switching sequence for this starter circuit is as follows:

power circuit operation	control circuit operation
manual closing of fused-isolator Q1	control circuit voltage available (e.g. 110V from control transformer)
closing KM1: star connection of transformer	press start button S2 to close KM1 interlocking of KM3 by KM1 closing of KA1 by KM1
closing of KM2: motor supply via transformer	closing of KM2 by KA1 hold-in of KM2
opening of KM1: star connection opens closing of KM3: direct supply to motor	opening of KM1 by KA1 (after time delay) closing of KM3 by KM1 interlocking of KM1 by KM3
(Note the mechanical interlock of KM1–KM3)	hold-in of KM3 opening of KM2 by KA1
KM3 contactors drops out, motor stop	Stop by S1 button or OCR trip F1

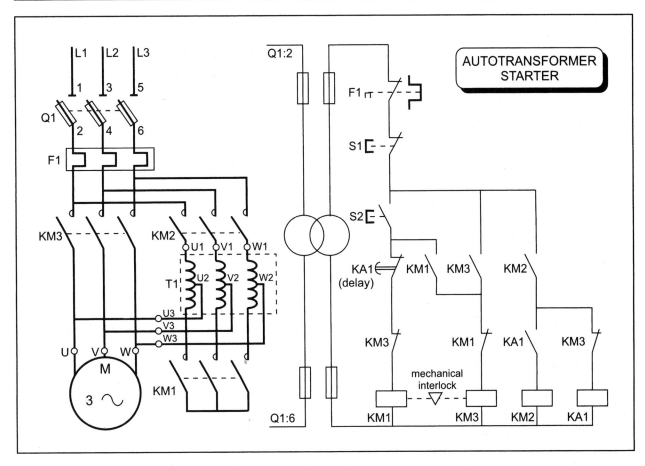

Fig. 4.11 Autotransformer starter circuit.

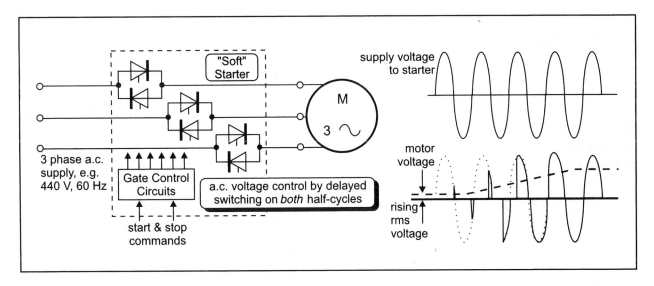

Fig. 4.12 "Soft" starter block diagram.

❏ "Soft" Starting

This method of supplying a gradually increasing a.c. voltage during start-up generally refers to an efficient *electronic* switching technique.

A basic method shown in Fig. 4.12, is to use back-to-back connected *thyristors* or *triacs* in the supply lines which are "gated" to delay "turn-on" within each a.c. half-cycle. This delayed switching applies a reduced average a.c. voltage to the motor.

The applied motor voltage is gradually ramped up by the starter software program until the full voltage level is reached. To achieve maximum efficiency, the electronic switching circuit can now be bypassed for normal running.

A *"soft"* starter may be further adapted to become a voltage controller over the motor operating load range. In this type of efficient *"energy manager"* application, the controller monitors the motor power factor which is a measure of the motor loading. On light load and full voltage, the power factor is low so the controller reduces the motor voltage which reduces current while improving power factor and efficiency. Note, this type of "soft-start/energy manager" is *not* a speed controller. To electrically change the speed of an induction motor it is necessary to vary the applied *frequency*. Motor speed control methods are outlined in a later section.

QUESTION

Estimate and compare the likely starting current surges for a motor that takes 200 A on full load when started:

(a) DOL

(b) Star-Delta

(c) Autotransformer with a 50% tapping.

ANSWER

(a) When starting DOL the initial surge current is about $5 \times FLC$, i.e. 1000 A.

(b) A *star-delta* starter reduces the initial starting surge to one-third of the equivalent DOL value, i.e. to about 330 A in this case.

(c) The autotransformer method reduces the initial starting surge to $(x)^2.I_{DOL}$ where x = tapping point.

In this example $x = 0.5$, so the surge current level is $0.5^2.1000 = 250$ A.

The DOL starter is simple and cheap but causes a large starting surge. *Star-delta* starting reduces the surge but is somewhat more complex, requiring three contactors and a timer. The autotransformer method can be arranged to match the motor surge current and run-up period to meet the supply limitations by a suitable choice of voltage tapping. This starter is considerably more expensive than the other two starter types.

4.7. Speed Control

The standard cage-rotor a.c. induction motor operates as an almost constant speed drive over its load range. This feature is satisfactory for most of the ship's auxiliary services supplying power to ventilation fans and circulating pumps.

Variable speed control is necessary for cranes, winches, windlass, capstans, forced-draught fans etc. Ship's electric propulsion with electronic speed control may use d.c. motors or a.c. induction motors for low/medium power applications. Large power electric propulsion, e.g. for a passenger cruise ship, will use a.c. synchronous motors – see Chapter Eight.

Two main forms of speed change/control are available:

- Pole-changing for induction motors to give two or more fixed speeds, e.g. 2-speed forced-draught fans and 3-speed winches

- Continuously variable speed control, e.g. smooth control of deck cranes, winches and electric ship propulsion using variable frequency

Fixed set speeds can be obtained from a cage-rotor induction motor by using a dual wound stator winding, each winding being designed to create a different number of magnetic poles.

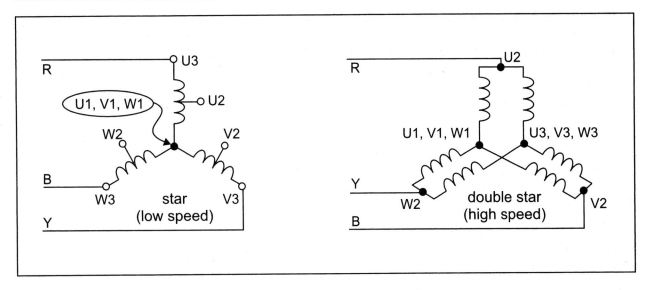

Fig. 4.13 Star-double star connections.

QUESTION

A dual-wound induction motor is arranged to create 6 pole and 10 pole stator magnetic fields. Estimate the rated speeds assuming that the rotor slips by 5% and the power supply is at a frequency of 60 Hz.

ANSWER

From $f = n_s \cdot p$ we get $n_s = f/p$
[where n_s is the synchronous speed of the rotating magnetic flux]
so, at high speed (6 poles, p = 3),
   $n_s = 60/3 = 20$ *rev/s or 1200 rpm*
but rotor runs at
   $n_R = 95\% \cdot 20 = 19$ *rev/s or 1140 rpm*

and, at low speed (10 pole, p = 5),
   $n_s = 60/5 = 12$ *rev/s or 720 rpm*
but rotor runs at
   $n_R = 95\% \cdot 12 = 11.4$ *rev/s or 684 rpm*

A 3-speed pole-change winch motor can be arranged by having two cage rotors mounted on the same drive shaft. One stator winding (usually 24-pole) gives a low speed while the other is dual wound to give medium speed (8-pole) and high speed (4-pole) outputs.

Speed control and drive direction are achieved by a set of switching and reversing contactors operated from the winch control pedestal. Remember that to reverse the rotation of an induction motor it is necessary to switch over two of the supply lines to the stator winding.

An alternative method giving two fixed speeds in a 2:1 ratio from a cage-rotor induction motor is to use a single stator winding which has centre-tap connections available on each phase. This method uses a starter with a set of contactors to switch the phase windings into either *single-star* (low speed) or *double-star* (high speed). The supply lines to the stator windings are shown in Fig. 4.13.

Note that two of the supply lines are interchanged in the *double-star* connection – this is to maintain the same direction of rotation as in the low speed connection.

A continuously variable speed range of motor control involves more complication and expense than that required to obtain a couple of set speeds. Various methods are available which include:

- Electro-hydraulic drive.
- Wound-rotor resistance control of induction motors.
- Ward-Leonard d.c. motor drive.
- Variable-frequency induction or synchronous motor control.

The electro-hydraulic drive, often used for deck crane control, has a relatively simple electrical section. This is a constant single-speed induction motor supplied from a *DOL* or *star-delta* starter. The motor runs continuously to maintain oil pressure to the variable-speed hydraulic motors.

A crude form of speed control is provided by the *wound rotor* induction motor. The rotor has a 3-phase winding (similar to its stator winding) which is connected to 3 sliprings mounted on the shaft as shown in Fig. 4.14. An external 3-phase resistor bank is connected to brushes on the rotor sliprings. A set of contactors or a slide wiper (for small motors) varies the amount of resistance added to the rotor circuit.

Increasing the value of external resistance decreases the rotor speed. Generally, the starters of wound-rotor motors are interlocked to allow start-up only when maximum rotor resistance is in circuit. This has the benefits of reducing the starting current surge while providing a high starting torque.

The wound-rotor arrangement is more expensive than an equivalent cage-rotor machine. It requires more maintenance on account of the sliprings and the external resistor bank which may require special cooling facilities.

Where continuously variable speed has to be combined with high torque, smooth acceleration, including inching control and regenerative braking, it is necessary to consider the merits of a d.c. motor drive. Speed and torque control of a d.c. motor is basically simple requiring the variation of armature voltage and field current.

The problem is: where does the necessary d.c. power supply come from on a ship with an a.c. electrical system?

A traditional method for lifts, cranes and winches is found in the *Ward-Leonard* drive as shown in Fig. 4.15. Here a constant speed induction motor drives a d.c. generator which in turn supplies one or more d.c. motors. The generator output voltage is controlled by adjusting its small excitation current via the speed regulator. The d.c. motor speed is directly controlled by the generator voltage.

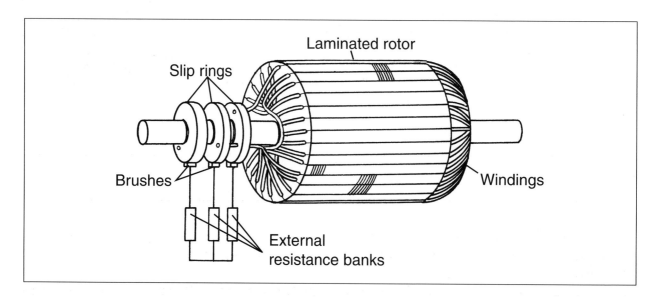

Fig. 4.14 Wound rotor construction.

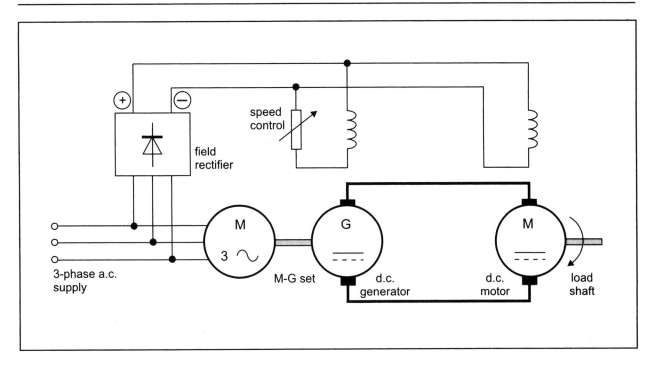

Fig. 4.15 Ward Leonard speed control method.

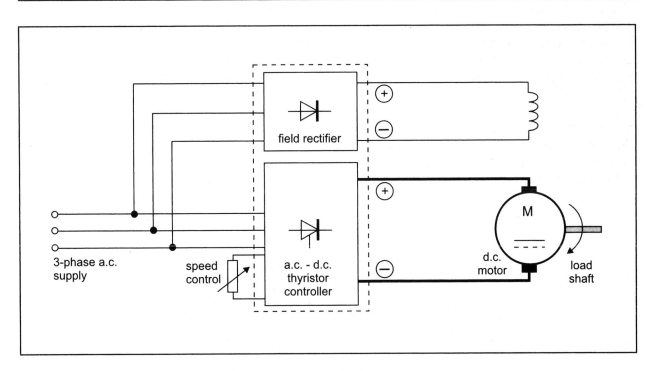

Fig. 4.16 Electronic control for a d.c. motor.

Obviously the motor-generator (M-G) set requires space and maintenance. An alternative is to replace the rotary M-G set with a static electronic thyristor controller which is supplied with constant a.c. voltage but delivers a variable d.c. output voltage to the drive motor as shown in Fig. 4.16.

Although the Ward-Leonard scheme provides an excellent power drive, practical commutators are limited to

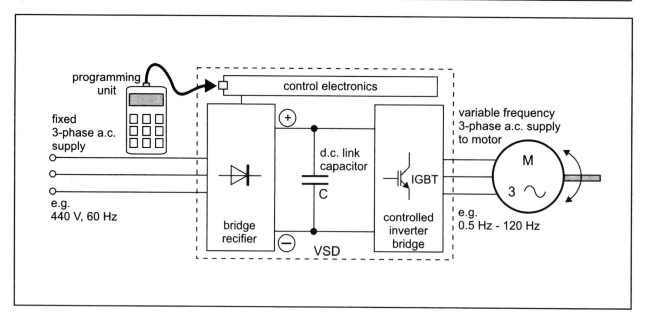

Fig. 4.17 Electronic VSD controller.

about 750 V d.c. maximum which also limits the upper power range. The commutators on the d.c. machines also demand an increased maintenance requirement.

To eliminate these problems means returning to the simplicity of the cage-rotor induction motor. However, the only way to achieve a continuously variable speed output by electrical control is to vary the supply *frequency* to the motor. A static electronic *transistor* or *thyristor* (high power) controller can be used to generate such a variable *frequency* output to directly control the *speed* of the motor as in the example diagram in Fig. 4.17.

In an electronic variable speed drive (VSD), the fixed a.c. input is rectified and smoothed by a capacitor to a steady *d.c. link* voltage (about 600 V d.c. from a 440 V rms a.c. supply). The d.c. voltage is then *chopped* into *variable-width*, but constant level, voltage pulses in the computer controlled inverter section using IGBTs (insulated gate bipolar transistors). This process is called *pulse width modulation* or PWM. See Fig. 4.18. By varying the pulse widths and polarity

of the d.c. voltage it is possible to generate an *averaged sinusoidal a.c.* output over a wide range of frequencies. Due to the smoothing effect of the motor inductance, the motor *currents* appear to be approximately sinusoidal in shape. By directing the currents in sequence into the three stator winding a reversible rotating magnetic field is produced at a frequency set by the PWM modulator.

Accurate control of shaft torque, acceleration time and braking are a few of the many operational parameters that can be programmed into the VSD, usually via a hand-held unit. The VSD can be closely *tuned* to the connected motor drive to achieve optimum control and protection features for the overall drive. Speed regulation against load changes is very good and can be made very precise by the addition of feedback from a shaft speed encoder.

VSDs, being digitally controlled, can be easily networked to other computer devices e.g. programmable logic controllers (PLCs) for the overall control of a complex process.

A disadvantage of *chopping* large currents with such a drive creates *harmonic voltages*

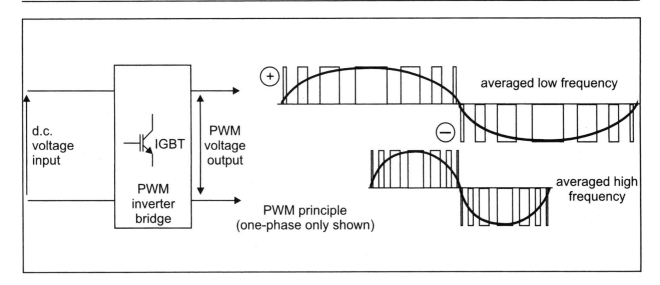

Fig. 4.18 PWM control method.

back into the power supply network. A harmonic voltage waveform is a *distorted* sinusoidal waveshape.

The analysis (not covered here) of a distorted waveshape reveals a set of sinusoidal *harmonic* voltages super-imposed upon the base (or fundamental) frequency. Harmonic frequencies are *integer* (whole number) multiples of the fundamental frequency. In an a.c. system, even numbered harmonics are conveniently self-cancelling as are multi-ples of *three* in a 3-phase network. This leaves harmonic numbered frequencies of 5, 7, 11, 13, 17, 19 etc. Fortunately, the higher the harmonic number the *lower* is the *amplitude* of the harmonic voltage. For a 60 Hz fundamental (1st harmonic), a 5th harmonic would be at a frequency of 300 Hz and a 7th harmonic would be at 420 Hz. The *amplitude* of a 5th harmonic may be up to about 20% of the fundamental while the 7th will be down to about 14% and so on.

Such harmonic voltage disturbances caused by current switching can interfere with other equipment connected to the power system. – e.g. progressive insulation breakdown due to high voltage spikes, flickering of the lighting, malfunction of low current devices such as electronic computers and instru-mentation/control circuits.

Minimising harmonic disturbance involves good circuit design and the fitting of *harmonic filters* adjacent to the VSD drive. A harmonic filter is a com-bination of inductance and capacitance units *tuned* to absorb the unwanted frequencies.

Be guided by the manufacturers' installation notes regarding the need for filters, acceptable cable rating and length, earthing and bonding etc. before fitting such a drive.

Very large drives use *thyristor* converters and *synchronous* motors, e.g. for ship's electric propulsion as outlined in Chapter Eight.

4.8. Motor Protection

The circuits in Fig. 4.19 show typical motor control circuits on LV and HV supplies.

In the HV motor protection scheme above, the back-up fuses are the *trigger* type. This type of fuse releases a trigger actuated by a spring held in tension until the element melts. When released,

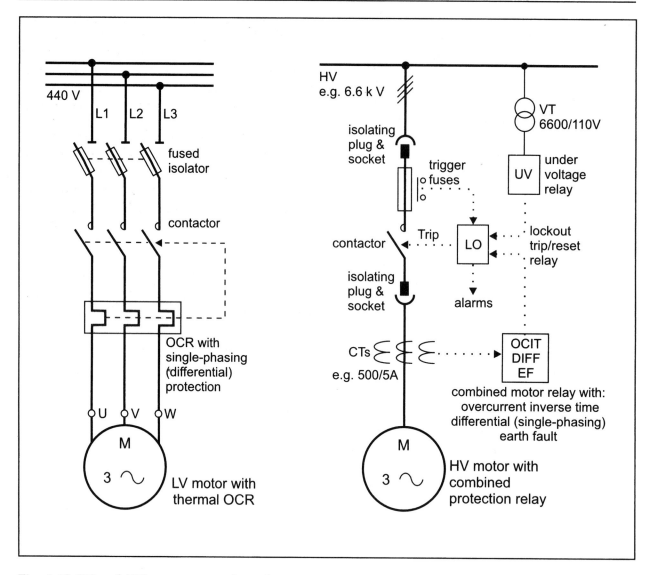

Fig. 4.19 LV and HV motor protection scheme.

the trigger may be used to indicate a blown fuse or to trip a circuit breaker or contactor. Trigger fuses are an additional protection against a single-phasing fault so that the motor is definitely tripped out when a single fuse blows.

Protecting an electric motor basically involves preventing the motor from getting too hot. Remember, every 10°C above the maximum recommended temperature of the insulation can reduce its working life by half. Obviously, the best way to protect a motor against overheating is to directly monitor the temperature of the motor windings. If the temperature exceeds the maximum

set value for the motor insulation its contactor is tripped to stop the motor and allow it to cool down.

Three main types of direct temperature sensors can be used. These are:

• Thermocouple

• Resistance temperature device (RTD)

• Thermistor

The *thermistor sensor* is probably the most common as its thermal characteristic more closely matches that of a motor than the other types. Thermistors are small pellets of semiconductor material which are embedded into the insulation of all three motor stator windings during manufacture. When a thermistor gets hot its resistance changes dramatically. They are connected so that if the motor temperature gets too high the starter contactor will be tripped by an electronic protection relay to stop the motor.

Direct thermistor protection is usually only fitted to large motors, e.g. bow thrusters, FD fans, air conditioning compressors, etc.

Most motors are protected by monitoring the temperature *indirectly* by measuring the current flowing in the supply lines. This method uses electronic, thermal or electromagnetic time-delayed overcurrent relays (OCRs) in the motor starter. The system is designed so that if the motor takes too much current because it is mechanically overloaded, the OCR will trip out the contactor coil, after a pre-set time delay, *before* severe overheating can occur.

The largest *overcurrent* possible is the current taken when the motor has stalled. This, of course, is the starting current of the motor which will be about five times the full load current. The contactor is capable of tripping this stalled current quickly and safely.

If a *short-circuit* occurs in the motor, the starter, or the supply cable, then a huge *fault* current will flow. If the

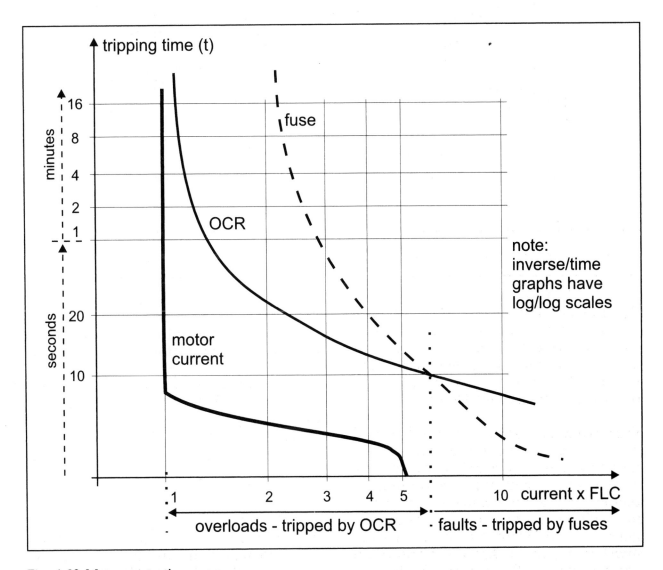

Fig. 4.20 Motor protection curves.

contactor tries to open under short-circuit conditions, serious arcing will occur at its contacts such that it may fail to *interrupt* the fault current. The prolonged short-circuit current will cause serious damage to the motor, starter and cable with the attendant risk of an electrical fire. To prevent this, a set of fuses or a circuit breaker is fitted upstream of the contactor which will trip out almost instantaneously thereby protecting the contactor during a *short-circuit* fault.

It is important that the tripping characteristics, as shown in Fig. 4.20, of the OCR and fuses/circuit breaker are co-ordinated so that the contactor trips on *thermal overcurrent* while the fuses/circuit breaker interrupt short-circuit fault currents. This *contactor + fuse* arrangement is usually called *back-up* protection.

QUESTION

At what value of current should the OCR be set?

ANSWER

To protect a modern CMR (Continuous Maximum Rating) motor the thermal OCR should be set at the full-load current (FLC) rating of the motor. This will ensure that tripping will not occur within 2 hours at 105% FLC. At 120% FLC tripping will occur within 2 hours.

It must be emphasised that the motor fuses are not chosen for their rated current but for their *inverse* current/time (I/t) characteristic. This means that the current rating of fuses used to protect a motor does not appear to have any direct relationship to the FLC rating of the motor.

Fuses used for back-up protection for motor circuits have a special time/current characteristic. They are generally carrying steady currents well below their rated capacity to allow for short duration DOL starting currents without *blowing*. Consequently they do not protect against normal overloads but do protect the motor and supply system against a *short-circuit* fault. Fuses designed for motor circuit *back-up* protection have a restricted continuous current rating (called "M" rating) as compared with their fusing characteristic.

Hence a typical fuse designation for motor circuits could be "32M63" which indicates a continuous rating of 32 A but a rating of 63 A for the starting period.

QUESTION

A motor is protected by a thermal OCR and back-up fuses. Can the motor exceed its rated temperature without being tripped by the protection?

ANSWER

Yes!
Although overheating is usually indicated by the current drawn by the motor rising above its rated value, a number of other situations can contribute to motor overheating.

For example: very high ambient temperature; inadequate ventilation; a *star-delta* starter stuck in the *star* connection; stopping and starting too often; worn or dry shaft bearings.

The motor windings can only be protected against these conditions by using *direct thermal* protection.

There are three types of overcurrent relay (OCR) used for motor protection:

- Electronic

- Thermal

- Electromagnetic

Electronic OCIT (overcurrent inverse time) relays have largely superseded

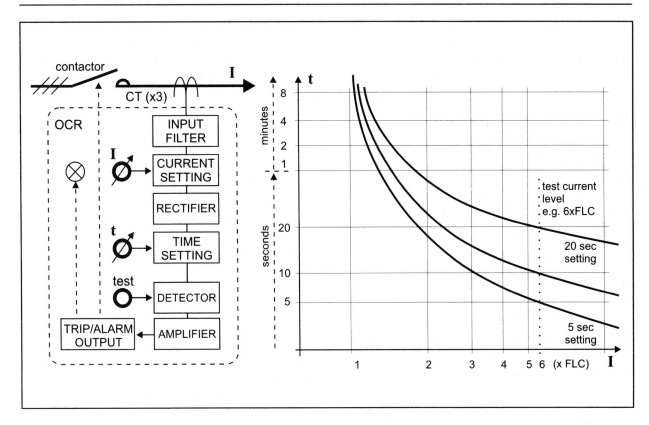

Fig. 4.21 Electronic overcurrent relay and I/t curves.

electromagnetic types as they have no moving parts (except for their output trip relay) and their very reliable tripping characteristics can be closely matched to the motor circuit. Such relays are robust, smaller and lighter than the equivalent electromagnetic type.

A block diagram of such an electronic OCR is shown in Fig. 4.21.

The block diagram of the electronic OCIT relay shows that the current and time settings can be adjusted over a limited range to match the motor FLC and run-up time. A self-test of the OCR performance can usually be applied with a fixed setting of, typically, 6 x FLC and the tripping-time can be measured and compared against the manufacturers current/time characteristics.

Although electromagnetic devices with time delays can give adequate protection against large, sustained overloads to motors which are operated well below their maximum output and temperature,

they have been found to be inadequate for continuous maximum rated (CMR) motors.

Most LV motors are protected by less expensive *thermal* OCRs. Inverse-time thermal OCRs usually work with bi-metal strips as shown in Fig. 4.22. The strips are heated by the motor current and bend depending on the temperature. If the motor takes an overload current, the strips operate a normally-closed (NC) contact which trips out the line contactor to stop the motor.

The minimum tripping current of such a device can be adjusted over a small range. This adjustment alters the distance the strips have to bend before operating the trip contact.

For larger motors, the heaters do not carry the full motor current. They are supplied from current transformers (CTs) which proportionally step-down the motor current so that smaller heater components may be used.

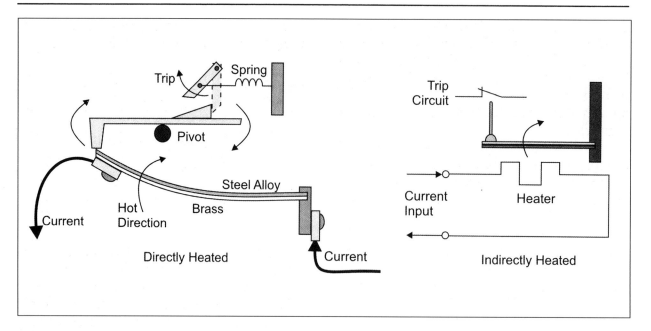

Fig. 4.22 Bi-metallic overcurrent action action.

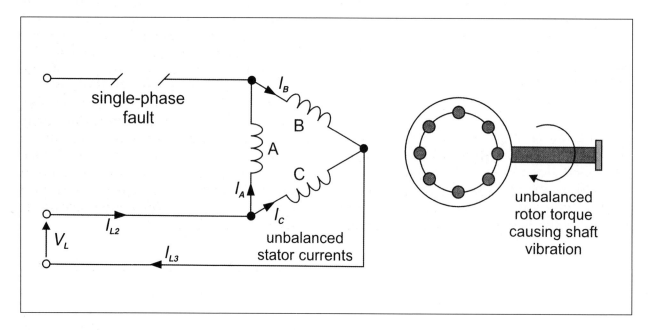

Fig. 4.23 Single-phasing fault.

To operate correctly, induction motors must be connected to a three phase a.c. supply. Once started they may continue to run even if one of the three supply lines becomes disconnected. This is called *single-phasing* and can result in motor burn-out.

Single-phasing, as shown in Fig. 4.23, is usually caused when one of the three

back-up fuses blows or if one of the contactor contacts is open-circuited. The effect of single-phasing is to increase the current in the two remaining lines and cause the motor to become very noisy due to the uneven torque produced in the rotor.

An increase in line current due to single-phasing will be detected by the protective OCR. The three thermal elements of an OCR are arranged in such a way that *unequal* heating of the bi-metal strips causes a differential movement which operates the OCR switch contacts to trip out the motor contactor.

For large HV machines a separate device, called a *negative phase sequence* (NPS) relay, is used to measure the amount of *unbalance* in the motor currents.

For *star* connected motor windings the phase and line currents are equal so the line connected OCR is correctly sensing the winding current. If the overcurrent setting is exceeded during a single-phase fault the motor will be tripped off.

The situation is not so simple with a *delta* connected motor. Normally the line current divides phasorally between two phases of the motor windings.

The phase current is just over half the line current as

$$I_{PH} = \frac{I_L}{\sqrt{3}} = 0.577\, I_L.$$

When one of the lines becomes open-circuited a balanced three phase condition no longer exists. Now the sets of line and phase currents are no longer *balanced*.

The table below shows typical values of line and phase currents at various levels of motor loading during a single-phasing fault as shown in Fig. 4.23.

Healthy condition (balanced)	Single-phasing fault condition (unbalanced)		
% of rated FLC	% of rated FLC		
	I_{L2} and I_{L3}	I_A and I_B	I_C
60	102	62	131
70	130	79	161
100	243	129	185

Particularly note that the current in winding C is considerably higher than that in the other two windings.

Look at the condition where the motor is at 60% of full load when single-phasing occurs: the line currents are 102% of the full-load value but the current in winding C is 131% of its full-load value. The 102% line current will probably *not* activate a line connected OCR and the motor remains connected. However, the local overheating in winding C of the motor will quickly result in damage.

Motors can he protected against this condition by using a *differential* type relay which trips out with *unbalanced* currents. In fact, most modern *thermal* OCRs for motors have this protection against single-phasing incorporated as a normal feature. A *differential* action is shown in Fig. 4.24.

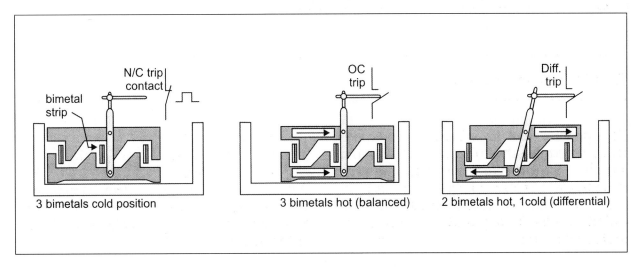

Fig. 4.24 Bi-metallic single-phasing protection (differential action).

If single-phasing occurs when in operation on light load, the motor keeps on running unless the protection trips the contactor. If the motor is stopped, it will not restart. When the contactor is closed, the motor will take a large starting current but develop no *rotating* torque. The OCR is set to allow the starting current to flow long enough for the motor, under normal conditions, to run up to speed. With no ventilation on the stationary motor, this time delay will result in rapid and severe overheating. Worse still, if the operator makes several attempts to restart the motor, it will burn out. If a motor fails to start after two attempts, you must investigate the cause.

Undervoltage protection is necessary in a distribution system that supplies motors. If there is a total voltage loss or *black-out*, all the motors must be disconnected from the supply. This is to prevent all the motors restarting together which would result in a huge current surge, tripping out the generator again. Motors must be restarted in a controlled sequence after a supply failure.

Undervoltage (UV) protection for LV motors is simply provided by the spring-loaded motor contactor because it will drop out when the supply voltage is lost. For large HV motor the UV protection function will be covered by a relay separate from the OCR function or it may be part of a special motor relay which incorporates all of the necessary protection functions.

When the supply voltage becomes available, the motor will not restart until its contactor coil is energised. This will usually require the operator to press the *stop/reset* button before initiating the start sequence.

For essential loads, the restart may be performed automatically by a *sequence restart* system. This system ensures that essential services are restarted automatically on restoration of supply following a blackout. Timer relays in the starters of essential motor circuits are set to initiate start-up in a controlled sequence.

4.9. Single Phase Motors

Low power motors for power tools, domestic equipment, refrigerators, vacuum cleaners etc are typically supplied at 220 V a.c. 50/60 Hz.

Common types are:

- Split-phase induction motor
- Capacitor start/run induction motor
- Shaded pole induction motor
- a.c. commutator motor

- Split-phase induction motor:

A single phase induction motor has a *cage* rotor similar to that used in a three phase type. A single stator winding produces a *pulsating* magnetic field when energised with single-phase a.c. current. This field cannot exert a *rotating* force on the cage rotor.

One method used to produce a rotational force is to employ *two* stator windings fitted 90° to each other with both connected across the same supply. This is the split-phase motor. To get the effect of a shifting magnetic field (and hence induce a rotating force into the rotor), one winding is electrically *phase-shifted* by adding capacitance in series with one of the windings.

- Capacitor start/run induction motor:

When the motor has started to run, the additional phase winding circuit may be disconnected and the rotor will continue to be pulsed around by the magnetic flux. This is called a *capacitor start* motor which is only useful for driving a very light load.

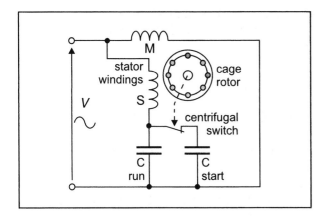

Fig. 4.25 Capacitor-start motor circuit.

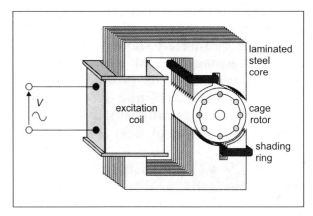

Fig. 4.26 Shaded-pole motor construction.

For starting *and* running, two capacitors are used in circuit as shown in Fig. 4.25.

During the starting period the two paralleled capacitors create a large phase angle to the "S" winding current. As the rotor runs up to speed a switch cuts out one of the capacitors. The switch may be a centrifugal type on the rotor shaft or a current-operated time-delay relay in the motor terminal box. This type of motor gives good starting and running torque with reasonable power factor. Most split phase motors are arranged for a 4-pole stator winding so at 50 Hz its synchronous (flux) speed will be 25 rev/s or 1500 rpm. As with all induction motors, the rotor will *slip* causing the shaft speed to be about 24 rev/s or 1440 rpm on no-load. On-load, a single-phase induction motor will run with greater slip and operate with less efficiency, than a three phase version.

• Shaded pole induction motor:

This is a low torque machine useful for low power drives such as small cooling fans in ovens and electronic equipment.

Fig. 4.26 shows how the face of each salient stator pole is partially split with one side carrying a thick copper wire called a *shading ring*. The pulsating a.c. flux divides into each half of the pole but is time delayed in the part with the

sshading ring. This is due to an induced current in the *ring* which opposes flux change in the *shaded* part. To the rotor, this delay appears as a flux *shift* across the overall pole face which drags the rotor with it by the normal induction motor action. Obviously, the developed torque is small and the machine is not very efficient but is an inexpensive drive for very low power applications. As with all induction motors the shaft base speed is fixed by the supply frequency, so at 50 Hz the maximum speed is 3000 rpm and shaft loading will cause the rotor to *slip* below this value.

• a.c. commutator motor:

This is basically a d.c. series motor. construction designed to operate very effectively on an a.c. voltage supply. See Fig. 4.27.

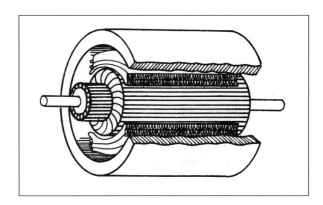

Fig. 4.27 Commutator motor construction.

The shaft torque produced is given by $T \propto \Phi.I$ where Φ is the flux produced by the series connected stator winding and I is the armature (and supply) current in the rotor. As Φ is produced by the same current the torque is essentially $T \propto I^2$ which makes this single phase a.c. motor more powerful than the induction types.

At 220 V a.c. the shaft speed on light load is typically 12,000 to 18,000 rpm and is easily controlled by an additional series resistance or an electronic voltage regulator. The speed falls rapidly with increased load torque.

This type of motor is mainly used intermittently in equipment's rated up to a few hundreds of watts. Typical examples would include power drills, sanders, jig-saws, food-mixers and vacuum cleaners.

The commutator and brush contacts will cause some sparking in normal operation which can cause radio/television interference so a high frequency voltage suppressor is usually fitted to this type of motor.

4.10. Maintenance

The maintenance requirements for cage-rotor induction motors are very simple:

- Keep insulation resistance high and contact resistance low

- Lubricate correctly and maintain a uniform air gap

- Ensure both the interior and exterior are always clean and dry

Provided these requirements are met, an induction motor should give trouble-free service during its long life.

QUESTION

What is the most common cause of induction motor failure?

ANSWER

Failure of stator insulation due to dampness is a major problem with marine motors.

Open ventilated motors are most at risk, particularly when they are not used for long periods.

Anti-condensation heaters should be regularly checked to see that they are actually working and keeping the motor dry.

For all motors, cleanliness is next to godliness. A regular cleaning routine is required to remove harmful deposits of dust, dirt, grease and oil from both inside and outside the motor. The cleaning of the external surface is especially important for totally enclosed motors which run continuously. The heat generated in these motors is removed through the external surface. A thick layer of dust will reduce the heat dissipation and result in very high temperatures. Internal dust and dirt in open ventilated motors must be regularly removed by blowing or extraction and ventilation screens and ducts cleared out.

If motors are to be blown out, the air used must be absolutely dry and the pressure should not be more than 1.75 bar. If the pressure is higher than this it forces the dust *into* the winding insulation rather than removing it.

When blowing out a motor remember to cover up other machines in the area to protect them from flying dust. Suction cleaning is better than blowing out.

QUESTION

How often should a motor be cleaned?

ANSWER

Basically this will be determined by the local conditions and the type of ventilation. Only the external surfaces of totally enclosed motors will require *regular* cleaning. But both the outside and inside of open ventilated motors will require routine attention. The inside of a totally enclosed motor can be cleaned if the motor has been dismantled for bearing replacement. Motors in areas where considerable amounts of air-borne dust are expected, hatch-cover motors are an example, will obviously require more frequent cleaning.

Contamination by oil and grease from motor bearings is often a cause of insulation failure. The insulation should be cleaned by brushing or spraying with one of the many proprietary brands of cleaning fluid which are available. Badly contaminated motors may require total immersion of the stator windings in cleaning fluid.

Broken or missing bearing covers must be repaired or replaced to prevent grease escaping.

When a motor has been dismantled for cleaning and overhaul it should be thoroughly inspected. In this way, faults can be detected *before* they evolve into a major breakdown.

- Stator

Look at the stator windings for damaged insulation caused by careless replacement of the rotor into the stator. Discoloured insulation is an indication that the winding has been overheated. The cause of overheating must be found and corrected before allowing the motor back into service.

Carefully examine the stator core for signs of *rubbing* with the rotor, usually caused by a worn bearing. Even slight rubbing of the rotor against the stator will generate enough heat to destroy the stator insulation. Replace the bearings before putting the motor back into service.

Laminated steel core plates which have been badly scored may cause a local hot spot to be generated when the motor is running. This is because the Fe (*iron*) losses will increase in the damaged area. After the motor has been put back into service with new bearings, check the motor running temperature. After a short period of service dismantle the motor and check for discolouration at the core damage which will indicate local heating. If you suspect core hot spots then the motor core will need to be dismantled for the laminations to be cleaned and re-insulated – *definitely* a shore job.

The insulation resistance reading is the best indication as to the presence of moisture in the motor windings. Breakdowns due to insulation failure usually result in an earth fault, short-circuited turns in a phase or phase-to-phase faults.

QUESTION

How do you check the insulation resistance between phases on an induction motor?

ANSWER

Larger motors are usually *six-terminal*, which means that all six ends of the stator windings are brought out to the terminal block. Links between the terminals are used to *star* or *delta* connect the motor. Disconnect the supply leads and remove the links. Test between phases with an insulation resistance tester as shown in Fig. 4.28.

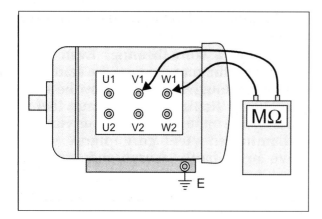

Fig. 4.28 Motor IR test.

A problem can arise on small, *three-terminal* motors where the *star* or *delta* connection is made inside the motor. Only one end of each winding is available at the terminal block. Phase-to-phase insulation resistance *cannot* be checked. If a three terminal motor is to be rewound, ask the repairer to convert it to a six terminal arrangement.

- Bearings

Induction motors are fitted with ball and/or roller bearings. These bearings are robust and reliable and should give very little trouble provided they are properly fitted, kept absolutely clean and lubricated correctly. Many engineers argue that if a bearing seems to be operating correctly it should not be tampered with.

Portable vibration detection results, sampled periodically and analysed can be a very useful way to recognise the onset of a bearing failure. Bearing temperature, e.g. using embedded detectors or with portable *Infra Red* (IR) spot checks, is another indicator the general health of a shaft bearing.

Otherwise, it is not easy to predict (with any degree of certainty) the unexpired life of bearings that have already run for some time. Also, inspection may not show damage to raceways and rolling elements in areas hidden from view. The best policy is to renew the bearings as part of a planned maintenance programme. If this is not possible because of cost or a shortage of replacements, then bearings should be removed, cleaned and inspected for signs of damage before a decision to refit or renew is taken.

Before opening up a bearing, make sure that the complete area around the housing is clean and dry. Manufacturers recommend that bearings should be removed from the shaft as seldom as possible, but cleaning and inspection is best done with the bearing *off* the shaft. If the correct size of wedges or pullers is used, then removal should not cause any damage. Bearings should be cleaned by immersion in a solvent such as clean white spirit or clean paraffin, then thoroughly dried in a jet of clean, dry compressed air. Bearings should not be spun by the air jet because skidding can damage the rolling elements and raceways.

Once dry, the bearing must be lightly oiled. Any traces of metal particles, such as brass, indicate cage wear and the bearing must be replaced. If there is no evidence of metal particles, carefully examine the raceways and rolling elements for signs of wear or damage. Hold the inner race in one hand and slowly turn the outer race. Any sticking or unevenness in the rotation requires a re-wash of the bearing and rotation in the cleaning fluid. If the sticking persists the bearing must be rejected. Similarly, bearings with visible signs of corrosion, overheating or damage, and those with a noticeable degree of roughness in rotation should also be replaced.

When fitting a bearing to a shaft, first clean the shaft and apply a thin film of light oil. Set the bearing square on the shaft and, with a tubular drift (pipe), force the bearing against the shaft shoulder. The drift should bear on the inner race as close to the shaft as possible. Large bearings can be heated for 10–15 minutes in clean mineral oil up to 80°C to facilitate fitting. Lubricate the bearings with the correct type and quantity of grease as recommended by the manufacturer. Fill the bearing about one third to one half full with grease. Overgreasing causes churning and friction which results in heating, oxidation of the grease and possible leakage through the seals.

On account of the high ambient temperature and excessive vibration which many marine motors endure, grease life can be short and fresh grease should be applied at regular intervals. Unless the bearing housing has a vent hole to allow excess grease to escape, it will be necessary to clean out the bearing housing before charging it with fresh grease. Because of the vibration on ships, bearings can be damaged when the motor is not running.

The shafts of *stationary* motors should be periodically rotated a quarter turn to minimise vibration damage to the bearings.

- Rotor

As you will have gathered, maintenance of cage-rotor induction motors tends to mainly involve the stator windings and bearings. Cage-rotors require little or no special care in normal service. Inspect for signs of damage and overheating in the cage winding and its laminated steel core. Make sure that all core ventilating ducts are clean and clear. If an internal fan is fitted it must be in good condition if it is to provide adequate cooling.

QUESTION

A cage-rotor induction motor has been flooded with sea water and its insulation resistance is down to zero MΩ. What is the procedure for putting the motor back into service?

ANSWER

The main problem is to restore the insulation resistance of the stator winding to a high value. This is achieved in three stages:

- Cleaning
- Drying
- Re-varnishing

Salt contamination can be removed by washing with clean, fresh water. Any grease or oil on the windings has to be removed using a degreasant liquid such as Armaclean.

Dry the stator windings with low power electric heaters or lamps with plenty of ventilation to allow the dampness to escape.

Alternatively, the windings can be heated by current injection from a welding set or from a special injection transformer. Be sure to keep the injected current level *well below* the motor's full load rating.

With the windings clean and dry, and if the IR test remains high over a few hours, apply a couple of coats of good quality air-drying insulating varnish.

The motor starter and other control equipment should be regularly inspected to check and maintain the following items:

✔ Enclosure:

Check for accumulations of dirt and rust. Any corroded parts must be cleaned and repainted. Examine the starter fixing bolts and its earth bonding connection — particularly where high vibration is present, e.g. in the steering flat and the forecastle.

✔ Contactors and relays:

Check for any signs of overheating and loose connections. Remove any dust and grease from insulating components to prevent voltage breakdown by surface tracking. Ensure that the magnet armature of contactors moves freely. Remove any dirt or rust from magnet faces which may prevent correct closing.

✔ Contacts:

Examine for excessive pitting and roughness due to burning. Copper contacts may be smoothed using a fine file. Copper oxide, which acts as a high resistance, can be removed using glass-paper. *Do not* file silver alloy contacts or remove silver oxide as it acts as a good conductor. A thin smear of electrical contact lubrication helps to prolong the life of all contacts. When contacts have to be replaced, always replace both fixed and moving contacts in pairs.

Check contact spring pressure and compare adjacent contact sets for equal pressure. Examine power and control fuse contacts for signs of overheating — lubricate the contact blades on fuse-holders.

✔ Connections:

Examine all power and control connections for tightness and signs of overheating. Check flexible leads for fraying and brittleness.

✔ Overcurrent relays:

Check for proper settings (relate to motor FLC).

Inspect for dirt, grease and corrosion and for freedom of movement (not possible with an electronic type of OCR).

A thorough OCR *performance test* can only be carried out by calibrated current injection.

✔ Control operation:

Observe the sequence of operation during a normal start-up, control and shut-down of the motor. Particularly look for excessive contact sparking (only possible with open-type contactors). Remember to check the operation of emergency stop and auto-restart functions.

Chapter Five
Ancillary Electrical Services

5.0. Introduction

To ensure a safe working environment, together with off duty comfort in the accommodation quarters on board your ship, a considerable proportion of the generated electric power is absorbed in the *ancillary services*.

Lighting of the ship's deck areas, engine room and accommodation to meet specified levels of illumination is provided by various light fittings (*luminaires*) designed to work safely in their particular locations.

The *hotel* services for food storage, preparation and cooking, together with accommodation air-conditioning and laundry services, are essential for the general maintenance of the mariner.

This chapter will examine ships' lighting and refrigeration/air conditioning together with galley and laundry services. Additionally, hull protection by the impressed current cathodic protection method and battery supplies are also included.

5.1. Ships' Lighting

Historically, the original application of electricity in ships was for lighting. Oil lanterns were a definite fire risk and the ship's lamp trimmer had great difficulty in maintaining his navigation lights in stormy weather.

To meet the safety and comfort levels of illumination required throughout your ship a wide range of lighting fittings (*luminaires*) are used. The power ratings of the lamps used will vary from a few watts for alarm indicator lamps to a few kW for deck floodlights and searchlights (e.g. a Suez Canal Projector Light).

The amount of light falling on a particular area can be checked with a *luminance* meter which is calibrated in *lux (lx)*. One lux is the illumination of one lumen/sq. metre (lm/m²) where a *lumen* is the unit of *luminous flux*.

For example, container loading requires a minimum illumination level of 50 lx while a main engine control room may be illuminated to a level of 500 lx.

The minimum illumination standards for crew spaces in UK registered ships are specified in "The Merchant Shipping (Crew Accommodation) Regulations".

The *luminous efficiency* of a light fitting is defined as the ratio of lumens/watt. This efficiency reduces in time mainly because the lamp deteriorates as the lumens emitted gradually get less while the watts input remains constant. Dirt on the lamp reflector and lamp-glass will also reduce its luminous efficiency.

Group replacement of lamps is often considered by shipping companies to be more economic and convenient than individual replacement following lamp failure. Cleaning of the fittings can also be carried out during group lamp replacement so maintaining a high luminous efficiency.

Lamp end caps are many and various but the most common types are *screw* and *bayonet* fittings. The old names, e.g. Goliath Edison Screw (GES) and Bayonet Cap (BC) are now re-designated to indicate the cap type and its dimensions.

A selection of old names and the current codes are listed below.

The first letter of the current code indicates the cap type (**E**dison or **B**ayonet). The first number indicates the nominal outer diameter of the cap barrel or screw in millimetres (mm). The next number gives the overall length and the final number (if listed) is the diameter of the flange.

Old Code	Description	Current Code
ES	Edison Screw	E27/27
GES	Goliath Edison Screw	E40/45
SES	Small Edison Screw	E14/23 × 15
MES	Miniature Edison Screw	E10/13
LES	Lilliput Edison Screw	E5/9
BC	Bayonet Cap	B22/25 × 26
SBC	Small Bayonet Cap	B15/24 × 17
MCC	Miniature Centre Contact	BA 9s/14

Broadly, the luminaires employ one of two general lamp types classified as:

• *Incandescent*

• *Discharge*

5.2. Incandescent Lamps

The most common lamp used for general lighting is the simple filament type as shown in Fig. 5.1. A current is passed through the thin tungsten wire filament which raises its temperature to around 3000°C when it becomes *incandescent* (it glows).

The glass bulb is filled with an inert gas such as nitrogen or argon which helps to reduce filament evaporation to allow an operating life expectancy of about 1000 hours. Lamp power ratings are available from 15 W to 1000 W.

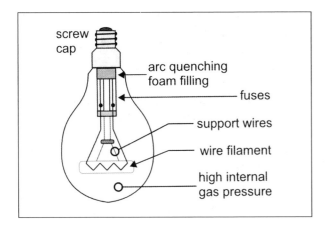

Fig. 5.1 Incandescent lamp construction.

The ordinary filament lamp is called a GLS (general lighting service) lamp. One variation of the basic lamp design has a special *coiled-coil* filament which increases the life expectancy of low power (up to 150 watt) lamps and are referred to as *double-life* lamps. Specially reinforced construction lamps (called *rough-service*) have a tough filament for use in areas where shock and vibration are expected – this type is useful with portable handlamps.

Other variations include: clear glass bulb, inside frosted glass bulb (pearl) to reduce glare, tubular construction, internal reflector lamps, decorative lamps (e.g. candle shape) and heating lamps.

Typical lamp power ratings and average light outputs (for a 240 V supply):

single-coil type		double-coil type	
Power(W)	Light (lm)	Power(W)	Light (lm)
15	150		
25	200		
40	325	40	390
60	575	60	665
		75	885
100	1160	100	1260
150	1960	150	2075
200	2720	For high vibration areas, single coil lamps are preferred as they are more robust than the double-coil type	
300	4300		
500	7700		
750	12,400		
1000	17,300		

QUESTION

Estimate the luminous efficiency of 100 W single-coil and coiled-coil lamps.

ANSWER

Efficiency = Output lumens/input watts
= 1160/100 = 11.6 lm/W and 12.6 lm/W

A popular variation of the incandescent lamp is the *tungsten-halogen* type. This lamp construction has a gas-filled quartz tube or bulb which also includes a halogen vapour such as iodine or bromine. When the filament is heated, evaporated tungsten particles combine with the halogen vapour to form a tungsten-halide. At the high filament temperature, the tungsten vapour re-forms onto the filament. This regenerative process continues repeatedly creating a self-cleaning action on the inner surface of the glass tube or bulb. In an ordinary GLS lamp the tungsten evaporation from the filament causes an internal blackening of the glass bulb which is eliminated in the tungsten-halogen lamp.

Two basic lamp forms for the tungsten-halogen design are the *linear double-ended* lamp (K class) and the *single-ended lamp* (M class) as shown in Fig. 5.2.

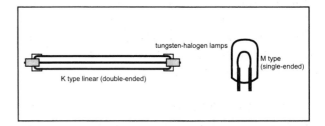

Fig. 5.2 K & M lamp construction.

Linear tungsten-halogen lamps must be used in the horizontal position otherwise the halogen vapour will concentrate at its lower end which results in rapid blackening of the tube and a reduced operating life. Both the linear and bulb type are particularly useful for display, floodlighting and spotlighting.

Examples of tungsten-halogen lamp details:

• Linear double-ended (240 V rated and life expectancy of 2000 hours):

Type	Power (W)	Light output (lm)
K9	300	5000
K1	500	9500
K2 & K3	750	15000
K4	1000	21000
K5	1500	33000
K6 & K8	2000	44000

• Single-ended:

Type	Voltage (V)	Power (W)	Life (hours)	Light output (lm)
M29	6	10	100	210
M30	6	20	100	420
M34	6	20	2000	350
M28	12	100	2000	2150
M32	12	50	2000	900
M35	12	20	250	450
M36	24	250	2000	5750
M38	240	300	2000	5000
M40	240	300	2000	8500

Tungsten-halogen lamps must be carefully handled when being fitted. If the outside surface of the quartz tube or bulb is touched with dirty or greasy hands, premature failure can occur due to fine surface cracks in the glass. Handle the tube by its ends only, or use a paper sleeve over the lamp during fitting. If accidentally handled, the lamp glass may be cleaned with a spirit solvent, carbon tetrachloride or trichlorethylene.

5.3. Discharge Lamps

The light output from a discharge lamp is generated by the flow of current in an electric arc between two electrodes through a gas and metal vapour inside a sealed glass bulb or tube.

The most common metal vapours employed in discharge lamps are:

❏ *Mercury* (as used in a fluorescent tube) and

❏ *Sodium*

Low and high-pressure types of *mercury* and *sodium* lamps are available.

A suitable voltage applied between the electrodes of a discharge lamp causes an arc discharge through the gas. This ionisation of the gas either creates visible light directly or by secondary emission from a phosphor coating on the inside wall of the lamp glass.

The discharge lamp current must be carefully *controlled* to maintain the desired light output and some form of current limiting *ballast* is required. This ballast is often an iron-cored inductor (*choke coil*) but special transformers and electronic regulator ballast circuits are also used. The ballast must *match* the lamp (e.g. a 20 W fluorescent tube must have a matching 20 W ballast unit) to ensure correct lamp operation for high luminous efficiency and long life.

❏ **Mercury Fluorescent**

These are manufactured as low pressure and high pressure lamp types.

• *Low-pressure* mercury fluorescent type

The most obvious example of this type is the popular fluorescent tube as shown in Fig. 5.3.

It is classified as an MCF lamp (M = mercury, C = low pressure, F = fluorescent coating).

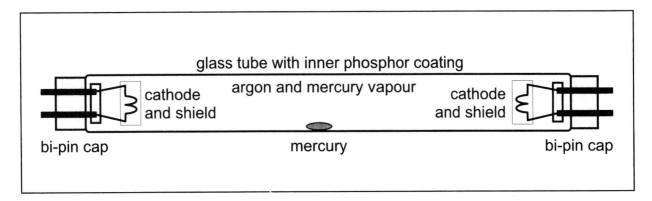

Fig. 5.3 Fluorescent lamp construction.

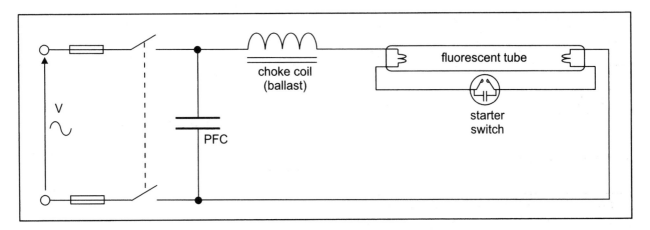

Fig. 5.4 Fluorescent lamp circuit and glow starter.

The inside surface of the glass tube is coated with a fluorescent phosphor which emits white light.

Variations of phosphor material create different light colours of which the most common are called:

- Warm White   Colour 29
- Warm White de luxe Colour 32
- Daylight   Colour 33
- White   Colour 35

Fluorescent tubes are available in lengths from 150 mm to 2400 mm with power ratings from 4 W to 125 W. The tube ends are usually fitted with bi-pin lamp caps or miniature bi-pin for the small tubes. Typical luminous efficiency for a fluorescent tube is about 70 lm/W with an average operating life of 5000 hours.

To *strike* a fluorescent tube, its gas filling (usually argon or krypton) must be ionised by a voltage between its cathodes that is slightly higher than that required to maintain the normal discharge. Two common methods are used to *strike* the tube:

- the switch-start circuit
- the transformer quick-start circuit.

The circuit in Fig. 5.4 shows a typical switch-start circuit.

The starting action is initiated by a *glow* type starter switch which is connected between opposite ends of the tube.

When the supply voltage is applied to the circuit, the full mains voltage appears across the starter switch. A glow

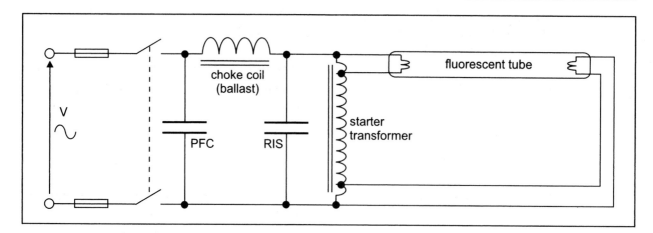

Fig. 5.5 Transformer-start fluorescent lamp circuit.

discharge occurs between the starter contacts which quickly heat up, bend and touch each other. This allows current to flow through the lamp cathodes which will cause the tube ends to heat up and glow before the tube actually strikes. The tube strikes when the starter switch re-opens as it cools down during its closed (non-glow) period. When the starter switch opens it interrupts an inductive coil (choke) circuit which produces a surge voltage across the tube which then *strikes*.

The tube is now *full-away* and the reduced arc voltage across it is not sufficient to re-start the glow discharge in the starter so its contacts remain open. In fact, in the normal running condition, the starter switch can be unplugged from its bayonet cap base and the lamp will function normally. The tube will not, of course, re-strike after switch off without the starter action.

Two or three *strikes* may be required to get the lamp running normally as the starter contacts may open before the cathodes are sufficiently heated. Such *cold-striking* reduces the lamp life by erosion of the cathode material which causes irregular lamp flashing.

In normal operation the choke coil acts as a series reactance to limit the lamp discharge current.

Severe blackening at the tube ends is a sure sign that its useful life is finished.

Each time the starter switch closes, a large current surges through the choke coil which increases its temperature. Excessive lamp flickering must, therefore, be swiftly corrected by lamp or starter replacement. Most choke coils are *potted* in a thermosetting polyester compound within a steel case.

While an earth fault is unlikely to occur within a choke, an open-circuit is possible and can be simply checked using an ohmmeter. No repair of a choke-coil is feasible so it must be completely replaced with an identically rated unit. Similarly, glow starters should only be replaced with an equivalent which matches the size of tube it is to be used with.

An example of a transformer quick-start circuit is shown in Fig. 5.5.

The lamp discharge begins as soon as the cathodes reach their operating temperature. A capacitive effect between the cathodes and the earthed metalwork of the fitting ionises the gas and the tube *strikes* very quickly.

Most tubes have a conducting path through the phosphor coating or, alternatively, a special metal earth strip running between the end caps which assists the starting process. The transformer ballast gives an immediate start but some difficulty can occur with low ambient temperatures, low supply voltage and poor earthing. Many other variations of quick-start circuits using transformers and resonant effects are used.

Capacitors are used with discharge tubes for:

- Power factor correction (PFC)
- Radio interference suppression (RIS).

The PFC capacitor is used to raise the *supply* power factor to around 0.9 lagging. Without this capacitor the power factor may be as low as 0.2 lagging due to the high choke-coil inductance to cause the supply current to be 4 to 5 times larger than normal. For a 125 W tube a PFC value of about 7.2 μF is typical.

Radio interference from discharge tubes is caused by the ionisation process of the discharge through the tube. This is suppressed by a capacitor fitted across the tube ends. In glow-switch circuits, the RIS capacitor is actually fitted within the starter. Typical RIS capacitor values are around 0.0005 μF.

Starter switches with an electronic time-delay can be used to eliminate flicker at switch on.

An *electronic ballast* circuit can be used to improve luminaire efficiency and supply power factor by increasing the lamp frequency to around 30 kHz.

QUESTION

What would happen if the RIS capacitor in a glow-switch failed to a short-circuit?

ANSWER

The tube would not strike but would glow at its ends while the choke may overheat and eventually fail. A similar result would occur if the bi-metal strips of the starter welded together.

- *High-pressure* mercury fluorescent type

A typical high-pressure lamp and its circuit is shown in Fig. 5.6.

This type of lamp is coded as MBF (M = Mercury, B = high pressure, F = fluorescent coating).

An additional suffix to lamp codes may be /U or /V meaning that the lamp is designed for fitting in a *Universal* or *Vertical* position respectively, e.g. MBF/U.

The high-pressure mercury lamp comes in sizes ranging from 50 to 1000 W and is fitted with Edison screw (ES) or Goliath Edison screw (GES) lamp caps. Its luminous efficiency is in the range of 40–60 lm/W with an average life of

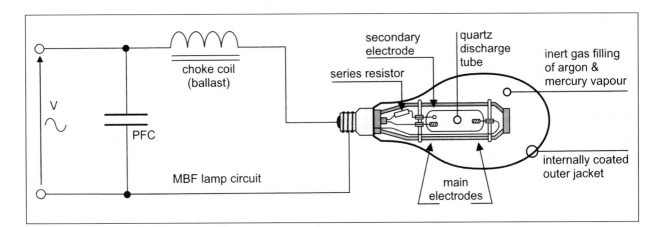

Fig. 5.6 HP mercury lamp and circuit.

around 7500 hours. The lamp takes several minutes to reach full brightness. It will not immediately re-strike when rapidly switched off then back on because the vapour pressure prevents this happening.

Re-striking will occur when the discharge tube has sufficiently cooled down.

Lamp gas ionisation is obtained between a secondary electrode fitted close to one of the main electrodes which warms up the tube and an arc strikes between the main electrodes. Mercury, which was condensed on the tube will now vaporise and the main arc passes through it. The secondary electrode ceases operation as the lamp pressure builds up.

□ **Sodium Vapour**

These, like the mercury lamps, come in low-pressure and high pressure versions.

• Low-pressure sodium vapour type

A low-pressure sodium lamp is coded as SOX (SO = sodium vapour, X = standard single-ended lamp of integral construction).

A typical lamp shape and its circuit is shown in Fig. 5.7.

The lamp has a U-shaped arc tube containing metallic sodium and an inert gas such as neon. Common lamp power ratings are 35 W, 55 W, 90 W, 135 W and 180 W with luminous efficiencies in the range of 120–175 lm/W with an average operating life of 6000 hours.

The low-pressure sodium lamp needs a high voltage (480–650 V) which requires a special transformer ballast or electronic ballast circuit.

When first ignited the SOX lamp gives a red glow as the discharge is initially through the neon gas. As the lamp warms up the sodium begins to evaporate to take over the discharge from the neon causing the lamp colour to change from red to yellow. The time taken to reach full brightness is between 6–15 minutes.

• High-pressure sodium vapour type

A typical lamp and its circuit is shown in Fig. 5.8.

The basic lamp type is coded as SON (SO = Sodium vapour, N = high pressure), but two other variations are labelled as SON-T (a tubular clear glass type) and SON-TD (a tubular double-ended clear quartz type).

The SON lamp gives a wide spread of illumination with a golden-white light. Lamp starting is achieved by a high voltage pulse from an electronic igniter circuit which ceases to function once the main arc has been struck.

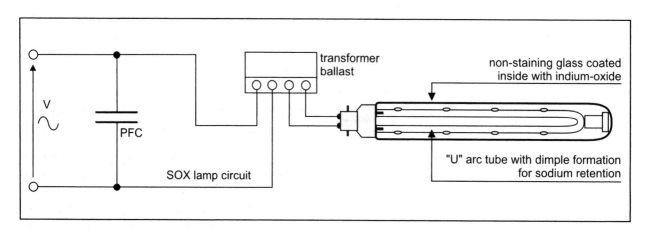

Fig. 5.7 SOX lamp and circuit.

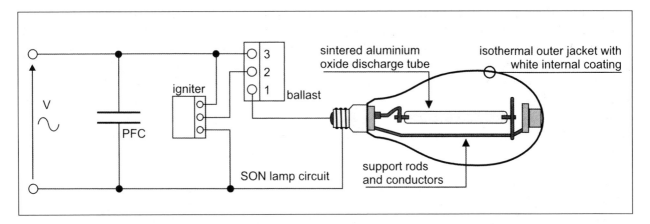

Fig. 5.8 SON lamp and circuit.

A start-up delay of about 5 minutes is required for the lamp to reach full brightness but will usually re-strike within 1 minute of extinction from the hot condition.

SON lamp power ratings range between 70 and 1000 W with corresponding luminous efficiencies being between 80 and 120 lm/W.

5.4. Voltage Effects on Lighting

Naturally, all lamps are designed to produce their rated luminous output at their rated voltage. An overvoltage on an incandescent lamp produces a brighter and whiter light because the filament temperature is increased. Its operating life is, however, drastically reduced. A 5% increase over its rated voltage will reduce the lamp life by 50%.

Conversely, a supply voltage reduction will increase the operating life of a GLS lamp but it produces a duller, reddish light. Lamps rated at 240 V are often used in a ship's lighting system operating at 220 V. This *under-running* should more than double the lamp life.

Similar effects on light output and operating life apply to discharge lamps but if the supply voltage is drastically reduced (below 50%) the arc discharge ceases and will not re-strike until the voltage is raised to nearly its normal value. A fluorescent tube will begin to flicker noticeably as the voltage is reduced below its rated value.

The normal sinusoidal a.c. voltage waveform causes discharge lamps to extinguish at the end of every half cycle, i.e. every 10 ms at 50 Hz or every 6.7 ms at 60 Hz. Although this rapid light fluctuation is not detectable by the human eye, it can cause a stroboscopic effect whereby rotating shafts in the vicinity of discharge lamps may appear stationary or rotating slowly which could be a dangerous illusion to operators.

QUESTION

Give 3 methods to alleviate a stroboscobic problem.

ANSWER

• Use a combination of incandescent and discharge lighting in the same area.

• Use *twin* discharge lamp fittings with each lamp wired as a *lead-lag* circuit, i.e. the lamp currents are phase displaced so that they go through zero at different times, hence the overall light output is never fully extinguished.

- Where a 3-phase supply is available, connect adjacent discharge luminaires to different phases (Red, Yellow, Blue) so the light in a given area is never extinguished.

5.5. Navigation and Signal Lights

The number, position and visible range of navigation lights aboard ships are prescribed by the International Maritime Organization (IMO) in their "International Regulations for Preventing Collisions at Sea". In the UK, the National Authority for maintaining marine safety standards is the MCA (Maritime and Coastguard Authority).

By far the most common arrangement is to have five specially designed navigation *running* lights referred to as *Foremast, Mainmast* (or *Aftmast*), *Port, Starboard* and *Stern*. See Fig. 5.9.

Two *anchor* lights, fitted forward and aft, may also be switched from the Navigation Light Panel on the bridge. The side lights are *red* for Port and *green* for Starboard while the other lights are *white*. For vessels length more than 50 metres, the masthead light(s) must be visible from a range of six nautical miles and the other navigation lights from three nautical miles.

To achieve such visibility, special incandescent filament lamps are used each with a typical power rating of 65 W but 60 W and 40 W ratings are also permitted in some cases.

Due to the essential safety requirement for navigation lights it is common practice to have two fittings at each position, or two lamps and lampholders within a special *dual* fitting.

Each light is separately supplied, switched, fused and monitored from a *Navigation Light Panel* in the wheelhouse. The electric power is provided usually at 220 V a.c. with a main supply fed from the essential services section of the main switchboard.

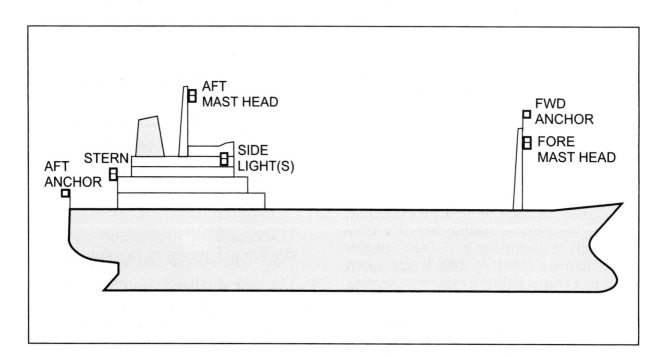

Fig. 5.9 Ship navigation lights arrangement.

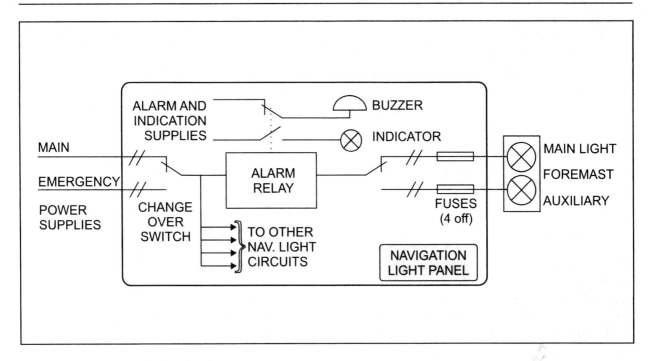

Fig. 5.10 Navigation light panel.

An *alternative* or *standby* power supply is fed from the emergency switchboard.

A changeover switch on the Navigation Light Panel selects the main or standby power supply.

The Navigation Light Panel has indicator lamps and an audible alarm to warn of any lamp or lamp-circuit failure. Each lamp circuit has an alarm relay which monitors the lamp current. The relay may be electromagnetic or electronic. A basic double navigation light scheme with alternative power supplies is shown in Fig. 5.10.

Various *signal* lights with red, green, white and blue colours are arranged on the signal mast as shown in Fig. 5.11. These lights are switched to give particular combinations to signal states relating to various international and national regulations.

Pilotage requirements, health, dangerous cargo conditions, etc., are signalled with these lights. White Morse-Code flashing lights may also be fitted on the signal mast.

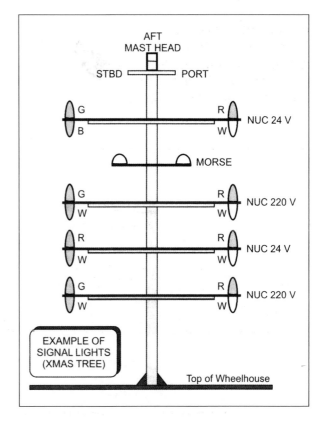

Fig. 5.11 Signal lights arrangement.

The NUC (*Not Under Command*) state is signalled using two all-round *red* lights vertically mounted at least 2 m apart. Such important lights are fed from the 24 V d.c. emergency supply but some ships may also have an additional NUC light-pair fed from the 220 V a.c. emergency power supply.

5.6. Emergency Lighting

Depending on the ship's classification, e.g. ferry, ro-ro, gas carrier, etc., and tonnage the Safety of Life at Sea (SOLAS) Convention prescribes minimum requirements for emergency lighting throughout the vessel.

Emergency light fittings are specially identified, often with a *red* disc, to indicate their function. Most of the emergency lighting is continually powered from the ship's emergency switchboard at 220 V a.c.

A few emergency lights may be supplied from the ship's 24 V d.c. battery, e.g. at the radio-telephone position in the wheelhouse, the main machinery spaces and the steering flat.

Some shipping companies now fit special battery-supported lighting fittings along main escape routes in the engine room, accommodation and at the lifeboat positions on deck. Generally, such emergency lights in the accommodation are arranged to produce light immediately on mains failure.

Boat station emergency lights are switched on when required. Inside the fitting a maintenance-free battery, usually nickel-cadmium, is continually *trickle-charged* from the normal mains supply

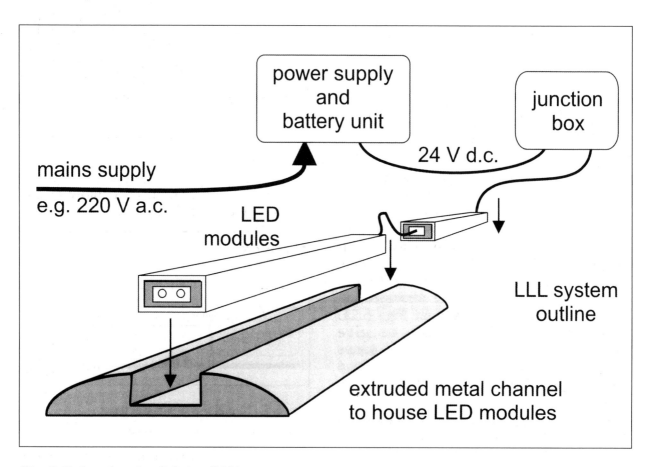

Fig. 5.12 Low location lighting (LLL).

via a transformer/rectifier circuit. The battery is then available to supply the lamp via a d.c. to a.c. inverter when the main power is absent. Usually the battery will only function for a few hours. This power supply arrangement is called an *uniterruptible power supply* or UPS. Such battery supported light fittings can be simply tested by switching off the normal mains power supply or, in some cases, by a test switch on the actual fitting.

Periodic inspection and testing of all emergency lights is an essential requirement on all ships.

A visible, illuminated escape route reduces uncertainty and assists orderly evacuation.

Passenger ships carrying more than 36 passengers are required by IMO resolution A752(18) to be fitted with *Low Location Lighting* (LLL) to identify escape routes where normal emergency lighting is less effective due to the presence of smoke. An LLL system must function for at least 60 minutes after activation and it should indicate a line along the corridors of an escape route.

The installation of LLL should be on at least one side of the corridor, either on the bulkhead within 300 mm of the deck or on the deck within 150 mm of the bulkhead. In corridors more than 2m wide, it should be installed on both sides.

The LLL light sources may be low power LED's, incandescent lamps or a photoluminescent material containing a chemical that stores energy when illuminated by visible light. Of these sources, the LED and incandescent lamp are the most effective. For hazardous areas such as car decks on a ferry, an intrinsically safe (Exia) version can be installed.

Fig. 5.12 indicates the main components of an LLL system where the LED's are wired onto a printed circuit board within a clear polycarbonate rectangular tube with connectors at each end. A similar arrangement is available using low power incandescent lamps.

5.7. Maintenance of Lighting Fittings

The performance of electric lamps will deteriorate with time. Eventually they fail and the lamps must be replaced. Simple lamp replacement becomes the most obvious maintenance task. When a luminaire fails to light-up when switched on, it is natural to suspect lamp failure. If this does not solve the problem, checks on the lamp control equipment and power supply must follow.

An incandescent lamp may be checked (out of circuit) for low-ohm continuity using a multimeter. If the lamp appears intact then the fault must lie in the supply or its connections. Voltage and continuity checks of the supply, fuse/ MCB and ballast circuit must be applied. Remember that a single earth fault on an insulated two-wire lighting supply *will not* blow a fuse. However, a similar earth fault on an earthed supply system (as used for a 110V transformer supply to deck sockets for portable tools and handlamps) will blow a fuse.

QUESTION

Why will a *single* earth fault blow a fuse in an *earthed* supply system?

ANSWER

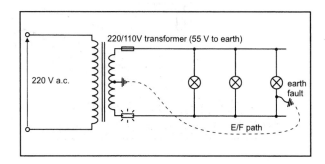

Fig. 5.13 Earth fault effect in an earthed supply system.

The single E/F completes a low resistance path back to the neutral or centrepoint of the supply with a resulting large fault current to rupture the fuse.

A maintenance check list:

- Remember that it is good practice to replace *both* fuses after clearing a fault which has ruptured only one of them.

- When replacing a lamp, ensure that the circuit is *dead* and *isolated* while removing the old lamp and inserting the new one. The glass bulb or tube of an old and corroded fitting may break loose from its end-cap while attempting to remove the lamp. If the supply is still connected, it is relatively easy to cause an accidental short-circuit during the removal process and the corresponding arc flash may cause blindness, burns and fire.

- Always replace a lamp with the correct size, voltage and power rating for the fitting it is housed in. Overheating and fire can easily result by using a higher powered incandescent lamp than the fitting was designed for. Check the lampholder wire connections behind the lampholder for signs of overheating (hard, brittle insulation on the wires) and replace if necessary.

- Take care when disposing of lamps, particularly discharge tubes, which should be broken (outdoors) into a container (e.g. a strong plastic bag) to avoid handling the debris.

- Remember that in a fluorescent lamp circuit the capacitor may remain charged for a while after switch off unless fitted with a discharge resistor. Play safe, discharge the capacitor with a screwdriver blade before touching its terminals.

- Cleaning of the lamp glass and reflectors is essential for safety and necessary to maintain the luminous efficiency of the luminaire.

- Particular care should be paid to the maintenance of the watertight integrity of exposed luminaires (e.g. for navigation, signal and deck lighting) at their flanged joints and cable gland entry. Similarly, a regular inspection of all portable handlamps and portable cargo light fittings, together with their flexible cables and supply plugs, should be undertaken.

Maintenance of *flameproof (Exd)* lighting equipment (e.g. in tanker pumprooms) is covered in Chapter Six.

5.8. Refrigeration and Air Conditioning

The basic electric power and control elements for refrigeration and air-conditioning are outlined below:

- Refrigeration

The safe storage of food necessitates that it is maintained at low temperatures which requires the process of refrigeration. For bulk foods one large industrial refrigeration plant will serve separate cold rooms for the storage of meat, fruit and vegetables, dairy products, etc. Smaller domestic sized refrigerators are used to meet the daily catering needs in the galley, pantries, duty messrooms and in cabins. The refrigeration process is also utilised in deep-freezers, water-chillers and air-conditioning plant. Large scale cargo space refrigeration is also necessary for the transportation of foods and certain liquid chemicals and gases.

Whatever the size or role of the ship's refrigerators, the basic principle is

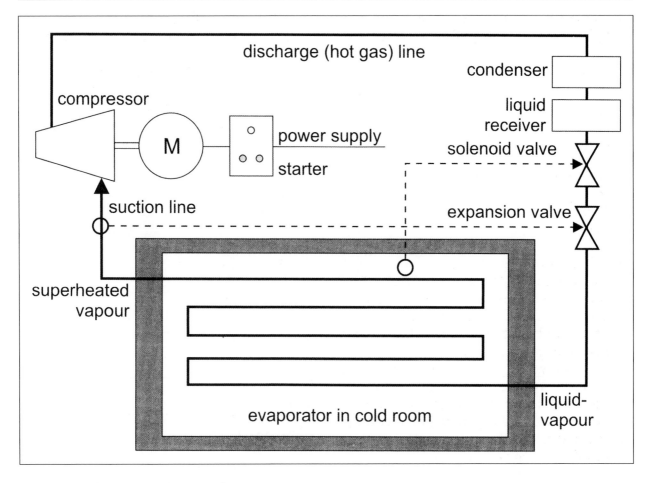

Fig. 5.14 Refrigerator scheme and main components.

common to them all. Each will have an evaporator (cooling unit), a refrigerant compressor and a condenser.

The refrigerant is generally Freon-12 (CCl_2F_2) or Freon-22, but ammonia is also used in large systems. Freon refrigerants in general use are colourless and almost odourless, while also being non-toxic, non-corrosive and non-flammable. However, when exposed to an open flame, a highly toxic phosgene gas is produced.

Additional components to the basic refrigerant cycle may include filter-driers, heat exchangers, accumulators and pre-coolers. Also required are the operating and protective controls such as thermostats, relays, defrost controls and overcurrent trips.

Above the domestic sized refrigerator, the compressor motor will invariably be

a 3-phase type driving a reciprocating compressor. The domestic version will usually be a single-phase motor driving a rotary compressor.

The basic refrigerant circuit of a *direct* (*or primary*) expansion system used for the cooling of meat and vegetable rooms is outlined in Fig. 5.14.

Each cold room is fitted with a thermostat which operates a solenoid valve between set temperature limits. The quantity of refrigerant flowing in the system is regulated by the expansion valve. This valve is controlled by a liquid phial connected by a capillary tube attached to the vapour return pipe at the outlet of the evaporator.

When the room temperature falls to the pre-set level, the thermostat de-energises the solenoid valve to stop

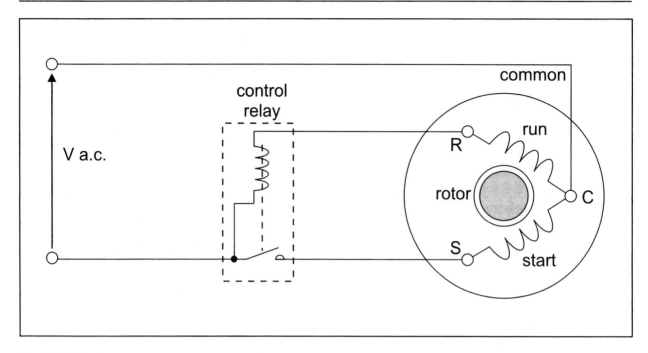

Fig. 5.15 Basic compressor motor control.

circulation of the refrigerant. The resulting pressure drop in the compressor suction line will operate a low-pressure cut-out valve and stop the compressor.

The rooms or compartments are cooled by natural air circulation through the evaporator coils or by forced-air from a fan blowing across a bank of cooling tubes.

In a domestic refrigerator the cooling effort is controlled by using a control thermostat to switch the compressor on or off.

The hermetically sealed compressor motor is the split-phase type having two separate windings – *start* and *run* as shown in Fig. 5.15.

The motor is accelerated by connecting both start and run phase windings to the supply. When the motor reaches about 80% of its rated speed, the start winding is tripped out of circuit. For compressor drives, this switch is usually in the form of a current-operated relay which is fitted adjacent to the compressor.

QUESTION

If the motor terminal markings are unknown, how could you identify the start, run and common terminal connections?

ANSWER

The start winding (being short-time rated) has a higher resistance than the run winding so a resistance check should identify the terminals as follows:

Using a multimeter on the low resistance range, find the two terminals that have the highest resistance between them. These are the start and run terminals. The remaining terminal must be the "common".

Connect one lead of the meter onto the common terminal and touch the other meter lead onto the other terminals in turn and note the readings.

The highest reading indicates the *start* winding terminal. The other remaining terminal is the *run* connection. Typically, the run winding is 1.5–6 Ω and the start winding is 6–22 Ω.

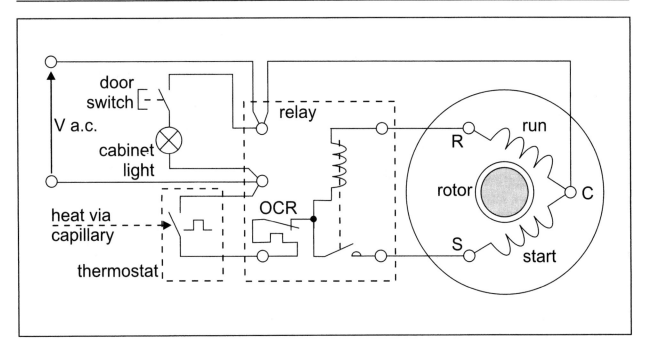

Fig. 5.16 Domestic refrigerator electric circuit.

The main temperature control device in the refrigerator is the thermostat which senses the evaporator temperature via a capillary tube. The *set* temperature is adjusted by a control knob which tensions the control spring against the pressure of the bellows.

For motor protection a bimetallic overcurrent relay (OCR) trip is included as part of the control relay alongside the compressor. The motor supply current either passes directly through a bi-metal strip or disc or the bi-metal is heated indirectly from a small resistance heater alongside it. A motor overcurrent will cause the bi-metal to deflect and cause a snap-action switch to open.

Fig. 5.16 shows the complete circuit of a simple domestic refrigerator (i.e. without timers, automatic defrost or air-circulation fans).

When the evaporator temperature rises, the thermostat switch closes allowing current to flow through the motor *run* winding and the relay solenoid coil. This current is initially high causing the solenoid to close the relay switch to allow current into the *start* winding.

The motor will now begin to accelerate from standstill causing its run winding current to reduce to a level where the start-relay will drop off. The motor will now run continuously on the *run*-phase only. When the evaporator reaches its set temperature the thermostat resets and the motor is switched off.

The most common way to achieve automatic defrosting of the evaporator is to use a time-switch to cut out the refrigeration circuit and initiate a defrost heater circuit. The timer may be a small motor with a cam driven changeover switch or an electronic timer with relay changeover contacts.

A bimetallic defrost thermostat controls the defrost heater in or below the evaporator. Most defrost thermostats close at 20°F ± 5° and open at 55° ± 5°. Defrost periods may vary from 15 to 45 minutes with up to four defrost cycles in 24 hours depending on the fridge/freezer design.

Some refrigerators and freezers may have electric heaters fitted for various duties such as a dewpoint heater (to prevent sweating on the cabinet in the freezer area) and a compartment divider panel or *stile* heater (to prevent sweating on the panel).

Additionally there may be condenser and evaporator fans which are driven by single-phase *shaded-pole* type motors.

• Air Conditioning

Air conditioning is a process which heats, cools, cleans and circulates air together with the control of its moisture content. The air must be delivered to a room with a definite temperature and specified relative humidity.

For *summer duty*, the usual method is to cool the incoming air to a temperature below the *dew point* to allow condensation to occur until the mixture has the desired specific humidity then heating the air to the required delivery temperature and relative humidity. In winter, the incoming air may have to be heated and have water added to achieve the correct inlet conditions. In most plants the bulk of the mixture is re-circulating

air with fresh air intake forming about one third of the total required. The amount of make-up air is a statutory requirement which is typically between 17 m³/hr and 28 m³/hr.

The electrical aspects of accommodation air conditioning (A/C) comprises the power equipment of motors and starters for the compressor(s), fans and sea-water cooling pumps. Associated control equipment will include electric solenoid valves, high and low-pressure and temperature switches together with safety cut-outs for overcurrent, loss of refrigerant, low compressor oil pressure, etc.

The usual air-conditioning system used for the accommodation spaces of cargo ships is the central single-duct type, shown in Fig. 5.17. In its simplest form a single compressor serves the whole accommodation.

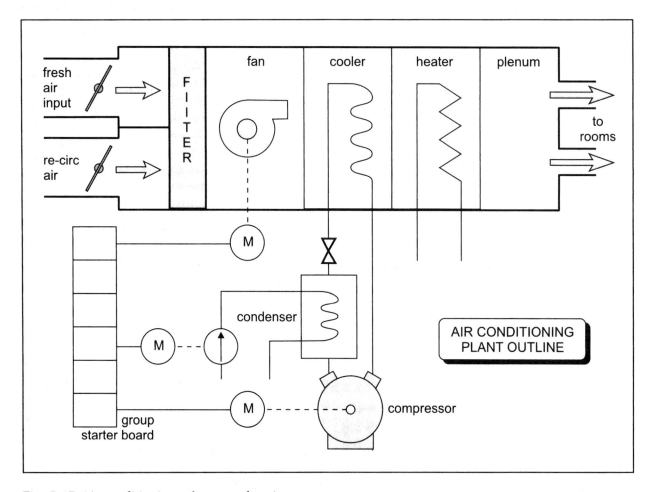

Fig. 5.17 Air-conditioning scheme and main components.

The compressor is generally a multi-cylinder reciprocating type with a power rating in the range of 50–200 kW, although rotary-vane or screw-action compressors may also be encountered. Large passenger vessels may have a total power requirement of more than 5 MW for the AC compressor drives to maintain air delivery to the hotel and staff accommodation areas. Capacity control of the reciprocating compressor is by automatic unloading of cylinders by valve control using servo oil pressure.

The compressor, air fan and sea water pump are driven by simple fixed speed, 3-phase a.c. induction motors each with its own starter and supplied from a distribution board fitted in the air-conditioning plant room.

Routine electrical maintenance and fault finding on the motors and starters will involve cleaning, checking of connections, IR (megger)/continuity tests and running tests as described in Chapter Four.

Inspection of connections and correct operation of any electric heaters must also be performed. Such heaters may be used for heating the compressor crankcase oil and for separating the refrigerant (Freon R12 or R22) from the oil in an oil reservoir.

Regular inspection and testing of control and safety thermostats and pressurestats should be carried out in accordance with the manufacturer's instructions. In particular the compressor's low oil pressure alarm and trip circuit should be tested periodically for correct operation.

5.9. Galley and Laundry

The following section outlines the basic power and control units utilised for galley and laundry services:

• Galley

The electrical power in a galley is largely absorbed in producing heat.

Ovens, deep fryer pans, water boilers and the hotplates on the galley range all employ resistive heating elements which are usually controlled by bimetallic thermostats. Other miscellaneous electrical galley equipment may include oven air circulating and range exhaust fans, meat slicers, food mixers and grinders, dishwashers, potato peelers and garbage disposal units. Most of this equipment will utilise small electric motors together with the necessary control switches, safety interlocks and indicator lamps.

Because of the large power requirement for food preparation and cooking, the major galley items are supplied from the 3-phase a.c. 440 V system. Smaller galleys may be supplied from the low-voltage 220 V a.c. system. The electrical equipment has to work safely in the usual galley atmosphere of high humidity and high temperature.

Catering staff have been known to wash down ovens and ranges with an enthusiasm that demonstrates a scant regard for Ohm's Law! All in all, the galley electrics work in a tough area so be prepared for faults caused by the environmental hazards of grease, dust and dampness.

Heating elements are usually formed from Nichrome-wire insulated with a magnesium-oxide (MgO) powder within an inconel tube which forms the outer sheath. Power ratings vary from 1 kW to about 4 kW and some elements are arranged to be switched to give varying levels of heat.

The simplest arrangement is obtained using a 3-heat, 4-position switch to control 2 elements within a single hotplate on a single-phase supply. The two resistance elements are interconnected by the switch to give a choice of OFF, LOW, MEDIUM and HIGH settings as shown in Fig. 5.18.

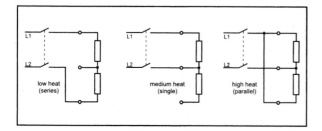

Fig. 5.18 Three-heat switching circuit.

For larger heating power control using 440 V 3-phase a.c., three heating elements can be interconnected into *star* and *delta* configurations.

Closer control of heating elements is obtained by using *simmerstat* switches and electronic switching. The simmerstat switch type shown in Fig. 5.19, houses a bi-metallic switch which *cycles* the heating element on and off at a rate determined by the switch setting. Average hot-plate temperature is fixed by the ratio of time that the element is *on* to the time it is *off*. Circuit current heats the bi-metal which operates the control switch.

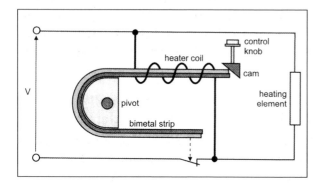

Fig. 5.19 Simmerstat controller circuit.

Oven simmerstat controls have a similar switching action but a temperature sensing capillary tube, located in the oven, deflects a diaphragm or bellows which activates the switch.

Electronic switching devices such as *transistors*, *thyristors* and *triacs* may also be used for temperature control of ovens

and hot-plates. Be careful not to megger test low-voltage electronic components during maintenance and fault finding. Check the manufacturer's instructions and drawings before fault chasing around electrical control circuits.

The most likely fault in a heating element is a simple open-circuit. Earth faults within the element or on the wires supplying it are also probable. Loose wire connections cause localised overheating with the wire burning away to leave an open-circuit at least, but the possibility of a short-circuit or earth fault also arises.

The connecting wires lying close to heating elements should be covered with high-temperature silicone or fibre glass sleeving or with ceramic beads.

QUESTION

What would be the continuity resistance of a healthy 2 kW, 220 V heating element?

ANSWER

The element current is:

$$I = \frac{P}{V} = \frac{2000 \ W}{220 \ V} = \underline{9.1 \ A}$$

and $P = I^2.R$ so, $R = \dfrac{P}{I^2} = \dfrac{2000}{9.1^2} = \underline{\underline{24.2 \ \Omega}}$

When measured cold, the resistance value may be lower than the calculated value. High power ovens and hotplate ranges are often supplied from the 3-phase, 440 V a.c. supply. Thermostats control the on-off heating cycle. A simple oven circuit is shown in Fig. 5.20 as an example of contactor control. Many and varied circuits occur in practice and the manufacturer's drawings must be checked in a particular case.

Microwave ovens provide rapid defrosting and cooking of foods.

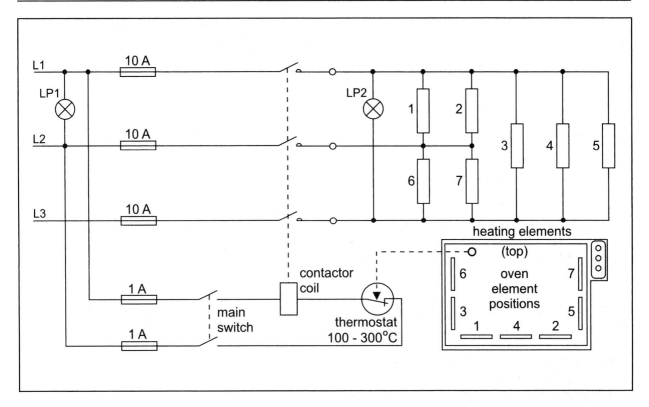

Fig. 5.20 Basic oven temperature control.

The microwaves are produced by a special valve called a *magnetron* operating at around 4000 V with a frequency of 2450 MHz. Specialised knowledge is required for the repair of this type of oven and internal fault finding is not recommended without the manufacturer's guidance.

Inspection and maintenance of galley equipment is most important. The main objective is to keep the electrical parts clean and free of water, oil, dust and grease. Pay particular attention to all connection points in high current heating circuits where loose connections cause overheating and future problems. For operator safety, all enclosure metalwork must be earthed and regular checks of earthing straps must be given priority.

Insulation resistance (IR) tests on heating elements, when cold, may reveal surprisingly low values (10–100 kΩ) even with new elements. This is because the element insulation (magnesium-oxide powder) is somewhat hygroscopic (absorbs moisture). The insulation resistance value of a healthy heating element should rise rapidly after being operated for a few minutes. Obviously, if the IR value of an element remains low when hot it is defective and must be replaced.

• Laundry

Washing machines, spin dryers and tumble dryers utilise heat and mechanical rotation during their laundry processes.

The sequence of events is controlled by timers which are often simple electric timer motors driving cam-operated switches. Alternatively, electronic timers with relay switching or solid state electronic switching using *thyristors* or *triacs* may be employed.

Small washing machines operating on a single-phase supply have motors which are usually the split-phase type of the *capacitor-start, capacitor-run* variety.

Larger washing machines operate from the 3-phase a.c. power supply with a 3-phase induction motor drive.

Control items in a washing machine include water level switches, temperature switches (bi-metallic) and solenoid valves in the inlet and outlet water lines. Lid and door switches interrupt the main power supply if operated after the washing sequence has begun.

Spin dryers have a safety door interlock that prevents it being opened while the drum is still revolving. Tumble dryers often only have one motor with a double-ended shaft for drum and blower fan drives.

Lint and fluff collects on the motor and wiring which causes no trouble while it remains dry and in small quantities. Periodic removal of the fluff will help prevent faults arising where dampness may combine with the fluff to cause conductive tracking between live conductors and to earth. Small single-phase motors are sometimes protected by a thermal cut-out attached to the stator end windings.

5.10. Cathodic Protection

The outer surface of a ship's hull is subjected to electro-chemical attack by corrosive currents that flow between areas of the hull which are at slightly different electric potentials.

Dissimilar metals, variations in structural and chemical uniformity in hull plates and welding, differences in paint thickness and quality, water temperature, salinity and aeration all combine to cause areas of the hull to become either *anodic* (positive) or *cathodic* (negative).

Fig. 5.21 shows that in the hull, electrons flow from anode to cathode leaving positively charged iron ions at the anodic area. At the cathode the effect of the arrival of electrons is to produce negatively charged hydroxyl ions (OH) by electrolysis of the sea water. These negative ions flow through the sea to the anodic area where they combine

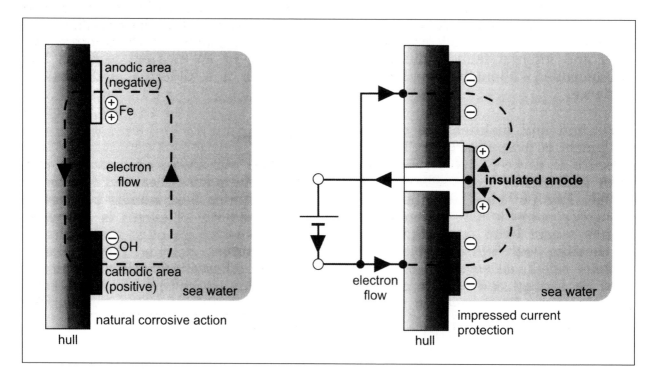

Fig. 5.21 Cathodic protective action.

with the positive iron ions to form ferrous hydroxide $Fe(OH)_2$. This ferrous hydroxide is further oxidised by dissolved oxygen to form ferric hydroxide $Fe(OH)_3$ which is *rust*. Thus the anodic area is gradually corroded away whilst no corrosion takes place at the cathodic area.

This naturally corrosive action can be overcome if the complete hull is made cathodic, i.e. electrons are allowed to arrive at the hull surface and produce negative hydroxyl ions but no electrons leave the hull to produce positive iron ions. This is achieved by fitting insulated lead or platinised titanium anodes to the hull and applying a positive d.c. potential to them with respect to the hull.

The negatively charged hydroxyl ions (OH) now pass to the insulated lead anodes causing the lead surface to change to lead peroxide PbO_2.

The potential is of such a value that it just overcomes the original corrosion current and gives rise to an impressed protection current which flows in the complete circuit. The value of protection current must be critically controlled to just prevent corrosion, as beyond this value the increase in the rate of release of hydroxyl ions will cause sponginess and flaking of the anti-fouling paint.

Initially the electrolytic action will form lead peroxide (PbO_2) on the surface of the anodes and when this skin is formed the action reduces. The anodes take on a rich brown appearance (positive lead-acid battery plate) and in service are expected to last 7–10 years.

The correct value of protection current can be determined by reference electrodes. These are either of zinc or silver attached to the hull, but insulated from it, below the waterline.

The voltage measured between the hull and reference electrodes of an unprotected ship with sea water as an electrolyte is:

- Zinc electrode   (450 mV *negative* to hull)
- Silver electrode   (600 mV *positive* to hull)

When satisfactorily protected, the protection current will make the hull 200 mV more negative, i.e. a zinc reference electrode will register 250 mV negative to hull and silver 800 mV positive to hull as shown in Fig. 5.22. The reference electrode voltage may, therefore, be used to monitor the protection, but more important, is used as the signal source to automatically regulate the value of protection current.

Cathodic protection systems fitted in ships consist of a number of anodes (lead or platinised titanium) fitted to the hull at selected places below the waterline, and control equipment which automatically regulates the anode current to the required value. Direct current is supplied to the anodes, after transformation and rectification, from the ship's 440 V 60 Hz 3-phase a.c. distribution system. The control equipment comprises reference electrodes, an amplifier assembly and one or more transformer rectifier units.

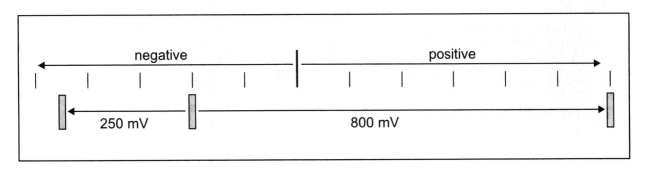

Fig. 5.22 Protection voltages.

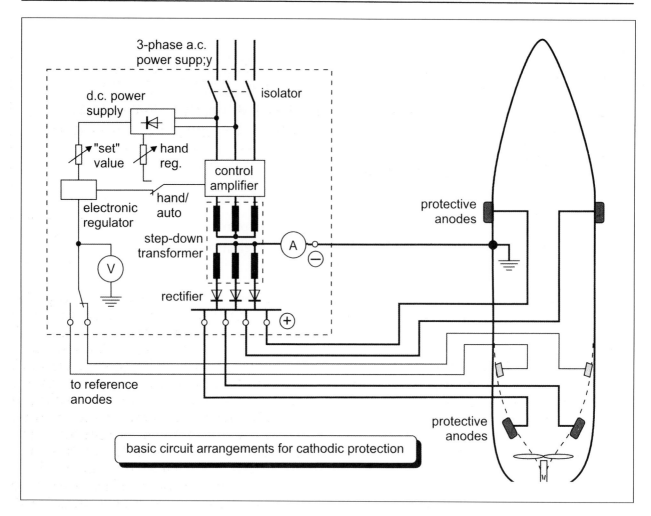

Fig. 5.23 Ship anodes and impressed current control system.

The anode current control is usually regulated by electronic thyristor controllers and the diagram in Fig. 5.23 outlines a typical scheme.

The control equipment automatically monitors the size of anode current required which will vary with the ship's speed, water temperature and salinity, condition of paint work etc. Typical anode current densities range from 10 mA/m^2 to 40 mA/m^2 for the protection of painted surfaces and 100 to 150 mA/m^2 for bare steel surfaces.

The total impressed current for a hull in good condition may be as low as 20 A. Maximum controller outputs may be up to about 600 A at 8 V.

Cathodic protection does not appear to deter molluscular growth on the ships hull, so a top coat of anti-foul (poisonous) paint is still necessary.

Typical reference and main anode outlines are shown in Fig. 5.24.

Monitoring facilities in the cathodic protection control cabinet may provide measurements of:

- Reference electrode voltage (hull potential)

- Amplifier output voltage

- Total anode current

- Individual anode current

Measurements should be regularly logged together with the ship operating conditions, e.g. location, draught, water

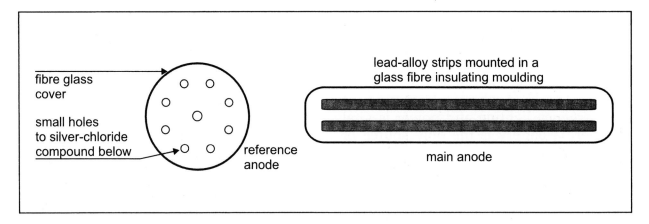

Fig. 5.24 Reference and main anode construction outlines.

temperature, etc. Changes in underwater hull area, speed, water temperature/salinity and paint condition will all cause the anode currents to vary. The hull potential should, however, remain constant in a properly regulated system.

Although the reference electrodes and the monitoring facilities give a reasonable day to day check they are only measuring in the vicinity of the fitted electrodes.

When the ship is moored singly or stopped at sea, voltage readings can be taken between a portable silver or zinc test electrode and the ship's hull. This portable electrode is lowered 2–3 metres below the water surface and as close as possible to the hull at specified positions around the ship.

Check the manufacturer's instructions regarding the storage and setting up of the portable electrode. Some have to be immersed in a plastic bucket of sea water for about 4 hours before the hull test. With the cathodic protection switched on and working normally, the voltage measured between hull and a silver/silver chloride portable electrode should be 750–850 mV using a high resistance multimeter (e.g. analogue or digital type); the electrode being positive with respect to hull.

When dry docked, ensure that the main anodes and reference electrodes are covered with paper tape to prevent paint contamination.

To ensure that the rudder, propeller screw and stabiliser fins receive the same degree of cathodic protection as the hull it is necessary to electrically *earth-bond* these items to the hull. The rudder stock may be bonded by a wire braid linking the top of the stock to the deckhead directly above it. Carbon brushes rubbing on the rotating main propulsion shaft effectively bond the shaft to the hull. A periodic inspection of such earthing is worthwhile as the brushes wear away and may occasionally stick in their brush holders.

5.11. Battery Supplies

A properly maintained storage battery will instantly supply electric power when required. This feature makes a battery the key element in the provision of essential and emergency power supplies on board ships.

Essential routine power supplies, e.g. for radio equipment, telephone exchange, fire detection, general alarm circuits etc., are often supplied from two sets of batteries worked on a regular charge/discharge cycle.

Emergency battery supplies, e.g. for emergency generator start-up and emergency lighting, are used in a *standby* role to give power when the main supply fails.

Ships' batteries are usually rated at a nominal voltage of 24 V d.c. In some cases a battery system of 110 V or 220 V d.c. may be used where a large amount of emergency lighting and power is vital or where a battery is the only source of emergency power.

The two main types of rechargeable battery cell are:

• Lead-acid

• Alkaline

The nominal cell voltages of each type are 2 V for lead-acid and 1.2 V for alkaline. Hence, twelve lead-acid cells or twenty alkaline cells must be connected in series to produce a nominal 24 V. More cells may be connected in parallel to increase the battery capacity which is rated in Ampere-hours (Ah). The battery capacity is usually rated in terms of its discharge at the 10 hour rate. A 350 Ah battery would be expected to provide 35 A for 10 hours. However, the battery will generally have a lower capacity at a shorter discharge rate. The manufacturer's discharge curves must be checked for such details.

After a 10 hour discharge a lead-acid cell voltage will have fallen to approximately 1.73 V. The equivalent figure for an alkaline cell is 1.14 V.

Battery installations for both types of battery are similar in that the battery room should be well ventilated, clean and dry. Both types generate hydrogen gas during charging so smoking and naked flames must be prohibited in the vicinity of the batteries.

Steelwork and decks adjacent to lead-acid batteries should be covered with acid-resisting paint and alkali resisting paint used near Ni-cad cells.

Acid cells must never be placed near alkaline cells otherwise rapid electrolytic corrosion to metalwork and damage to both batteries is certain For similar reasons, *never* use lead-acid battery maintenance gear (e.g. hydrometer, topping up bottles, etc.) on an alkaline installation or vice-versa.

Battery maintenance includes keeping the cell tops clean and dry, checking the tightness of terminal nuts and applying a smear of petroleum jelly to such connections to prevent corrosion. Be most careful when handling the battery electrolyte (e.g. when using a hydrometer to check its specific gravity). Use protective rubber gloves and eye goggles when handling electrolyte. Insulated spanners should be available for use on cell connections to prevent accidental *short-circuiting* of battery terminals. Such a short-circuit across the terminals of just one cell of a battery will cause a blinding flash with the probability of the cell being seriously damaged.

QUESTION

An alkaline cell has an electrolyte of potassium hydroxide while a lead-acid cell uses sulphuric acid. Both are diluted with distilled water.

What first aid treatment would you apply should you be splashed with either electrolyte?

ANSWER

In both cases rapidly wash eyes and skin with plenty of fresh water. The electrolyte of alkaline cells causes skin burns which should be treated with boracic powder and the eyes washed out with a solution of boracic power — one teaspoonful to a pint of water.

Sulphuric acid splashes can be washed with a saline solution — two teaspoonfuls of household salt to one pint of water.

For both types of battery first aid equipment should be in the battery compartment.

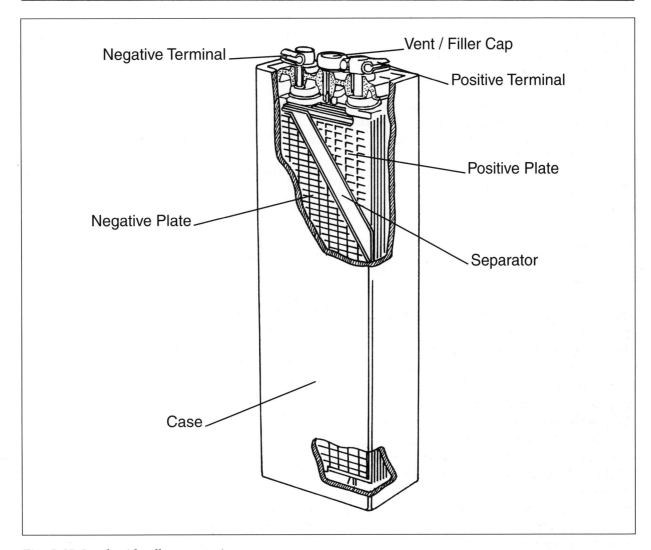

Fig. 5.25 Lead-acid cell construction.

The diagram in Fig. 5.25 outlines the principal features of a *lead-acid* cell.

The state of charge held by a *lead-acid* battery is best indicated by a test on the electrolyte specific gravity (SG) by using a *hydrometer* as shown in Fig. 5.26. A fully charged lead-acid cell has an SG of about 1.27–1.285 (often written as 1270–1285) which falls to about 1.1 (or 1100) when fully discharged. The cell voltage also falls during discharge and its value can also be used as an indication of the state of charge.

A lead-acid battery may be safely discharged until the cell voltage drops to approximately 1.73 V (measured while delivering load current).

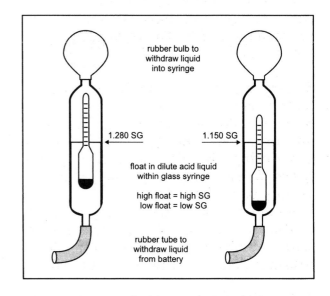

Fig. 5.26 Hydrometer testing.

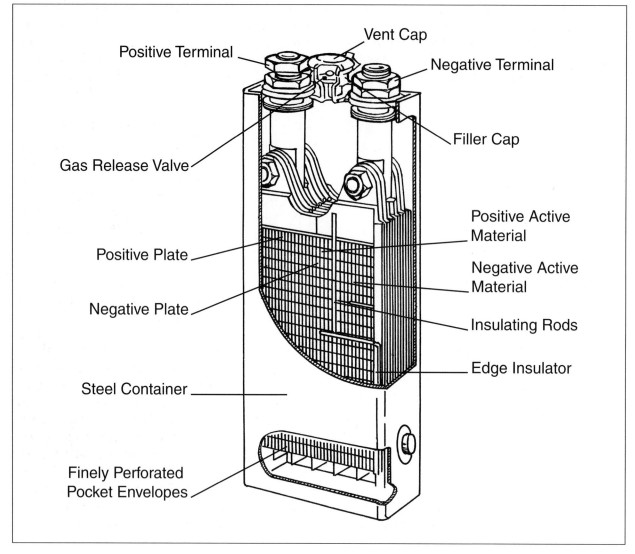

Positive Terminal

Vent Cap

Negative Terminal

Gas Release Valve

Filler Cap

Positive Plate

Positive Active Material

Negative Active Material

Negative Plate

Insulating Rods

Edge Insulator

Steel Container

Finely Perforated Pocket Envelopes

Fig. 5.27 Alkaline cell construction.

The *open-circuit* (no-load) battery voltage readings can be misleading as a high value does not necessarily indicate that the cells are in a healthy charged state.

Note, the SG values quoted above for lead-acid cells are based on an ambient temperature of 15°C. Corrections to the SG value at any other ambient temperature are as follows:

- *Add* 0.007 to reading for each 10°C above 15°C

- *Subtract* 0.007 from reading for each 10°C below 15°C.

e.g. a hydrometer reading taken during an ambient temperature of 25°C is 1.27.

The equivalent SG value at 15°C is 1.27 + 0.007 = 1.277 (or 1277)

Fig. 5.27 outlines the principal features of an alkaline cell.

The state of charge of an *alkaline* battery cell *cannot* be determined from its SG value. The electrolyte density does not change during charge/discharge cycles but gradually falls during the lifetime of the battery.

New alkaline cells have an SG of around 1190. When this reduces to about 1145 (which may take 5–10 years depending on the duty cycle) the electrolyte must be completely renewed or the battery replaced. Discharge of alkaline cells should be discontinued when the cell voltage has fallen to about 1.1 V.

Battery charging equipment uses a transformer/rectifier arrangement to supply the required d.c. voltage to the cells. The size of voltage depends on the battery type (lead-acid or alkaline) and the mode of charging, e.g. charge/discharge cycle, boost charge, trickle or float charge. Check the manufacturer's instructions for details of the required charging voltages.

Do not allow electrolyte temperatures to exceed about 45°C during charging.
    A lead-acid cell will gas freely when fully charged but an alkaline cell gases *throughout* the charging period. The only indication of a fully charged alkaline cell is when its voltage remains at a steady maximum value of about 1.6–1.8 V.

Generally, alkaline cells are more robust, mechanically and electrically, than lead-

acid cells. Nickel cadmium cells will hold their charge for long periods without recharging so are ideal for standby duties. Also they operate well with a *float-charge* to provide a reliable emergency supply when the main power fails.

For all rechargeable batteries (other than the sealed type) it is essential to replace lost water (caused during gassing and by normal evaporation) with the addition of *distilled* water to the correct level above the plates. Exposure of the cell plates to air will rapidly reduce the life of the battery.

On all ships and offshore platforms there are particular essential services which are vital during a complete loss of main power. Such services include switchgear operation, navigation lights, foghorns, fire and gas detection, internal communications, some radio communications, alarm systems. To avoid the loss of essential services they are supported by an *uninterruptible power supply* or UPS. These can be for battery supported *d.c.* supplies or *a.c.* supplies both of which can be configured as *continuous* UPS or *standby* UPS. Fig. 5.28 shows an a.c. supported UPS arrangement:

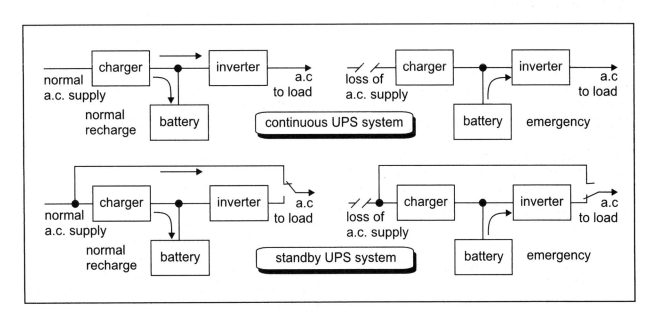

Fig. 5.28 UPS systems.

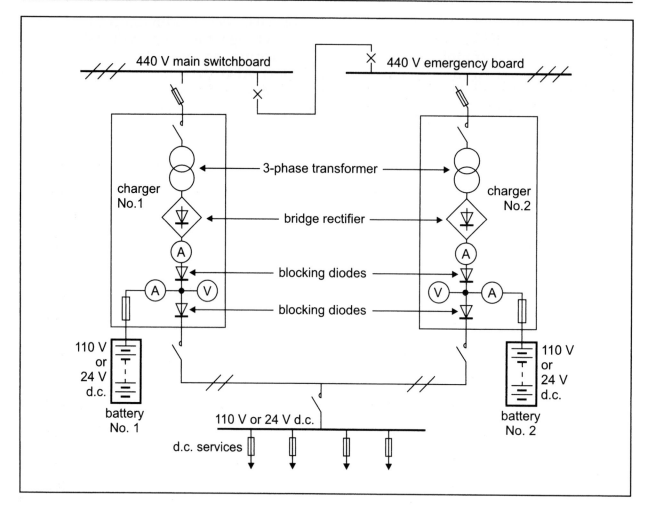

Fig. 5.29 UPS d.c. battery charger.

The arrangement shown in Fig. 5.29 is typical of a *continuous* UPS d.c. supported supply system.

The essential d.c. services are normally supplied from the 440 V main power system through charger 1 which continuously *trickle charges* its battery. During a loss of main power, battery 1 maintains a transitional supply while the emergency generator restores power to the emergency board and hence to charger 2. Either battery is available for a few hours if both main and emergency generators are unavailable.

Some critical emergency lights have an internal battery supported UPS within the luminaire where its battery charge is continuously maintained during non-emergency conditions.

Chapter Six
Special Electrical Practice for Oil, Gas and Chemical Tankers

6.0. Introduction

Ships and offshore installations that transport, process and store bulk quantities of oil, gas and liquid chemicals are subject to special codes of practice regarding their electrical installations. Statutory authorities and classification societies generally base their recommendations on Publication 92 of the International Electrotechnical Commission (IEC).

The object of all such guidance is to prevent the hazards of fire and explosion occurring on board these tank ships.

Spaces in tankers where explosive gas-air mixtures may be expected to be present are called *dangerous* or *hazardous*. All other areas being regarded as *safe*.

The best way to avoid explosions caused by electrical equipment is simply *not* to install such equipment in the hazardous areas. However, special electrical equipment is permitted and this chapter will provide a guide to the range and maintenance of such explosion (Ex) protected equipment.

6.1. Tanker Classification

Shore practice for hazardous areas is to divide the areas into three zones (0,1,2) which recognises the degree of hazard by indicating the likelihood of an explosive gas-air mixture being present. This practice is not used on tankers. However, electrical equipment is manufactured on the basis of such zones.

On tankers, areas are designated as either *dangerous* or *normally-safe* spaces.

A *dangerous* space is defined as an area where flammable gas-air mixtures would normally be expected to occur. The degree of hazard or danger presented by a dangerous space is determined, initially, by the nature of the flammable cargo of the tanker.

On this basis, four types of tanker are recognised as:

❑ Type A

Oil tankers intended for the carriage in bulk of non-boiling oil cargoes having a flash point (closed test) of 60°C or less. These include crude oil carriers, gasoline carriers, etc.

❑ Type B

Oil tankers intended for carriage in bulk of non-boiling oil cargoes having a flash point (closed test) in excess of 60°C. These include tankers for carrying bituminous or asphalt products, or for carrying diesel or fuel oils.

❑ Type C

Gas carriers intended for the carriage in bulk of liquefied petroleum gas (LPG) or liquefied natural gas (LNG).

❑ Type D

Tankers for the carriage in bulk of other flammable liquid cargoes.

This includes those cargoes which are potentially more dangerous than those conveyed by Type A and Type C tankers, and those products which exhibit chemical instability.

❑ **Type A Tankers**

Dangerous Spaces:

✳ Cargo tanks.

✳ Cofferdams adjoining cargo tanks.

✳ Cargo pump rooms.

✳ Enclosed or semi-enclosed spaces immediately above cargo tanks, or having bulkheads above and in line with the cargo tank bulkheads.

✳ Enclosed or semi-enclosed spaces immediately above cargo pumprooms, or above vertical cofferdams adjoining cargo tanks, unless separated by a gastight deck and suitably mechanically ventilated.

✳ Spaces, other than cofferdams, adjoining and below the top of the cargo tanks, e.g. trunks, passageways and holds.

✳ Areas on open deck, or semi-enclosed spaces on open deck, within at least 3 m of any cargo oil tank outlet or gas or vapour outlet.

✳ Areas on open deck over all cargo tanks, including all ballast tanks within the cargo tank block and to the full width of the vessel plus 3 m forward and aft on open deck, up to a height of 2.4 m above the deck.

✳ Compartments for cargo hoses.

✳ Enclosed or semi-enclosed spaces having a direct opening into any of the spaces or areas mentioned above.

Electrical equipment and cables should only be located in dangerous spaces when it is absolutely necessary.

Only *intrinsically safe* (Exi) electrical equipment is allowed inside cargo tanks. Electric motors are not permitted in cargo pump rooms.

Flameproof (Exd) or *pressurised* (Exp) luminaires may be used in pumprooms. The switches and fuses for the luminaires must be located in a normally safe space outside the pumproom. At least two independent circuits must be provided for the lighting. If maintenance is carried out on the luminaires of one circuit this circuit must be de-energised while the other circuit provides sufficient light for the work to be safely completed.

QUESTION

Tanker pumprooms require two separate lighting circuits. How can the circuits be arranged so that the luminaires can only be opened up when the correct circuit has been isolated?

ANSWER

Many tankers use the following arrangement:

The luminaires on one of the circuits have bolts with a different size or type of head to those on the luminaires supplied by the other circuit. Typically, these would be two different types of triangular bolt head.

The keys to remove the bolts are actually the operating handles of the circuit isolators. A key can only be removed from its trapped position on the switch after the circuit has been isolated. This key can only open up those luminaires connected to the circuit which has been isolated.

Cable runs are permitted through most dangerous spaces except cargo tanks, provided they are continuously monitored for earth leakage.

Flameproof (Exd) or *pressurised* (Exp) luminaires are permitted in enclosed or semi-enclosed spaces immediately above a cargo tank, above a cargo pump room and in compartments for storing cargo hoses. The switches and fuses must be located in a normally safe area and must switch both lines of the circuit (i.e. double pole switching).

❏ Type B Tankers

Dangerous spaces are not defined for vessels of this type, but it is recommended that care be exercised so that potential sources of ignition are reduced as far as possible. Also, the following practices should be followed:

✳ Use *intrinsically safe* (Exi) for any monitoring or instrumentation equipment which is in direct contact with oil in the cargo tanks or in the oil circuits.

✳ Cargo pump motors should be *increased safety* (Exe) type if they are located in the cargo pump room.

✳ All portable electrical equipment used in the cargo tanks must be suitably *explosion protected* (Ex).

❏ Type C Tankers (Gas Carriers)

Dangerous Spaces:

✳ A space in the cargo area which is not equipped with approved arrangements to ensure that its atmosphere is at all times maintained in a safe condition.

✳ An enclosed space outside the cargo area through which any piping terminates, unless approved arrangements are installed to prevent any escape of product vapour into the atmosphere of that space.

✳ A cargo containment system with cargo piping:

(a) a hold space where cargo is carried in a cargo containment system requiring a secondary barrier;

(b) a hold space where cargo is carried in a cargo containment system not requiring a secondary barrier.

✻ A space separated from a hold space described in (a) above by a single gastight steel boundary.

✻ A cargo pump room and cargo compressor room.

✻ A zone on open deck, or semi-enclosed space on open deck, within 3 m of any cargo tank outlet, gas or vapour outlet, cargo piped flange, cargo valve or of entrances and ventilation openings to a cargo pumproom and cargo compressor rooms.

✻ The open deck over the cargo area and 3 m forward and aft of the cargo area on open deck up to a height of 2.4 m above the weather deck.

✻ A zone within 2.4 m of the outer surface of a cargo containment system where such surface is exposed to the weather.

✻ An enclosed or semi-enclosed space in which pipes containing products are located.

✻ A compartment for cargo hoses.

✻ An enclosed or semi-enclosed space having a direct opening into any dangerous space or area.

The recommendations for the use of electrical equipment in dangerous spaces are the same for this type of vessel as they are for **Type A** tankers. There are, however, two important additional recommendations for gas carriers:

✻ Cargo Pump Motor

Submerged cargo pump motors and their cables are permitted in cargo tanks subject to the atmosphere of the tank being controlled to prevent presence of a gas-air mixture when the motors are energised.

✻ Gas Compressor Motors

These motors are allowed, under certain circumstances, to be sited in the same space as the compressors. In these instances the motors are required to be pressurised (Exp) with air, inert gas or water.

Alternatively, an *increased safety* (Exe) motor within a *flameproof* (Exd) enclosure may be used and marked overall as Exe d.

❏ **Type D Chemical Carriers**

The products carried in these vessels may produce explosive gas-air mixtures and can also be intensely corrosive.

In cases like this electrical equipment must not only be explosion protected but also designed to withstand corrosion.

These products are categorised as follows in order to give guidance on the electrical equipment which would be suitable.

Types of chemical product:

✻ Products which have similar properties to those carried by vessel types A, B and C. The recommendations given for those vessels would apply.

✻ Products which are considered to be more hazardous than those above. The extent of dangerous areas is increased from 3 m to 4.5 m.

✻ Products which are susceptible to chemical instability which creates flammable gases. Special arrangements would be required for this type of product.

✻ Products which will damage any electrical equipment with which they come into contact. Materials and enclosures must resist the corrosive effect of these products.

6.2. Hazardous Zones

Hazardous areas ashore are classified into *zones* which indicate the probability of an explosive gas-air mixture being present and, therefore, the likelihood of an explosion occurring.

✳ Zone 0

In which an explosive gas-air mixture is continuously present, or present for long periods.

✳ Zone 1

In which an explosive gas-air mixture is likely to occur in normal operation.

✳ Zone 2

In which an explosive gas-air mixture is not likely to occur in normal operation and, if it occurs, will exist for only a short time.

An area which is not classified Zone 0, 1 or 2 is assumed to be a *non-hazardous* or *safe* area. Examples of this zoning applied to ships could be:

✳ Zone 0

Interior spaces of oil cargo tanks, pipes, pumps, etc.

✳ Zone 1

Enclosed or semi-enclosed spaces on the deck of a tanker, the boiler firing area on a gas carrier using methane boil-off as a fuel and battery rooms.

✳ Zone 2

Open spaces on the deck of a tanker.

The cargo pump rooms of tankers are, at present, considered as falling somewhere between Zone 0 and Zone 1.

6.3. Electrical Ignition of Gas

In practice, three essential components must be present to start a fire or cause an explosion:

✳ A flammable gas or vapour (hazard)

✳ Air or oxygen to support combustion (oxidiser)

✳ Something to start the explosion (source of ignition)

When all three of these components are brought together ignition can take place, often with devastating results.

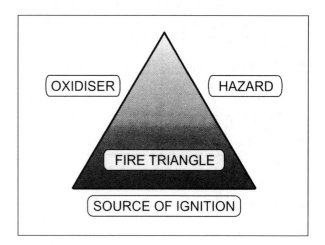

Fig. 6.1 Fire triangle.

The occurrence of a fire or ignition depends on the *probability* of the simultaneous occurrence of all three components shown in the *fire triangle* diagram shown in Fig. 6.1.

Gases, when concentrated above the *Lower Flammable Limit* (LFL), can be ignited by heat generated from various electrical sources e.g.:

✳ Arcing between switch contacts.

✳ Arcing between a live conductor and earth.

✳ An internal arcing fault within an electrical enclosure.

✳ Overheating causing hot spots.

✳ An electrostatic spark discharge between charged bodies or between a charged body and earth.

✳ Chemical action.

✳ Lightning strikes.

As might be expected, the *flammability* of a gas/air mixture is dependent upon the *ratio* of gas to air. A ratio of 100% gas/air concentration will not burn and, as can be expected, 0% will also not burn.

Furthermore, each gas is quite different and the *flammability range* depends on the gas type as shown in the table below:

Gas	Flammable Limits Lower %	Higher %
Acetylene	1.5	100
Hydrogen	4	75.6
Methane	5	15
Butane	1.5	8.5

The terms used to describe these limits are called: LFL, *lower flammable limit*, and UFL, *upper flammable limit* (previously called LEL and UEL, lower and upper *explosive* limits).

This is still not all that must taken into consideration; there is also the amount of minimum ignition *energy* required to ignite the gas, and the *temperature* at which the gas *automatically* ignites. Some examples are shown in the table below:

Gas	Auto-Ignition Temperature (°C)	Minimum ignition energy (mJ)
Acetylene	305	0.02
Butane	365	0.25
Hydrogen	560	0.02
Methane (firedamp)	595	0.29

The above table shows that hydrogen has a very low *ignition energy*, but a very high *ignition temperature*. Acetylene, however has a low ignition energy and low ignition temperature (beware, it is very easy to ignite). Methane with its very high ignition temperature and high ignition energy can prove quite difficult to ignite. (Natural gas igniters are difficult to design!)

On the other hand, the amount of energy *released* (in MJ/m^3) by a given volume of gas does vary, methane containing three times as much energy as Hydrogen and Butane eleven times as much (see table below). A medium size camping gas cylinder of butane can contain more than enough energy to destroy an average-sized household garage.

Gas	Net Calorific Value MJ/m^3
Acetylene	51
Butane	112.4
Hydrogen	10.2
Methane	34

6.4. Apparatus Gas Groups

The flammable gases in which explosion protected electrical equipment may have to operate are grouped according to the *amount* of electrical *energy*, in the form of an arc, which is needed to ignite the gas.

Gases associated with the mining industry are fire-classed as GROUP **I**, all other industrial gases are classed as GROUP **II** which are listed in three sub-groups according to their ease of ignition.

It should be noted that equipment certified for use in group IIC may also be used for IIA and IIB. Equipment certified for IIB may be used for IIA.

Equipment certified for IIA may be used with no other group.

Groups (BS4683 Part 21971)

Apparatus Gas Group	Gas or Vapour		
I	Methane (Firedamp)		
IIA	Ammonia Industrial methane Blast furnace gas Carbon monoxide Propane Butane Pentane Hexane Heptane	iso Octane Decane Benzene Xylene Cyclohexane Acetone Ethyl methyl ketone Methyl acetate Ethyl acetate n-Propyl acetate Butyl	acetate Amyl acetate Chloroethylene Methanol Ethanol iso Butanol n-Butanol Amyl alcohol Ethyl nitrite
IIB	Buta-1, 3 diene Ethylene Diethylether Ethylene oxide Town gas		
IIC	Hydrogen		

The gas grouping can affect the design and construction of some types of *explosion protected* equipment (Exd and Exi)

6.5. Temperature Class

This defines the *maximum surface temperature* of the components in the electrical equipment under normal and fault conditions. This maximum surface temperature must not exceed the gas ignition temperature.

The temperature class is stated with reference to a maximum ambient temperature of 40°C, should any other reference temperature be adopted, regulations require that this temperature be shown on the equipment.

It is important to note that the apparatus gas grouping and temperature class are not related. For instance, hydrogen requires very little spark energy to ignite, but the surface temperature necessary for ignition is very high (560°C).

The following table relates the temperature class to the maximum surface temperature under fault conditions.

Temperature Class	Maximum surface temperature
T1	450°C
T2	300°C
T3	200°C
T4	135°C
T5	100°C
T6	85°C

For example, an electric motor may have a maximum surface temperature of 120°C and would be classed as T4. Temperature Classifications and Apparatus Groups for all Group II gases can be found in BS 5345 Part 1.

6.6. Types of Explosion Protection

There are a number of different constructional techniques employed in preventing electrical equipment causing explosions in hazardous areas. Some techniques, such as *flameproof* enclosures, have long been established but others, such as *intrinsic safety* and *increased safety*, are the result of developments in material and electrical/electronic circuit design.

Fig. 6.2 Ex identification marks.

It has been internationally agreed that explosion protected equipment be identified by the symbol "Ex" followed by a letter indicating the type of protection employed.

The following table lists the *types* of protection:

Symbol	Type of Protection
Exd	flameproof enclosure
Exi	intrinsic safety
Exe	increased safety
Exn	non-sparking
Exq	powder filled (*not applicable to ships*)
Exo	oil immersed (*not applicable to ships*)
Exp	pressurisation
Exs	special protection

Some equipment may use more than one of these types of protection in its construction. In this case, the primary type of protection is quoted first. For example, an *increased safety* motor with a *flameproof* terminal box would be marked Exe d. Equipment may also be marked with a prefix "E" which denotes compliance with European Standards e.g. EExe d.

6.7. Exd Flameproof Enclosure

Type 'd' protection, code EExd, uses a flameproof enclosure to contain the electrical apparatus. The internal apparatus may include parts which arc and surfaces which become hot. Gas may be inside the enclosure so it must fulfil three conditions:

- The enclosure must be strong enough to withstand an internal explosion without suffering damage.

- The enclosure must prevent the flame and hot gases from being transmitted to the external flammable atmosphere.

- The external surface temperature of the enclosure must remain below the ignition temperature of the surrounding gas under all operating conditions.

The transmission of flame and hot gases from a flameproof enclosure is prevented because all joints, such as flanges, spigots, shafts and bearings are closely machined to achieve a small gap which is less than a defined maximum. The pressure of an internal explosion is then released through the small gap between machined faces which *cools* the gas sufficiently to prevent it from igniting any external flammable atmosphere.

The maximum permitted gap depends upon three factors:

- The type of gas with which the apparatus is safe for use. This is indicated by *Apparatus Group*.

- The width of the joint (L).

- The volume of the enclosure (V).

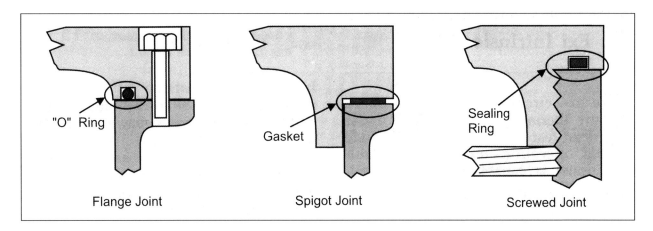

"O" Ring   Gasket   Sealing Ring

Flange Joint   Spigot Joint   Screwed Joint

Fig. 6.3 Exd flamepaths.

These factors are illustrated in Fig. 6.3 for a flanged enclosure:

QUESTION

A ship's battery room is fitted with a flameproof luminaire marked Exd IIC T4. Is this luminaire certified for use in the battery room?

ANSWER

Yes.
The hazard is *hydrogen* gas from the batteries which requires apparatus designed for use in apparatus gas group IIC. The ignition temperature of hydrogen is 560°C and the tenperature classification of the luminaire is T4. This means that it's surface temperature will not exceed 135°, so the temperature classificatio is satisfactory.

The cable entry into an Exd enclosure must also be maintained *flameproo by using a certified Exd gland. This type of gland, shown in Fig. 6.4, has a compound filling which forms a barrier between the individual conductors and prevents entry of explosive products from the enclosure entering the cable.*

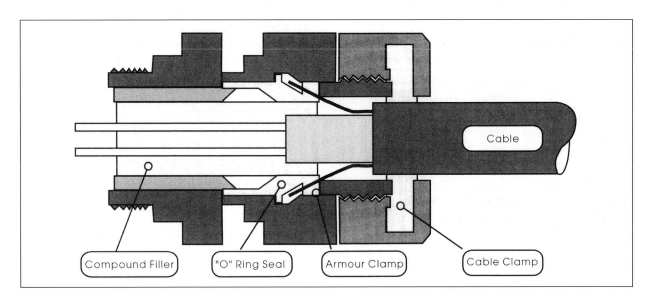

Cable

Compound Filler   "O" Ring Seal   Armour Clamp   Cable Clamp

Fig. 6.4 Exd cable gland.

6.8. Exi Intrinsic Safety

These are circuits in which no spark nor any thermal effect produced under prescribed test conditions (which include normal operation and specified fault conditions) is capable of causing ignition of a given explosive atmosphere. Generally, this means limiting the circuit conditions to less than 30 V and 50 mA. Naturally, this restricts the use of Exi protection to low power instrumentation, alarm and communication circuits.

The design of the circuit will depend on the type of gas present (gas grouping).

In the UK, two grades of *intrinsic safety* are recognised based on the safety factor of the equipment involved:

✳ Exia

the highest category based on a safety factor of 1.5 with *two* faults on the circuit.

✳ Exib

based on a safety factor of 1.5 with *one* fault on the circuit.

In addition to apparatus in the hazardous area being rated as intrinsically safe, an electrical safety barrier may also be fitted to the circuit.

The purpose of such a barrier is to *limit voltages* and *currents* in the hazardous area when faults occur on the circuit.

A separate barrier is required for each Exi circuit and they must be fitted *outside* the hazardous area. See Fig. 6.5.

A safety (or zener) barrier comprises:

✓ A fuse to limit the maximum current through the shunt (zener) diodes.

✓ A set of resistors to limit the maximum current into the hazardous area.

✓ A set of shunt connected zener diodes to limit the maximum voltage appearing on the circuit within the hazardous area.

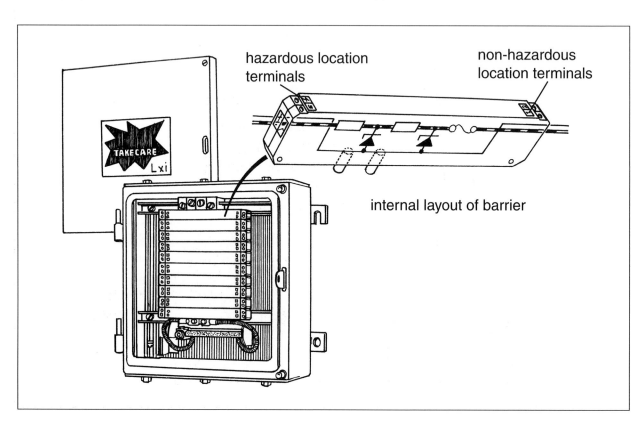

Fig. 6.5 Exi barrier construction.

All components are sealed into a compact package with clearly marked terminals at each end of the barrier.

The circuit in Fig. 6.6 shows a single-channel zener barrier. It illustrates the preventive action in the event of a high voltage being accidentally applied to the non-hazardous terminals.

The zener diode characteristic shows that when connected with reverse bias

it has an approximately constant voltage across it irrespective of the size of current flow. In normal operation the instrumentation circuit has a supply voltage lower than the U_z voltage rating of the zener diodes so no current flows through them.

When an accidental high voltage appears at the input to the barrier, the diodes conduct to clamp their voltages to their U_z rating. This then limits the maximum

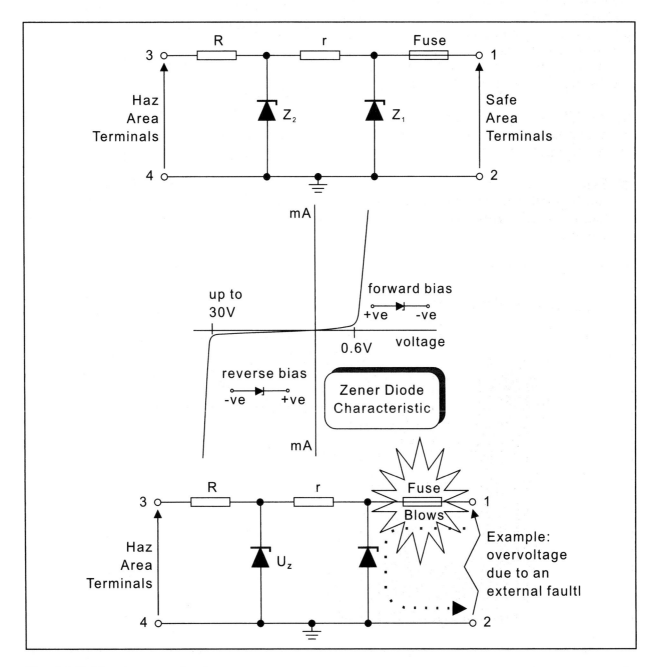

Fig. 6.6 Exi barrier operation.

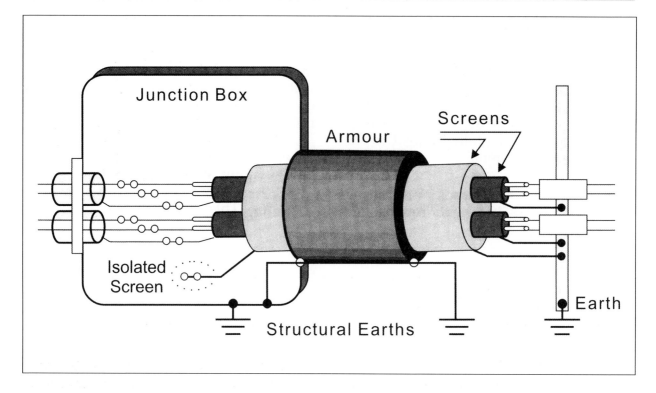

Fig. 6.7 Exi cable terminations.

voltage appearing on the hazardous area wiring. While the zeners are conducting, the current level is designed to blow the fuse which now isolates the circuit to maintain safety in the hazardous area.

In the event of a short-circuit on the hazardous area wiring or equipment, the in-line resistors within the barrier will limit the size of fault current while the fuse blows. Two or three zener-resistor combinations are used within a barrier to provide back-up voltage *anchors* while the fuse is blowing.

After clearing a fault, the complete zener barrier must be *replaced* with an identical unit. No alterations to the original is allowed – remember this is a *certified Ex* safety device.

Cables for intrinsically safe circuits aboard ships should be *separated* from power cables and the crossing over of such cables should be at 90°. This is to minimise electromagnetic interference from the power cables affecting the intrinsically safe circuits.

The metallic cable *screens* of *intrinsically safe* circuits should be earthed at the power supply end only to prevent circulating currents within the sheath. See Fig. 6.7.

Power and intrinsically safe cable runs should be *separately identified*. i.e. by labels or by using cables with a distinctive colour (typically blue for Exi).

6.9. Exe Increased Safety

Increased safety equipment is based primarily on the elimination of *open sparking* as at relay and switch contacts or on the commutators or slip-rings of motors and generators, and on the close control of surface temperatures.

Also, the construction of the equipment is to a very high standard to prevent faults developing. Extra insulation is used, creepage distances between bare

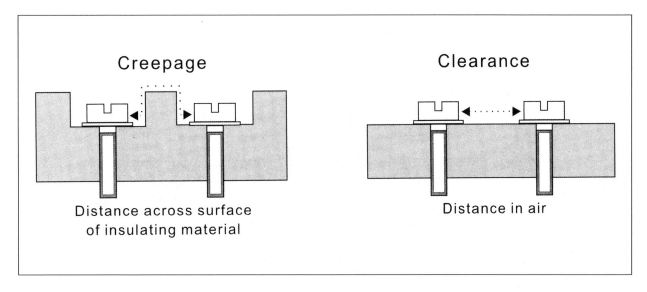

Fig. 6.8 Creepage and clearance distances.

terminals are made longer and special enclosures to protect against damage due to entry of moisture and mechanical damage are also specified. See Fig. 6.8.

The enclosure is made to withstand impact and to prevent ingress of solids and liquids.

Applications include cage-rotor induction motors, luminaires and connection boxes. Special Exe cable glands, metal or plastic, are used with Exe apparatus.

6.10. Exn Non-Sparking

Similar to Exe, the designation Exn applies to equipment which has no arcing contacts or hot surfaces which could cause ignition.

The Exn requirements are less stringent than for Exe, and designs are very close to that of normal electrical apparatus.

The main consideration is extra care to ensure locking of terminal connections to avoid any risk of electric sparking or flashover.

6.11. Exp Pressurised Enclosure

Clean, dry air or an inert gas is supplied to the equipment slightly above atmospheric pressure to prevent entry of the external flammable gas. This method is sometimes used for motors, instrumentation enclosures and lighting.

The diagrams in Fig. 6.9 show that the internal pressure may be maintained by leakage compensation or by continuous circulation. A pressurisation system requires a *purge* flow before the internal electrical equipment is permitted to operate. Also, the pressurised enclosure must be fitted with alarm and trip

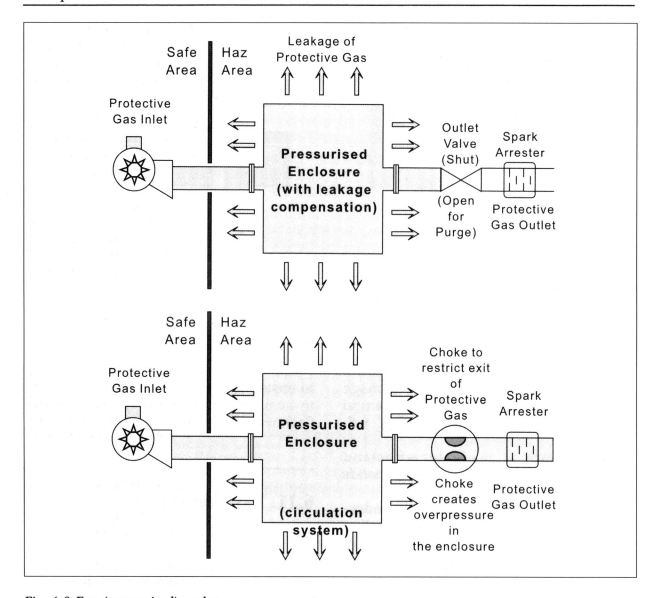

Fig. 6.9 Exp (pressurised) enclosure arrangements.

signalling for a reduction of pressure which in turn will switch-off the enclosed electrical circuits.

6.12. Exs Special Protection

This includes precautions taken to prevent explosions which are not specifically covered by the previous designations.

The table below shows the type of protection which is allowed in the three hazardous zones:

Zone	Type Of Protection
0	Exia Exs (specially certified for use in Zone 0)
1	Any type of protection suitable for Zone 0 and: Exd Exib Exp Exe Exs
2	Any type of protection suitable for Zone O or 1 and: Exn, Exo, Exq

6.13. Certification and Identification

When a manufacturer produces an item of explosion protected equipment, it must be tested and inspected to ensure that it complies with the required standards relating to that type of protection.

In the UK this work is carried out by BASEEFA (British Approvals Service for Electrical Equipment in Flammable Atmospheres) and SCS (SIRA Certification Service).

BASEEFA/SCS issue a certificate for each explosion protected device they test.

The BASEEFA certificate number is shown on the equipment name plate.

Some other national certification authorities:

USA: There is no national certifying body in the USA. Two separate insurance based organisations carry out tests on equipment and issue approvals (listings) of apparatus and equipment acceptable to their published standards. The organisations are:
FM Factory Mutual Research Corporation.
UL Underwriters Laboratories.

Canada: CSA The Canadian Standards Association is the national body responsible for certifying equipment for hazardous areas.
CSA have an arrangement with BSI to allow U.K. equipment which has a BASEEFA approval to be certified to CSA Standards in the U.K.

Australia: SAA The Standards Association of Australia is responsible for certification in Australia. SAA has an arrangement with BSI to help U.K. organisations to obtain SAA Approval.

South Africa: SABS South African Bureau of Standards.

Germany: PTB PTB are the testing and certification authority, certifying either to CENELEC Standards or to VDE Standards. (VDE is the German equivalent of BSI).

Denmark: DEMKO Danmarks Eleclriske Material-Kontrol.
Denmark also recognises the CENELEC Standards.

Norway: DNV Det Norske Veritas: an approvals body similar to Lloyds.

The following example gives a reminder of the meaning of the Ex identification marks on a rating label for an item of explosion-protected apparatus:

Example: **EExia IIC T4 No.** BASEEFA Ex 78229X					
E	**Ex**	**ia**	**IIC**	**T4**	**No.**
to European Standard EN50 020	Explosion Protection	Type of protection	Apparatus Group	Temperature Class	Certifying Authority and Certificate Number

QUESTION

Explain the meaning of the Ex label listed above

ANSWER

Intrinsically safe (Exi) to the highest safety factor (a) which is suitable for installation in Zone 0. Apparatus group (IIC) is suitable for hydrogen. Temperature class (T4) allows a maximum surface temperature of 135°C.

The certifying authority is the UK test house BASEEFA.

6.14. Electrical Testing in Hazardous Areas

All electrical apparatus and associated circuits are required to be tested periodically in accordance with a definite testing routine with recorded test results.

Insulation resistance, earth loop resistance and earth continuity resistance tests are required to be made, the last two in relation to the setting or rating of the protective devices associated with the apparatus and its circuitry.

It is important that insulation resistance tests are NOT made in such a way that the safety devices and insulation used in intrinsically safe apparatus and circuits are damaged by excess test voltages.

No apparatus should be opened in a danger area until it has been made dead and effective measures (e.g. locking-off the isolating switch) have been taken to prevent its being made live again inadvertently.

Where, for the purpose of electrical testing, it is necessary to restore the power supply before the apparatus is reassembled, tests should be made using a suitable *gas detector* and continued during the operation to ensure that the combustible does not approach the explosive limit.

Unless the hazardous area can be made *gas-free* or otherwise safe, or the electrical equipment is removed from the area, then insulation resistance testing should be carried out using a 500 V d.c. tester of *certified intrinsically safe (Exi)* design.

The testing and maintenance of *flameproof* or *intrinsically safe* equipment should be entrusted only to competent persons who have received instruction in the special techniques involved.

The body material of instruments and tools required for maintenance purposes should be designed so that they will not make a hot spark when dropped.

The *energy* output of all *intrinsically safe* instruments should be so small that they do not produce hot sparks. An insulation tester has a *drooping* characteristic to prevent high currents and may be intrinsically safe when applied to circuits of small inductance or capacitance but a risk may arise when such energy-storing properties of a circuit have an appreciable value.

Where such instruments are used the test leads should be firmly connected throughout and on completion of the test they should *not* be detached until the circuit has been discharged through the testing instrument (leave the tester for one minute after test is finished).

6.15. Maintenance of Ex-protected Apparatus

The previous sections covering zoning, gas grouping, temperature classification and the various types of protection methods show that the design of electrical equipment for hazardous areas is very special.

Maintenance of such apparatus must not, in any way, cause its operation to be less safe than in its original certified state.

This most important point means that the maintenance must be carried out by a competent person. Temporary *lash-ups*, refitting with wrong sized components (e.g. lamps), failing to employ the correct number of cover bolts etc., is absolutely *forbidden*.

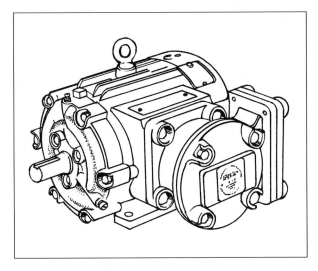

Fig. 6.10 Exd (flameproof) motor construction.

The inspection and maintenance of Exd (*flameproof*) enclosures for luminaires, switches, junction boxes, push-buttons, etc., requires meticulous care.

The following example gives a guide to the inspection and maintenance points as applied to a *flameproof luminaire*:

✔ Corrosion

This will reduce the enclosure strength. To ascertain the extent of corrosion, remove dirt, loose paint and surface corrosion with a wire brush. If only the paintwork is deteriorating, the enclosure should be repainted to prevent further corrosion.

✔ Bolts

Make sure that there are no missing bolts. This is particularly important on flameproof luminaires because a missing bolt will invalidate the certification. Replacement bolts must be of equivalent strength as originals (usually high tensile steel).

✔ Mountings

Ensure all mountings are secure. Corrosion and vibration are severe on ships and can cause premature failure.

✔ Flamepaths

Examine the flamepath for signs of corrosion or pitting. If the flamepath needs cleaning, this should be done with a non-metallic scraper and/or a suitable non-corrosive cleaning fluid.

✔ Cement

Examine the cement used around lamp-glass assemblies both inside and outside. If the cement is eroded, softened or damaged in any way, advice should be sought from the manufacturer regarding repair. If deterioration of the cement has occurred, a complete new lampglass assembly should be fitted.

✔ Lampglass

Check lampglass; if cracked or broken a complete new lampglass assembly should be fitted. Clean the lampglass.

When re-assembling an *Exd enclosure* you must ensure that the following points are covered:

✔ Lightly grease all flamepaths and threaded components with an approved form of non-setting silicone grease. Care must be taken to ensure that blind tapped holes are free from accumulated dirt or excessive grease which can prevent the correct closure of flamepaths, or cause damage to the tapped components. Fit new lamp of the correct rating.

✔ Ensure bolts are not over-tightened as this can distort flamepaths, cause excessive stress on lampglasses or distort weather proofing gaskets, if fitted, allowing the ingress of liquids and dusts.

✔ Check the luminaire is installed in accordance with the requirements of the installation, particularly the classification of the area if it is hazardous and that the correct rating of lamp is fitted.

✔ Remove any build-up of dust on the luminaire, this can cause overheating as well as acting as a corrosive agent.

Before attempting any maintenance work on Exd equipment check for any particular inspection and overhaul instructions given by the manufacturer.

Chapter Seven
Electrical Survey Requirements

7.0. Introduction

The electrical equipment aboard ship is inspected and tested during the complete engine survey which occurs every four years. Such a survey is prescribed under the Rules and Regulations for the Classification of the Ship.

The electrical survey guidance given in this chapter is based on the periodical Survey regulations of Lloyds Register of Shipping, London. Other classification societies have their own rules which, although similar to Lloyds, should be consulted prior to an electrical survey.

7.1. SOLAS

The International Maritime Organization (IMO), which met for the first time in 1959, is a specialised agency of the United Nations devoted to maritime affairs. Its main interests can be summed up in the phrase *"safer shipping and cleaner oceans"*.

Of all the international conventions dealing with maritime safety, the most important is the International Convention for the Safety of Life at Sea, better known as SOLAS, which covers a wide range of measures designed to improve the safety of shipping.

The Convention is also one of the oldest of its kind: the first version was adopted in 1914 following the sinking of the *Titanic* with the loss of more than 1,500 lives.

Since then there have been four more versions of SOLAS. The present version was adopted in 1974 and entered into force in 1980.

The Convention in its consolidated edition dated 1997 has eleven chapters.

Electrical regulations are part of Chapter II-1 which outlines the requirements for *Ship construction − sub-division and stability, machinery and electrical installations*.

This Chapter has five Parts as follows:

✧ Part A *General*
✧ Part B *Sub-division and stability*
✧ Part C *Machinery installations*
✧ Part D *Electrical installations*
✧ Part E *Additional requirements for periodically unattended machinery spaces*

The electrical installations (Part D) is sub-divided into regulations as:

✧ Regulation 40 *General*
✧ Regulation 41 *Main source of electrical power and lighting systems*
✧ Regulation 42 *Emergency source of electrical power in passenger ships*
✧ Regulation 42–1 *Supplementary emergency lighting for ro-ro passenger ships*
✧ Regulation 43 *Emergency source of electrical power in cargo ships*

✧ Regulation 44 *Starting arrangements for emergency generator sets*
✧ Regulation 45 *Precautions against shock, fire and other hazards of electrical origin*

7.2. Classification Societies

Some of the main Classification Societies for ships are:

• American Bureau of Shipping, New York.

• Bureau Veritas, Paris.

• Germanischer Lloyd, Hamburg.

• Nippon Kaiji Kyokai, Tokyo.

• Det Norske Veritas, Oslo.

• Registro Italiano Navale, Genoa

Electrical equipment and services aboard ship must also meet the minimum standards specified by various national and international organisations.

For British registered ships in particular, it is necessary to comply, with:

• Regulations for the Electrical and Electronic Equipment of Ships − Institution of Electrical Engineers (IEE). In conjunction with the British Standards Institute (BSI) these Regulations are being combined with the Recommendations for the Electrical and Electronic Equipment of Offshore Installations.

• The Merchant Shipping Rules − Maritime and Coastguard Agency (MCA)

• Safety of Life at Sea (SOLAS) − IMO Convention

• British Standards (BS)

• International Electrotechnical Commission (IEC).

The standards specified by the above organisations are met when the ship is designed, built, approved and classified.

It is for the shipowner and the operating staff to maintain the vessel and its electrical installation to the requirements of the Classification Society throughout the ship's lifetime.

The periodical electrical survey is, therefore, to check that the installation is maintained to the Rules of the Classification Society.

7.3. Main Electrical Survey Items

The following survey items apply in general to all ships:

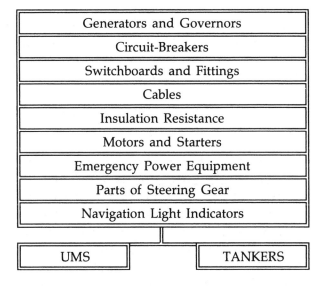

Generators and Governors
Circuit-Breakers
Switchboards and Fittings
Cables
Insulation Resistance
Motors and Starters
Emergency Power Equipment
Parts of Steering Gear
Navigation Light Indicators

UMS	TANKERS

For UMS operation, a survey of the associated alarms, controls and fire detection is required.

For tankers/gas carriers and other ships transporting flammable cargo, an additional survey of all electrical equipment in hazardous areas is carried out during each docking survey and annual survey. This means that hazardous area electrical equipment is surveyed every year.

7.4. Generators and Governors

The surveyor will require that main and emergency generators are clean, respond correctly to controls and load changes, and show stable operation when required to run in parallel with other generators.

Generator windings on stator and rotor must be free of dust, oil and moisture. See Fig. 7.1. A visual check will be made for any obvious deterioration, abrasion or cracking of the insulation around the end winding coils on the stator.

An insulation test to earth and between stator phase windings (if the neutral point can be disconnected at the terminal box) should be carried out while the machine is still hot after running on load. See Fig. 7.2.

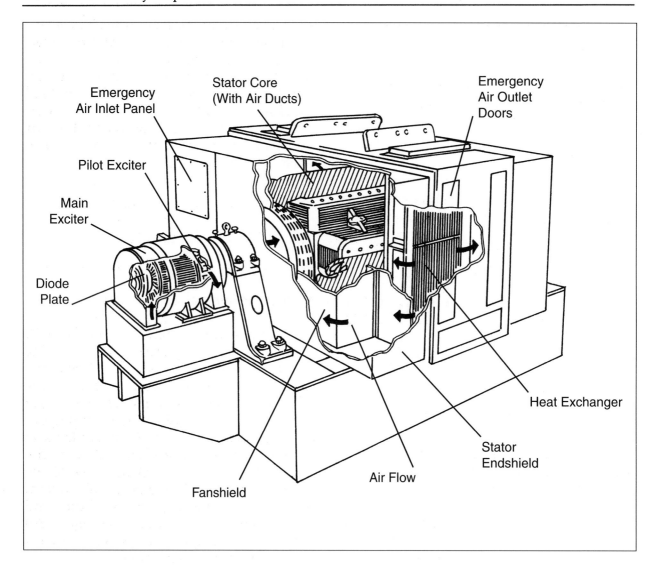

Fig. 7.1 Generator construction.

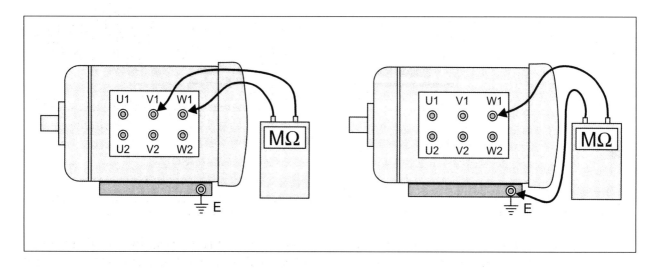

Fig. 7.2 Insulation resistance (IR) test.

QUESTION

Would an IR test result of 0.5 MΩ to earth be acceptable for a 440 V main generator?

ANSWER

Although a minimum of 1.5 MΩ is generally specified for new equipment, Lloyds rules suggest that 0.1 MΩ is acceptable in special cases. However, most surveyors would insist on at least 1 kΩ/volt, i.e. 440 kΩ, say, 0.5 MΩ as a reasonable minimum value for a 440 V generator. For HV equipment the usual recommended minimum IR level is (kV + 1) MΩ. e.g. for a 6.6 kV motor, the acceptable minimum IR would be 7.6 MΩ.

Remember to disconnect all AVR equipment, instrument connections and generator heater supplies when testing for IR.

The rotor circuits must also be tested for insulation value, taking care to short out the rotating shaft diodes of a *brushless* excitation system as the diodes usually have a low PIV (Peak Inverse Voltage) rating.

Special attention to the contact surface of any commutator or slip-rings is required. The contact surfaces must be smooth and concentric without any signs of pitting or deep grooves. Carbon brushes must be of adequate length, maintained at the correct spring pressure and properly contoured onto its rotating commutator or slip-ring. Be sure to remove any excess carbon dust in the vicinity of the brush gear and around rotor coils.

Generator running tests, on load, should confirm the proper operation of governor and AVR controls with correct voltage, frequency and current values indicated on the generator control panel. Governor droop and its response to sudden load changes must be within the declared specification for the prime mover/generator combination. Stability of load sharing of kW and kVAr (or load current/power factor) between two or more generators running in parallel must be demonstrated.

7.5. Circuit Breakers

A visual examination of circuit-breakers (e.g. as shown in Fig. 7.3) in main, emergency and section boards will usually precede operational tests. The surveyor will particularly check the condition of main, arcing and auxiliary contacts for signs of wear, misalignment and overheating. A similar inspection of fixed and moving isolator contacts at the rear of a circuit-breaker will be made.

Arc chutes must be clean, free of arc debris and correctly aligned. All internal wiring should be in good condition and its end connections must be tight. All mechanical linkages will be checked for any signs of wear or stress.

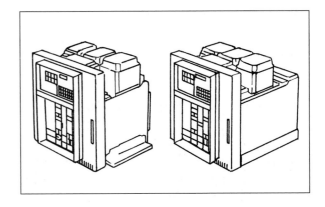

Fig. 7.3 Air-break circuit breaker outlines.

Tests on a circuit-breaker will include *close* and *trip* operations while in its *isolated* position (i.e. not connected in circuit). The racking mechanism for moving the breaker from the service to the *isolated* position must be demonstrated to be free moving and the fixed main terminals must be seen to be shuttered off when the breaker is withdrawn. Emergency hand charging (if fitted) of the closing spring will be tested. Correct operation of the mechanical indicators to show whether the breaker is *open, closed* or *isolated*, is required.

The *undervoltage* release mechanism and *overcurrent* trip settings for level and time delay may have to be demonstrated to the surveyor's satisfaction. An overcurrent trip for a generator breaker is typically set for 130% of full load current (FLC) with a typical time delay of 3 s, but this has to suit the thermal capacity of the generator and be co-ordinated with the overall protection scheme for the power system.

Although the overcurrent and time delay settings on the breaker can be seen to be correctly adjusted to the desired values, only a proper *current injection test* will prove these settings against the manufacturer's I/t characteristics. In this test the circuit-breaker is isolated from the bus-bar and a set of calibrated currents from a current injection set are fed directly through the closed circuit-breaker (*primary injection*) or (more usually) through the overcurrent relay (*secondary injection*). This is generally a specialist task for an outside contractor.

Circuit-breaker time delay mechanisms with oil dash pots must have the pots filled to the correct level with clean oil of a type recommended by the manufacturer.

7.6. Switchboards and Fittings

An obvious survey requirement for any switchboard (as in Fig. 7.4), section board or distribution board is that they are clean. This includes all internal surfaces as well as the external panel surfaces, instrument faces and control switches. A thorough cleaning job on the inside of the main switchboard can only be safely carried out when the board is completely *dead* (all generators stopped and prime movers *locked-off*).

All the main bus-bar and auxiliary connections throughout the boards should be checked for tightness during the *dead* period of a major internal clean up. Overheating signs at a connection junction are probably due to a loose joint. Direct heat testing on load with an infra-red thermal camera is now a very useful technique for locating hot-spots.

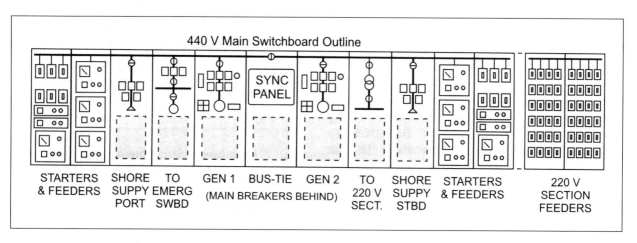

Fig. 7.4 Main switchboard arrangement.

Bus-bar supports will be examined for surface tracking and damage to the insulation material. All internal wiring within the switchboard panels must be securely fixed. Cable entries at the bottom of the switchboard should be sealed with a non-flammable material to exclude dirt and act as a fire stop.

The main switchboard *earth bar* must be securely bonded to both the frame of the board and, of course, to the ship's hull. One secondary terminal of each current transformer (CT) and the metal cases of instruments and relays should be wired to the main earth bar. Hinged panel doors should be bonded with an earth strap to the main switchboard frame.

QUESTION

What is the reason for earthing one end of the secondary winding of a CT?

ANSWER

Should the insulation between primary and secondary break down, the secondary circuit can be raised to full primary voltage; e.g. 440 V above earth which could damage the secondary insulation with a serious risk to personnel. By earthing one end of the CT, the circuit is *anchored* to zero volts. As a bonus, the earth connection will allow such a fault to be detected on the earth fault monitor.

Feeder isolator and fuse holder contacts must be checked for any mechanical wear or damage due to overheating or arcing at the contacts. A slight smear of a proprietary electrical contact lubricant on such moving contacts is usually recommended.

Operational tests on a main switchboard under this heading will focus on the synchronising controls and generator protection relays such as reverse power and preferential load shedding trips. Typical reverse power trip settings may range between 5–15% of the generator power rating, with a time delay of 0.5–2.5 s for a diesel drive. Equivalent settings for a turbo-generator may be 2–5% and 5 s.

Such time delay settings must allow for the operating practice on the ship. For example, cargo winches and cranes may, at times, feed power back into the supply network. Under light load conditions such regenerative feedback may cause a generator to trip on reverse power if its time delay was set too short.

7.7. Cables

Apart from an IR (*megger*) test on a main cable run (e.g. along the flying bridge

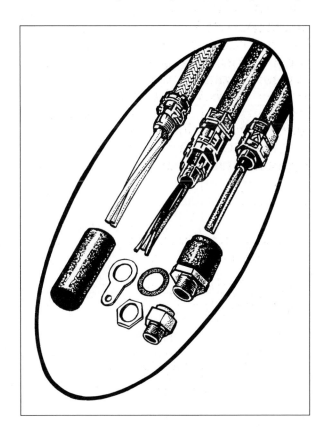

Fig. 7.5 Cable construction outlines.

of a tanker) the survey of cables and their installation is largely based on a close visual examination. Inspection would search for any external damage of a cable's outer sheath and wire or basket weave armouring (if fitted). The cable must, of course, be adequately supported along horizontal and vertical runs by suitable cable clips or ties.

Where cable-runs along an open deck have expansion loops, these must be examined for abrasion and wear.

Where cables pass though fire check bulkheads they must be correctly glanded or pass through stopper boxes which prevent the passage of fire between compartments.

Probably the most common ship-board cable insulations used are EPR (ethylene propylene rubber) or butyl rubber which is sheathed with either PCP (poly-chloroprene) or CSP (chlorosulphonated polyethelene).

QUESTION

What are the functions of EPR or butyl and PCP or CSP?

ANSWER

EPR or butyl rubber are good electrical insulators but are not mechanically strong or resistant to oil. This is why a sheath of PCP or CSP (which is stronger and has greater oil and fire resistance) is fitted around the inner insulation.

Where EPR/butyl cable terminations may be subjected to oil vapour it is usual to tape or sleeve the cable ends to prevent deterioration of the insulation. Check that such taping is secure.

Flexible cables to light fittings, power tools, etc., should be inspected for mechanical damage. In normal operation a flexible cable may be repeatedly dragged and chafed so reducing its safety. If in doubt replace flexible cables.

A copper strap or flexible earthing braid/wire is used to bond the steel frame of all electrical motors and other equipment to the ship's hull.

QUESTION

Why is such an earth bond required?

ANSWER

Without an earth strap, a loose internal wire may touch the frame causing it to become *live* at mains voltage with obvious danger to operators. The earth strap electrically *anchors* the frame to the ship's hull (zero volts) to eliminate the shock hazard to personnel.

7.8. Insulation Resistance

The surveyor will require a list which shows the results of recent insulation tests on all main 440 V and 220 V circuits.

Such a list should also indicate the test date's, weather conditions (hot, humid, etc.) together with any comments relevant to the test conditions (e.g. machine hot or cold).

An example of an IR log and its graphical trend for a motor is shown in Fig. 7.6.

For essential items such as generators and main motors, the surveyor will be more interested in the IR *trend*, so a set of past results showing the insulation history of such machines may be requested.

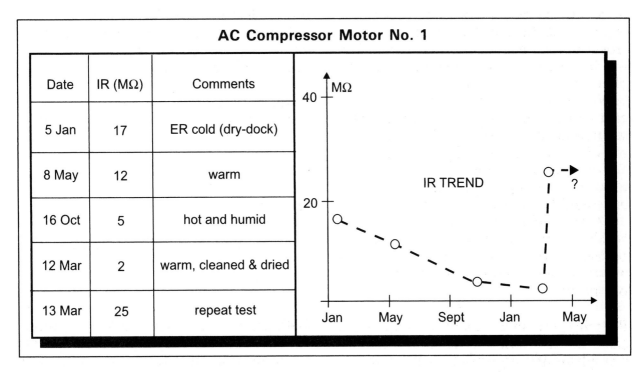

Date	IR (MΩ)	Comments
5 Jan	17	ER cold (dry-dock)
8 May	12	warm
16 Oct	5	hot and humid
12 Mar	2	warm, cleaned & dried
13 Mar	25	repeat test

Fig. 7.6 IR log and trend.

7.9. Motors and Starters

After checking through the IR test results list, a surveyor may ask to witness a repeat test on selected motors. A visual examination of a motor frame and terminal box will reveal any damaged or missing parts. General neglect will be suspected if the motor is covered with dirt, oil or rust.

Totally enclosed fan ventilated (TEFV) induction motors require little attention as their windings are protected against the external atmosphere. The surveyor will be more likely to concentrate on motors with *drip proof, weatherproof* and *deck-watertight* enclosures. It may be necessary to open up such motors to check for ingress of oil and water which could damage insulation and cause internal corrosion.

Special machines such as d.c. commutator or a.c. slip-ring types used, for example, on an electric windlass, must have their rotary contacts and brush gear checked.

Cargo cranes and winches are not strictly part of a survey as they are not considered essential to the safety of the ship.

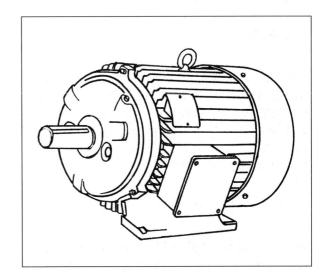

Fig. 7.7 Motor construction.

A running test on a motor will reveal any vibration problems, undue noise and worn out bearings. On-load, the motor running current (shown on the ammeter at the starter) should be checked against the value indicated on the motor rating plate.

With starters and associated control gear such as remote stop/start buttons, regulating resistors etc., an inspection will check mainly for badly burned and misaligned contacts. The general condition of starter equipment will also be examined. This would include an inspection for loose connections, worn *pigtails* on moving contacts, badly carbonised arc-chutes and signs of overheating on coils, transformers and resistors. Dust and weather-proof sealing features on a starter must be in place and in a serviceable condition.

Functional checks will test the normal operation of the starter from its local, remote and emergency control (if applicable) positions. Signal status lamps showing the motor/starter condition, e.g. *running, off, tripped*, etc., must be demonstrated as working correctly. Overcurrent trip settings should be compared with the motor full-load current (FLC) rating. Motor starter back-up fuse size and type may be checked against the ship's/manufacturer's drawings and the motor rating.

7.10. Emergency Power and Associated Equipment

This section surveys the *operation* of the emergency generator and/or battery power equipment (inspection of the emergency generator itself is covered under the heading of Generators and Governors).

The emergency generator must be started, manually or automatically, while the initiation sequence and operation of starting equipment is observed.

Electrical supplies taken from the emergency switchboard should be checked as receiving their rated voltage, current and frequency when powered from the emergency generator.

Emergency lighting, fire pump and other emergency electrical equipment must be functioning correctly. Electrical interlocking arrangements between main and emergency switchboard must be checked. Auto-start initiation relays, whether voltage or frequency operated, will be examined and tested.

The ship's emergency battery installation and its charging rectifier will be examined. In particular the battery environment must be dry and well ventilated. The battery tops must be clean with terminal posts and connections appearing free from corrosion. A typical lead-acid cell outline is shown in Fig. 7.8.

Grease all connections with petroleum jelly. Battery electrolyte should be at its proper level and have the correct value of specific gravity (SG) as checked on a hydrometer. Safety notices and personnel safety clothes (gloves, apron and goggles) should be available adjacent to the batteries. The ventilation arrangements for the battery locker will be checked.

Battery charging equipment should be given the normal checks for dirt, overheating, loose connections and correct functioning of indicators, instruments and alarms.

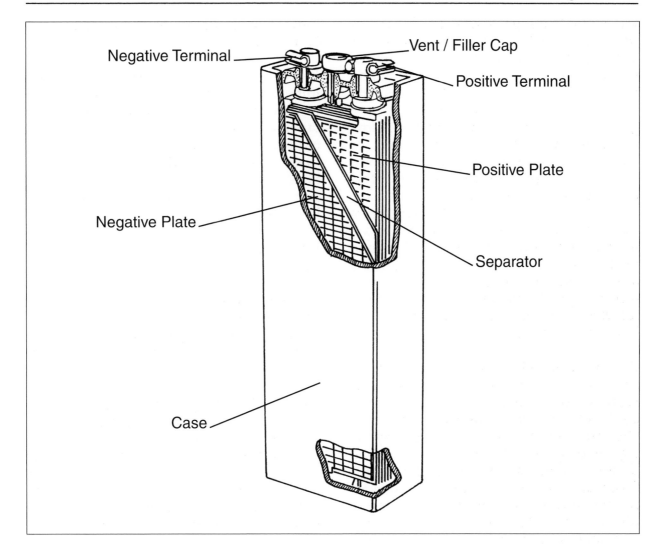

Fig. 7.8 Lead-acid cell outline.

7.11. Parts of Steering Gear

Fig. 7.9 indicates how an electrohydraulic steering gear system can be envisaged from the surveyor's viewpoint as being in three parts:

- Power unit
- Steering control
- Indications and alarms

The power unit comprises duplicate electric motors and starters supplied from either side of the main switchboard.

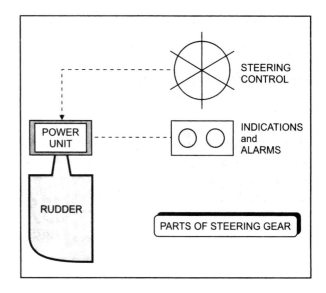

Fig. 7.9 Main steering-gear components.

On many ships one of the steering gear motors will be supplied via the emergency switchboard as recommended by the SOLAS requirements for certain vessel types, e.g. passenger ships and ferries.

The motors, starters and any changeover supply switch units will be inspected under the same criteria outlined earlier in the section on Motors and Starters.

Rudder control from the bridge position may be via an hydraulic telemotor or via an electric controller or both. Main and alternative electric supplies, including any changeover facilities for the electric control from the steering wheel and for the auto pilot, must be tested

The steering gear and its control must be functionally tested for its response. This is generally specified to be that the rudder must be swung from 32° port to 32° starboard in 28 seconds. Note, a fully loaded response can only be obtained when the ship is loaded and under way at sea. Steering gear status indications must be operating correctly in the steering flat, main control room and on the bridge. The rudder position indicators on the bridge may be checked during the functional testing of the steering gear. The bridge indication should be compared with the direct mechanical indicator on the rudder stock in the steering flat.

Motor overcurrent alarms can be initiated by simulating the action of the overcurrent relay. Remember that a steering gear motor does not have overcurrent trip protection; the only main circuit protection being from the back-up fuses which are essential for short-circuit protection. Hydraulic fluid low level alarms, if fitted, must be checked for correct initiation by the oil level sensors.

7.12. Navigation Light Indicators

Essentially, the surveyor will expect to prove that the navigation light indicator operates correctly and gives the appropriate alarms. A broken wire or lamp can be simulated by pulling the appropriate fuse.

The power supply for the navigation lights must be duplicated (usually the alternative supply is obtained from the emergency switchboard) and the changeover facilities must be checked. See Fig. 7.10.

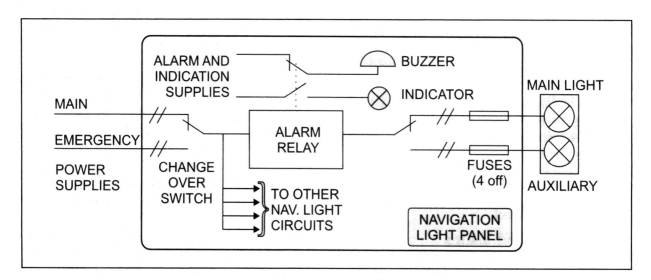

Fig. 7.10 Navigation light indicator panel.

Although the actual light fittings for navigation are part of the Safety Equipment Survey, the electrical survey will naturally include a check on the supply cables to the lights.

7.13. UMS Operation

If your ship is classified for Unattended Machinery Space (UMS) operation, the electrical survey will be extended to include all the alarms, fire detection, controls and fail-safe features of such an installation.

All alarms associated with the main engine, auxiliary machines, lubrication and cooling are to be tested for correct operation. Testing of the electrical circuits from the various sensors is relatively straightforward. This can be achieved by operating the sensor switch by hand or by simulating the switch action under the expected alarm condition. To prove that the overall sensor (pressurestat, flow switch, level switch, temperature switch, etc.) is functioning correctly is obviously more involved. Often, specialist contractors may be called upon to service and calibrate the sensors and alarm annunciators.

Particular attention will be paid to the main engine and auxiliary generators in respect of their alarms for lubrication and cooling. Initiation and action of automatic shut-down features will be tested. Essential drives for lubrication, cooling and fuel supply are duplicated and arranged so that one pump can be selected on a duty/standby basis. Loss of pressure at the duty pump should automatically start up the standby unit.

Automatic start-up of the emergency generator must be demonstrated. The initiation of the undervoltage or under-frequency relay can usually be accomplished by pulling the fuses in the detection unit. The emergency generator should then run up to speed and supply voltage to the emergency switchboard.

UMS requirements demand that a standby main generator starts automatically on loss of the duty generator. The standby generator is to start and close onto the dead bus-bars within 45 seconds.

This is followed by automatic sequential re-starting of essential auxiliaries for lubrication, cooling, fuel and steering. The correct functioning of the system will be tested. The duplicate bilge level alarms together with automatic bilge pumping must be proven to the surveyor's satisfaction.

The main and standby electric power supplies to the overall alarm monitoring system must be inspected and tested. The standby power arrangement usually includes battery back-up. It will be necessary to inspect the general condition of the battery and its trickle-charger.

Tests are made on the UMS alarm system to verify:

✔ that alarms displayed on the main console in the engine control room are relayed to the smaller group alarm panel on the bridge;

✔ that the duty engineer call system is operating in the accommodation areas, i.e. in the cabin of the selected duty engineer and in the duty mess and lounges;

✔ that the selected duty engineer is allowed 2–3 minutes to respond to a machinery alarm. If the engineer has not reached the control room and accepted the alarm within this time, a *dead man* alarm should be sounded generally in the alleyway adjacent to the engineers' accommodation.

A complete inspection and test of the fire detection apparatus must be performed.

All smoke, heat and flame sensors must function correctly to initiate the appropriate audible and visual alarms on the bridge, in the main control room and in the accommodation.

Hand operated fire-alarm switches of the *break-glass* type must also be examined and tested to be in proper working order.

Fig. 7.11 Break-glass switch.

Main engine controls must function correctly and will be tested from the bridge position, local position (engine control room) and at the emergency position alongside the engine.

The operational features of the electrical equipment for main engine control and indication will be best demonstrated during a full engine test during an engine survey. Such electrical equipment and connections associated with engine control will be examined as usual for wear and tear, insulation level, cleanliness, loose connections and overheating.

7.14. Tankers

Electrical equipment in the hazardous areas of oil/gas carriers and other ships carrying potentially dangerous cargo will be surveyed during the normal engine survey (every four years) and during docking and annual surveys.

Consequently, the *hazardous area electrical equipment* is effectively surveyed every year.

The most common form of hazardous area electrical equipment is the *flameproof* enclosure type (marked Exd on the equipment certification label). This type of enclosure will be found on light fittings, motors, starters, push-buttons and alarm bells within the hazardous zones.

The flameproof enclosure will be inspected for surface cleanliness (which affects the surface temperature), corrosion and secure mountings. On lighting fittings the cement that bonds the lamp glass to its frame must be closely inspected for cracks or indentations. All bolts must be in place, evenly torqued-up and of the correct type.

The edges of flamepath flanged joints must not be painted over or impeded in any way. Exposed flameproof equipment on deck must be adjudged weatherproof with the correct (approved) gaskets or "O" rings in place.

An Exd fitting may be opened up to check the condition of its *flamepath* surfaces for corrosion, pitting or scratch marks as shown in Fig. 7.12.

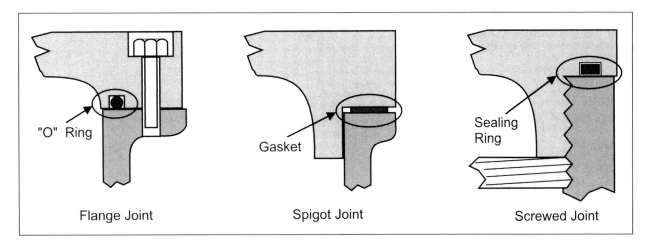

Fig. 7.12 Exd flamepaths.

The Ex Certification label and equipment rating label must not be painted over.

Remember that no alterations to the Exd equipment are allowed without permission from the Certification Authority. This applies also to the *lamp size* and its rating for a particular light fitting — it must have the correct lamp fitted.

Some pump rooms have *pressurised* light fittings (marked Exp on the Certification label). Here it is necessary to confirm that the fittings are *purged* and *pressurised* before the light is allowed to be switched on. Similarly the lights should automatically be switched off if the air pressure drops below its set value.

Electrical instrumentation and communication equipment used in hazardous areas must be *intrinsically safe* (marked Exi on the Certification label). In most cases, zener barriers, as shown in Fig. 7.13, are connected in line with intrinsically safe circuits and are fitted in a *safe* area just outside the hazardous area.

The surveyor cannot easily test zener barriers in situ as this would involve special equipment and it is generally accepted that such protection equipment will function correctly when circuit fault conditions arise. This is no different to accepting that a fuse will blow when a short-circuit occurs.

However, the surveyor will visually inspect the zener barrier *installation*. The barriers must have secure connections and be properly bolted to an earth strap, which in turn, must be solidly bonded to the ship's hull.

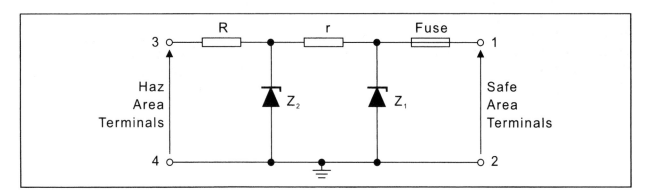

Fig. 7.13 Exi barrier circuit.

Chapter Eight
Electric Propulsion and High Voltage Practice

8.0. Introduction

The earliest electric propulsion for ships was demonstrated in Russia in 1832 with a d.c. motor powered from a battery. In 1886 an electrically propelled vessel called the *Volta* crossed the English Channel. By 1888 the improvements to batteries and motors led to the first commercial applications in passenger launches on the River Thames in London.

As with road transport, electric river boats were soon eclipsed by the arrival of the internal combustion engine.

Electric propulsion for many new ships is now re-established as the popular choice where the motor thrust is governed by electronic switching under computer control.

The high power required for electric propulsion usually demands a high voltage (HV) power plant with its associated safety and testing procedures.

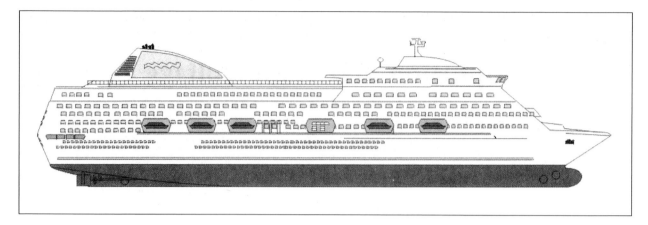

Fig. 8.1 Passenger cruise ship with electric propulsion.

8.1. Electric Propulsion Scheme

Electric propulsion of ships has a long but somewhat chequered history. There have been periods when it has enjoyed popularity, with a significant number of installations being undertaken, whilst at other times it has been virtually ignored as a drive system.

Passenger ships have always been the largest commercial vessels with electric propulsion and, by their nature, the most glamorous. This should not, however, obscure the fact that a very wide variety of vessels have been, and are, built with electric propulsion.

Early large passenger vessels employed the turboelectric system which involves the use of variable speed, and therefore *variable frequency*, turbo-generator sets for the supply of electric power to the propulsion motors directly coupled to the propeller shafts. Hence, the generator/motor system was acting as a speed reducing transmission system. Electric power for auxiliary ship services required the use of separate *constant* frequency generator sets.

A system that has generating sets which can be used to provide power to both the propulsion system *and* ship services has obvious advantages, but this would have to be a *fixed* voltage and frequency system to satisfy the requirements of the ship service loads. The provision of high power variable speed drives from a fixed voltage and frequency supply has always presented problems. Also, when the required propulsion power was beyond the capacity of a single d.c. motor there was the complication of multiple motors per shaft.

Developments in high power static converter equipment have presented a very convenient means of providing *variable speed* a.c. and d.c. drives at the largest ratings likely to be required in a marine propulsion system.

The electric propulsion of ships requires electric motors to drive the propellers and generator sets to supply the electric power. It may seem rather illogical to use electric generators, switchgear and motors between the prime-movers (e.g. diesel engines) and propeller when a gearbox or length of shaft could be all that is required.

There are obviously sound reasons why, for some installations, it is possible to justify the complication of electric propulsion and some of the reasons advanced are:

- Flexibility of layout
- Load diversity between ship service load and propulsion

- Economical part-load running
- Ease of control
- Low noise and vibration characteristics

Flexibility of layout
The advantage of an electric transmission is that the prime-movers, and their generators, are not constrained to have any particular relationship with the load as a cable run is a very versatile transmission medium. In a ship propulsion system it is possible to mount the diesel engines, gas turbines etc., in locations best suited for them and their associated services, so they can be

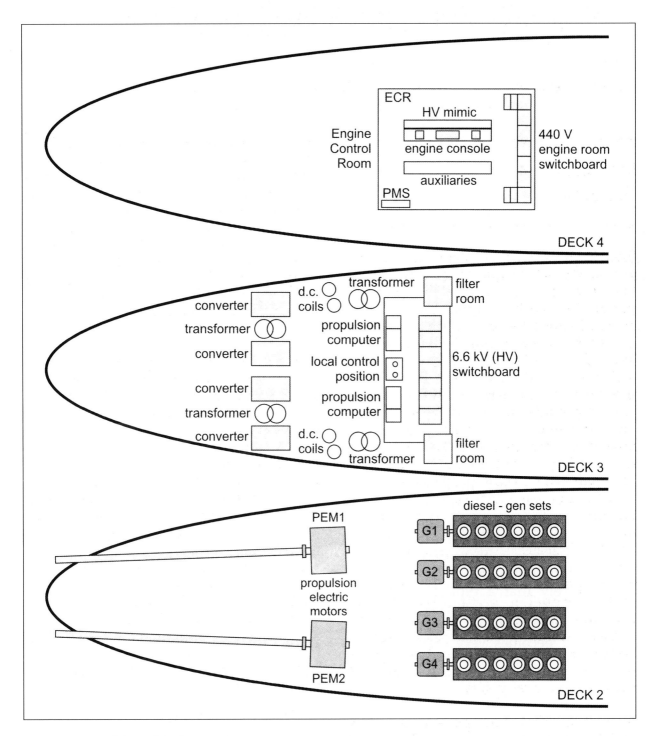

Fig. 8.2 Propulsion plant layout.

remote from the propeller shaft. Diesel generator sets in containers located on the vessel main deck have been used to provide propulsion power and some other vessels have had a 10 MW generator for ship propulsion duty mounted in a block at the stern of the vessel above the ro-ro deck. An example of an electric propulsion plant layout (for a large cruise ship) is shown in Fig. 8.2.

Another example of the flexibility provided by an electric propulsion system is in a semi-submersible, with the generators on the main deck and the propulsion motors in the pontoons at the bottom of the support legs.

Load diversity

Certain types of vessels have a requirement for substantial amounts of electric power for ship services when the demands of the propulsion system are low. Tankers are one instance of this situation and any vessel with a substantial cargo discharging load also qualifies. Passenger vessels have a substantial electrical load which, although relatively constant, does involve a significant size of generator plant. There are advantages in having a single central power generation facility which can service the propulsion *and* all other ship loads as required.

Economical part-load running

Again this is a concept that is best achieved when there is a central power generation system feeding propulsion *and* ship services, with passenger vessels being a good example.

It is likely that a typical installation would have between 4–8 diesel generator sets and with parallel operation of all the sets it becomes very easy to match the available generating capacity to the load demand. In a four engine installation for example, increasing the number of sets in operation from two that are fully loaded to three partially loaded will

result in the three sets operating at a 67% load factor which is not ideal but also not a serious operating condition. It is not necessary to operate generating sets at part-load to provide the spare capacity to be able to cater for the sudden loss of a set, because propulsion load *reduction* may be available instantaneously, and in most vessels a short time reduction in propulsion power does not constitute a hazard.

The propulsion regulator will continuously monitor the present generator capability and any generator overload will immediately result in controlled power limitation to the propulsion motors. During manoeuvring, propulsion power requirements are below system capacity and failure of one generator is not likely to present a hazardous situation.

Ease of control

The widespread use of controllable pitch propellers (cpp) has meant that the control facilities that were so readily available with electric drives are no longer able to command the same premium. Electric drives are capable of the most exacting demands with regard to dynamic performance which, in general, exceed by a very wide margin anything that is required of a ship propulsion system.

Low noise

An electric motor is able to provide a drive with very low vibration characteristics and this is of importance in warships, oceanographic survey vessels and cruise ships where, for different reasons, a low noise signature is required. With warships and survey vessels it is noise into the water which is the critical factor whilst with cruise ships it is structure borne noise and vibration to the passenger spaces that has to be minimised.

An overview of practical electric drive options is shown in Fig. 8.3.

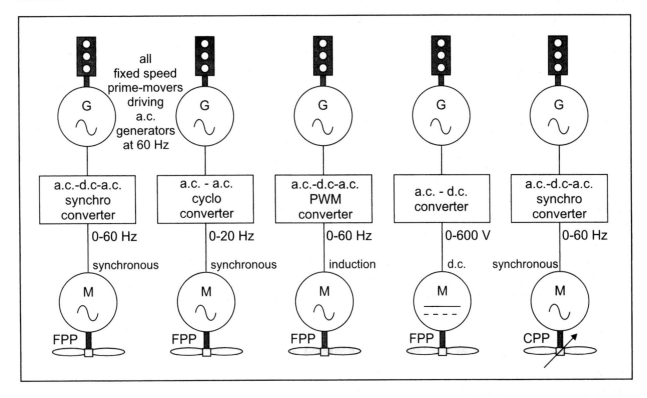

Fig. 8.3 Electric propulsion options.

For very high power, the most favoured option is to use a pair of high efficiency, high voltage a.c. *synchronous motors* with fixed pitch propellers (FPP) driven at variable speed by *frequency control* from electronic converters. A few installations have the combination of controllable pitch propellers (CPP) *and* a variable speed motor.. Low/medium power propulsion (1–5 MW) may be delivered by a.c. *induction motors* with variable frequency converters or by d.c. motors with variable voltage converters.

The prime-movers are conventionally constant speed *diesel engines* driving a.c. generators to give a fixed output frequency. Gas turbine driven prime-movers for the generators are likely to challenge the diesel option in the future.

Conventionally, the propeller drive shaft is directly driven from the propulsion electric motor (PEM) from inside the ship. From experience obtained from smaller *external* drives, notably from ice-breakers, some very large propulsion motors are being fitted within rotating *pods* mounted outside of the ships hull. These are generally referred to as *azipods*, as shown in Fig. 8.4, as the whole pod unit can be rotated through 360° to apply the thrust in any horizontal direction, i.e. in *azimuth*. This means that a conventional steering plate and stern side-thrusters are not required.

Ship manoeuvrability is significantly enhanced by using azipods and the external propulsion unit releases some internal space for more cargo/passengers while further reducing hull vibration.

Gradual progress in the science and application of superconductivity suggests that future generators and motors could be super-cooled to extremely low temperatures to cause electrical resistance to become zero. In this condition, the electrical power losses (I^2R) are also zero so it is possible to drive extremely large currents (> 100,000 A) through very thin wire coils to create an exceptionally large magnetic field. The combination of a large current and a large magnetic field will produce a very large electromagnetic

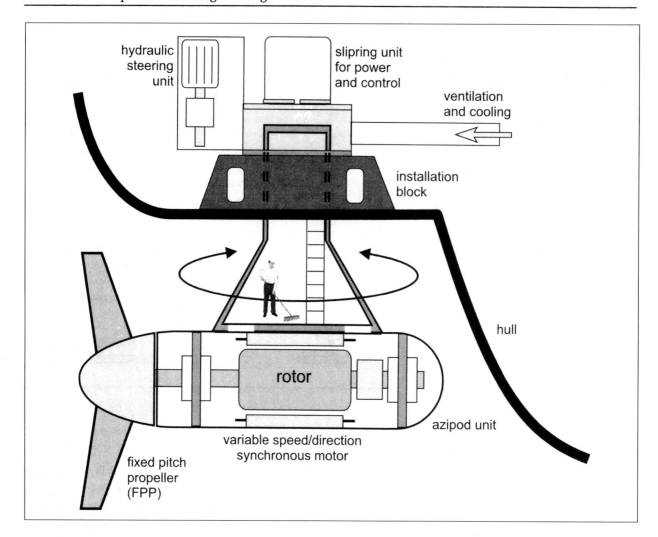

Fig. 8.4 Azipod drive unit.

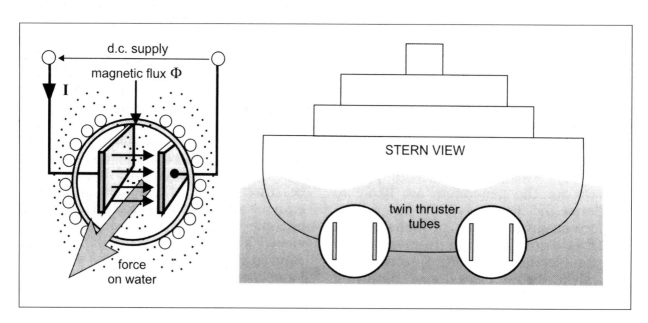

Fig. 8.5 Linear electric propulsion.

force as $F \propto \Phi.I$. One way of applying such a direct force into the water for ship propulsion (a long-term ongoing experiment in Japan) is outlined in Fig. 8.5.

A large d.c. current is driven between metal plates mounted in a open tube below the hull. The conductor for this current is the sea water. Coils of wire at a superconducting temperature (e.g $-269°C$ cooled by helium) are fitted around the propulsion tube to create a magnetic field $90°$ to the current flow. The combination of current and magnetic field produces a direct mechanical force on the conductor (water) to create a linear thrust without the need for a rotating propeller. By dividing port and starboard thrust tubes into short sections along the hull, the size and location of thrust can be distributed so that conventional steering and side thrusters are not required. This is a very interesting experiment into the direct application of electromagnetic force for ship propulsion.

8.2. Power Supply Network

As the demand for electrical power increases on ships (particularly passenger ferries, cruise liners, and specialist offshore vessels and platforms) the supply current rating becomes too high at 440 V. To reduce the size of both steady state and fault current levels, it is necessary to increase the system voltage at high power ratings.

Note: In marine practice, voltages below 1000 V are considered LV (low voltage). HV (high voltage) is any voltage above LV. Typical marine HV system voltages are 3.3 kV or 6.6 kV but 11 kV is used on some offshore platforms and specialist oil/gas production ships e.g on some FPSO (floating production, storage and offloading) vessels.

By generating electrical power at 6.6 kV instead of 440 V the distribution and switching of power above about 6 MW becomes more manageable.

e.g. A three phase 6 MW ships load on a 440 V system supplied by 3×2 MW, 0.8 pf diesel-generator units requires the switchboard *fault level* to be about 90 kA and each generator circuit breaker and system cabling has to handle a *full-load* current (FLC) of:
$I = 2,000,000 \ W/\sqrt{3}.440. \ 0.8 = 3300 \ A$
The same system at 6.6 kV requires the HV switchboard and cables to be rated for a fault level of about 9 kA with generator circuit breakers rated only for an FLC of 220 A.

The component parts of an HV supply system are now standard equipment with HV diesel generator sets feeding an HV main switchboard. Large power consumers such as thrusters, propulsion motors, air-conditioning (A/C) compressors and HV transformers are fed directly from the HV switchboard.

An economical HV system must be simple to operate, reasonably priced and require a minimum of maintenance over the life of the ship. Experience shows that a 9 MW system at 6.6 kV would be about 20% more expensive for installation costs. The principal parts of a ships electrical system operated at HV would be the main generators, HV switchboard, HV cables, HV transformers and HV motors.

An example of a high voltage power system is shown in Fig. 8.6.

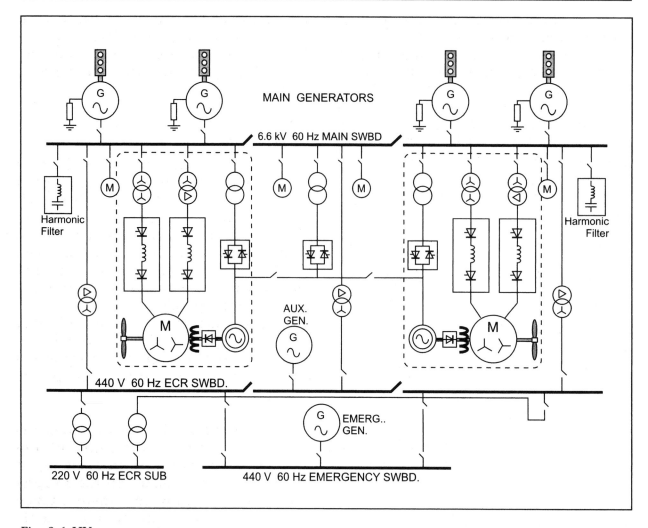

Fig. 8.6 HV power system.

In the example shown the HV generators form a central power station for all of the ship's electrical services. On a large passenger ship with electric propulsion, each generator may be rated at about 10 MW or more and producing 6.6 kV, 60 Hz three-phase a.c. voltages.

The principal consumers are the two synchronous a.c. propulsion electric motors (PEMs) which may each demand 12 MW or more in the full away condition. Each PEM has two stator windings supplied separately from the main HV switchboard via transformers and frequency converters. In an emergency a PEM may therefore be operated as a *half-motor* with a reduced power output.

A few large induction motors are supplied at 6.6 kV from the main board with the circuit breaker acting as a direct-on-line (DOL) starting switch. These motors are:

• Two forward thrusters and one aft thruster, and

• Three air conditioning compressors

Other main feeders supply the 440 V engine room sub-station (ER sub) switchboard via step-down transformers. An interconnector cable links the ER sub to the emergency switchboard. Other 440 V sub-stations (accommodation, galley etc.) around the ship are supplied from the ER sub. Some installations may feed the ships sub stations directly with HV and step-down to 440 V locally.

The PEM drives in this example are synchronous motors which require a controlled low voltage *excitation* supply current to magnetise the rotor poles. This supply is obtained from the HV switchboard via a step-down transformer but an alternative arrangement would be to obtain the excitation supply from the 440 V ER sub switchboard.

QUESTION

Assuming 100% efficiency, *calculate* the FLC then *estimate* the DOL starting current for a three phase, 100 kW, 0.9 p.f. induction motor supplied at:

(a) 440 V;

(b) 6.6 kV

ANSWER

(a) 145.8 A; 729 A

(b) 9.7 A; 49 A (*assuming $I_{DOL} = 5 \times I_{FLC}$*)

8.3. Review of Motor Operation

Electric motors for ship propulsion duty may be of the d.c. or a.c. type. The a.c. versions may be the *induction* or *synchronous* models. The following is a brief review of the basic action and control possibilities for the various types.

- d.c. motors

The d.c. motor drive is still used where very high torque and/or precise speed control is acquired. Traction drives such as electric trains, submarines and offshore drilling rigs use d.c. motors. The torque is governed by: $T \propto \Phi . I_A$ and the speed is due to: $n \propto V/\Phi$ where Φ is the magnetic field flux and I_A is the armature current. See Fig. 8.7.

As the armature current and field flux can be independently controlled, the d.c. motor is able to provide very useful torque/speed characteristics for power drives.

The major drawback of a d.c. motor is that the necessary switching of the armature current is achieved by a *mechanical "commutator"* on the rotating shaft. Apart from the maintenance required for the commutator and its carbon brushes, the applied voltage for the armature is limited to about 750 V d.c. Many regional "Metro" train systems run at 1500 V d.c. where two d.c. motors are connected in series across the supply voltage.

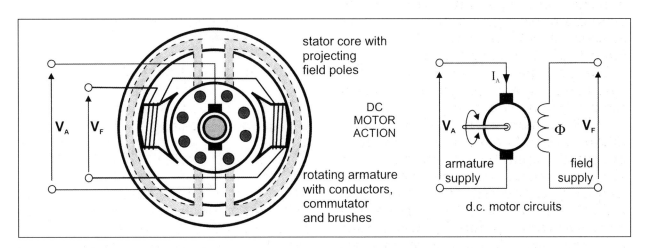

Fig. 8.7 d.c. motor circuit.

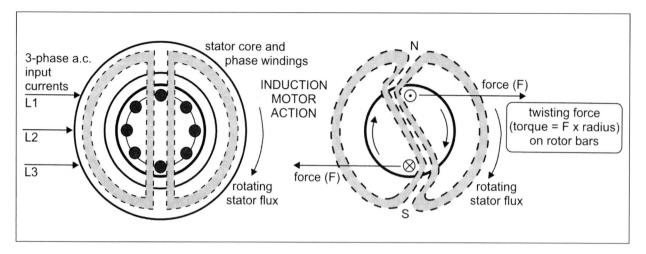

Fig. 8.8 Induction motor action.

- a.c. motors
❖ induction type

The most common motor drive is a three phase a.c. induction motor with a cage-rotor because it is extremely robust as there are no electrical connections to the rotor. See Fig. 8.8.

Three time-displaced supply currents to the three stator windings produce a rotating magnetic field which *induces* currents into the cage winding on the rotor. The interaction of stator flux Φ and rotor current I_R produces a torque on the shaft from $T \propto \Phi.I_R.\cos\phi$ where ϕ is the phase angle between Φ and I_R. To be able to induce currents into the rotor, its running speed must be slightly lower than that of the stator rotating field. This difference is called the *slip* speed and ranges between about 1–5% over the load range for a standard induction motor.

The speed n_s (synchronous speed) of the rotating flux produced by the stator is fixed by the number of winding pole-pairs "p" and the supply frequency "f" as: $n_s = f/p$ (rev/s).

An example:

for a motor designed for 4-poles (p = 2) to run on a 50 Hz supply with a full-load slip of 4%, the speed of the rotating flux is $n_s = 50/2 = 25$ rev/s (1500 rev/min) but the actual rotor speed will be $n_R = 96\%$ of 25 = 24 rev/s or 1440 rev/min.

While the cage-type induction motor is simple and low-cost it has some practical disadvantages. When supplied with a fixed voltage and frequency the motor runs at an almost constant speed and has a high starting current of typically 6 times its full load value.

If the motor in the above example is designed for 440 V with a full load rated output of 100 kW with an efficiency of 90% and a power factor of 0.8 lagging, its full load supply current will be found from the three phase power formula: $P = \sqrt{3}.V_L.I_L.\cos\phi$

So, the electric power input is 100/90% = 111.1 kW and $I_L = (111.1 \times 10^3)/\sqrt{3}.440.0.8 = 182.2$ A then the initial starting current surge is about 911 A!

❖ *synchronous type*

This is a three phase motor that produces a magnetic field rotating at a speed of $n_s = f/p$ (rev/s) just like the induction motor type.

The rotor has a set of magnetic poles with *d.c. excitation* which *locks* in synchronism with the stator *rotating* flux.

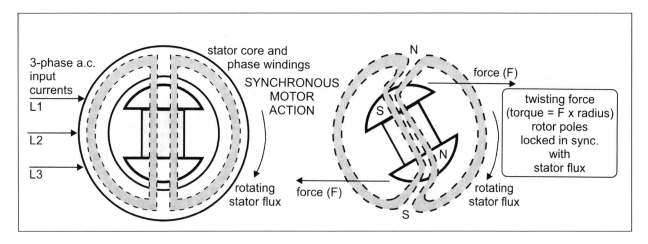

Fig. 8.9 Synchronous motor action.

This means that the shaft is always running at the synchronous speed set by the supply frequency. See Fig. 8.9.

To start the motor from standstill can be a problem – it is either:

• *Pulsed* forward at a very low frequency with the rotor poles excited, or

• *Dragged* up to slip speed as an induction motor with an embedded cage rotor then locked into synchronism by energising the d.c. rotor field.

For normal running, the operating power factor of a synchronous motor can be lagging or leading as this is determined by the size of the d.c. excitation field current.

• Basic speed control of motors

Many industrial installations can benefit from direct and smooth speed control of a drive which is moving the process material (water, compressed air, oil, conveyor belts, lifts etc.). Smooth, controlled acceleration and deceleration also reduces shock loading in the system. For a d.c. motor on a fixed voltage supply, this is easily achieved by using resistance in the armature or field circuits to control the armature current or field flux (or both). The disadvantage is the overall loss of efficiency due to the power losses in the external control resistance(s).

For an a.c. induction motor or synchronous motor on a fixed voltage and frequency supply, resistance control would only affect the size of operating current but the speed is constant due to the fixed supply frequency. This can only be overcome by changing the *frequency* of the stator supply currents. To prevent overheating (by over-fluxing) of the motor while frequency changing, the supply voltage must be changed in direct proportion.

• Advanced speed control

Computer controlled variable speed drives (VSDs) are now applied to d.c. and a.c. motor types of all sizes. The most popular application is for induction motors for the main industrial power range but synchronous motors are used in large installations e.g. marine electric propulsion.

The a.c. motor drives produce a variable frequency output by fast voltage switching from a transistor or thyristor converter which may be ac-dc-ac (PWM and synchroconverter) or ac-ac (cycloconverter). These drives use a mathematical model of the motor and the computer controls the converter output to precisely match the set inputs for speed, torque, acceleration, deceleration, power limits etc.

Such drives may even be *tuned* to create optimum conditions for run-up/down, braking and energy savings against the connected shaft load.

• Problems arising

The fast switching (or *chopping*) of the voltages to VSDs will produce a distorted waveform which includes high frequency *harmonic* components whose frequencies are exact multiples of the fundamental (base frequency) value.

For example a 7th harmonic of a 60 Hz fundamental will be at 420 Hz. Such harmonics create additional heating in equipment and possible interference (often called radio frequency interference or RFI).

Practical solutions to a harmonic problem include good initial system design, filtering and suppression. See later section on harmonics.

8.4. Controlled Rectification and Inversion

The generated three phase a.c. electrical power supply on a ship has a fixed voltage and frequency. This is generally at 440 V and 60 Hz but for high power demands it is likely to be 6.6 kV and 60 Hz.

Speed control for a propulsion motor requires variable voltage for a d.c. drive and variable frequency + voltage for an a.c. drive. The set bus-bar a.c. voltage must be converted by controlled rectification (a.c.→d.c.) and/or controlled inversion (d.c.→a.c.) to match the propulsion motor type.

A basic rectifier uses semiconductor diodes which can only conduct current in the direction of anode (A) to cathode (K) and this is automatic when A is more positive than K. The diode turns-off automatically when its current falls to zero. Hence, in a single-phase a.c. circuit a single diode will conduct only on every other half-cycle and this is called *half-wave rectification*. Other single-phase circuits using a bi-phase arrangement with two diodes and a centre-tapped transformer will create *full-wave rectification*. Similarly, four diodes in a bridge formation will also produce a full-wave d.c. voltage output. An equivalent three phase bridge requires six diodes for full-wave operation. A diode, having only two terminals, *cannot control* the size of the d.c. output from the rectifier.

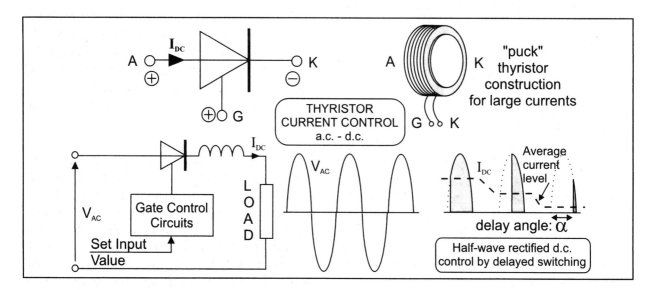

Fig. 8.10 Single-phase controlled rectification.

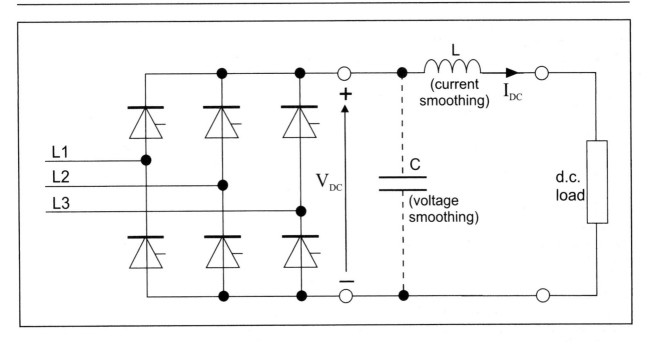

Fig. 8.11 Three-phase controlled rectifier bridge circuit.

- controlled rectification process

For *controlled rectification* it is necessary to use a set of three-terminal devices such as thyristors (for high currents) or transistors (for low – medium currents).

A basic a.c.→d.c. control circuit using a thyristor switch is shown in Fig. 8.10. Compared with a diode, a thyristor has an extra (control) terminal called the *gate* (G). The thyristor will only conduct when the anode is positive with respect to the cathode and a brief trigger voltage pulse is applied between gate and cathode (gate must be more positive than cathode). Gate voltage pulses are provided by a separate electronic circuit and the pulse timing decides the switch-on point for the main (load) current. The load current is therefore *rectified* to d.c. (by diode action) and *controlled* by delayed switching. In this circuit an inductor coil (choke) *smooths* the *d.c. load current* even though the d.c. voltage is severely *chopped* by the thyristor switching action. An alternative to the choke coil is to use a capacitor across the rectifier output which *smooths* the *d.c. voltage*.

Full wave controlled rectification from a three-phase a.c. supply is achieved in a bridge Circuit with six thyristors a shown in Fig. 8.11.

For a 440 V (r.m.s.) a.c. line voltage the peak voltage is $440 \times \sqrt{2} = 622$ V. The equivalent maximum d.c. *average* voltage output is taken to be about 600 V as it has a six-pulse *ripple* effect due to the three-phase input waveform.

- controlled inversion process

A d.c. voltage can be inverted (switched) repeatedly from positive to negative to form an alternating (a.c.) voltage by using a set of thyristor (or transistor) switches. A controlled three-phase thyristor bridge inverter is shown in Fig. 8.12.

The inverter bridge circuit arrangement is exactly the same as that for the rectifier. Here, the d.c. voltage is sequentially switched onto the three output lines. The rate of switching determines the output *frequency*. For a.c. motor control, the line currents are directed into (and out of) the windings to produce a rotating stator flux wave which interacts with the rotor to produce torque.

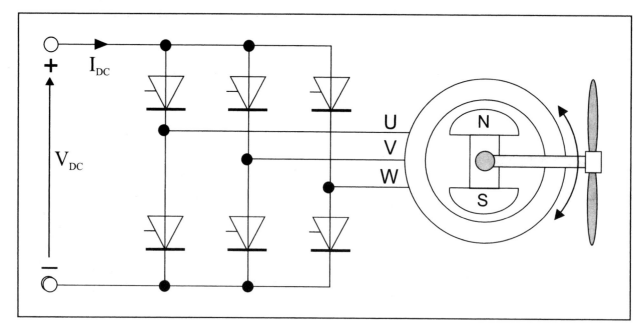

Fig. 8.12 Three-phase inverter circuit and a.c. synchronous motor.

8.5. Converter Types

The processes of controlled rectification and inversion are used in *converters* that are designed to match the drive motor. The principal types of motor control converters are:

- a.c.→d.c. (controlled rectifier for d.c. motors)

- a.c.→d.c.→a.c. (PWM for induction motors)

- a.c.→d.c.→a.c. (synchroconverter for synchronous motors)

- a.c.→a.c. (cycloconverter for synchronous motors)

These are examined below.

- a.c.→d.c. converter

This is a three phase a.c. controlled rectification circuit for a d.c. motor drive. Two converters of different power ratings are generally used for the separate control of the armature current (I_A) and

the field current which produces the magnetic flux (Φ). Some systems may have a fixed field current which means that the field supply only requires an uncontrolled diode bridge as shown in Fig. 8.13.

Motor torque is determined from $T \propto \Phi.I_A$ and the speed is controlled from $N \propto V_A/\Phi$. Shaft rotation can be achieved by reversing either the field current or the armature current direction. Ship applications for such a drive would include cable-laying, offshore drilling, diving and supply, ocean survey and submarines.

- a.c.→d.c.→a.c. PWM converter

This type of converter is used for *induction* motor drives and uses transistors as the switching devices. Unlike thyristors, a transistor can be turned on *and* off by a control signal and at a high switching rate (e.g. at 20 kHz in a PWM converter). See Fig. 8.14.

The input rectifier stage is not controlled so is simpler and cheaper but the converter will not be able to allow power from the motor load to be

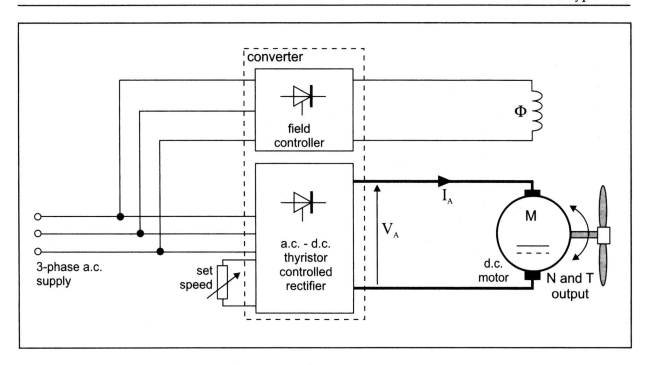

Fig. 8.13 Controlled rectification converter and d.c. motor.

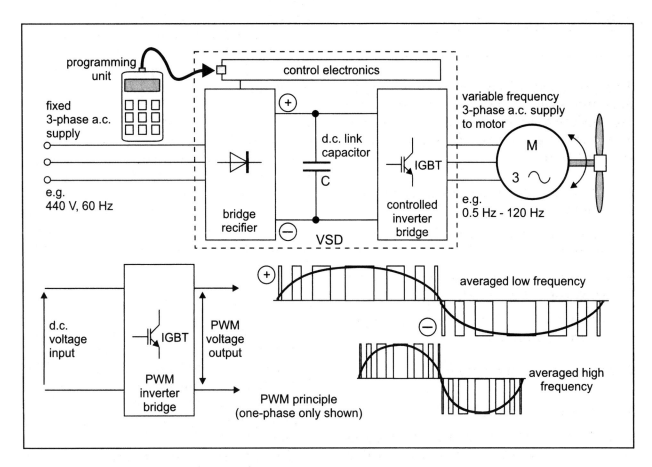

Fig. 8.14 PWM converter and a.c. induction motor.

regenerated back into the mains supply during a braking operation. From a 440 V a.c. supply, the rectified d.c. (link) voltage will be smoothed by the capacitor to approximately 600 V.

The d.c. voltage is *chopped* into *variable-width*, but constant level, voltage pulses in the computer controlled inverter section using IGBTs (insulated gate bipolar transistors). This process is called *pulse width modulation* or PWM. By varying the pulse widths and polarity of the d.c. voltage it is possible to generate an *averaged sinusoidal a.c.* output over a wide range of frequencies typically 0.5–120Hz. Due to the smoothing effect of the motor inductance, the motor *currents* appear to be nearly sinusoidal in shape. By sequentially directing the currents into the three stator windings, a reversible rotating magnetic field is produced with its speed set by the output frequency of the PWM converter.

Accurate control of shaft torque, acceleration time and resistive braking are a few of the many operational parameters that can be programmed into the VSD, usually via a hand-held unit. The VSD can be closely *tuned* to the connected motor drive to achieve optimum control and protection limits for the overall drive. Speed regulation against load changes is very good and can be made very precise by the addition of feedback from a shaft speed encoder.

VSDs, being digitally controlled, can be easily networked to other computer devices e.g. programmable logic controllers (PLCs) for overall control of a complex process.

- a.c. → d.c. → a.c. synchroconverter

This type of converter is used for large a.c. synchronous motor drives (called a synchrodrive) and is applied very successfully to marine electric propulsion.

A synchroconverter, as shown in Fig. 8.15, has controlled rectifier *and* inverter stages which both rely on natural turn-off (line commutation) for the thyristors by the three phase a.c. voltages at *either* end of the converter. Between the rectification and inversion stages is a current-smoothing reactor coil forming the *d.c. link*.

An operational similarity exists between a synchrodrive and a d.c. motor drive.

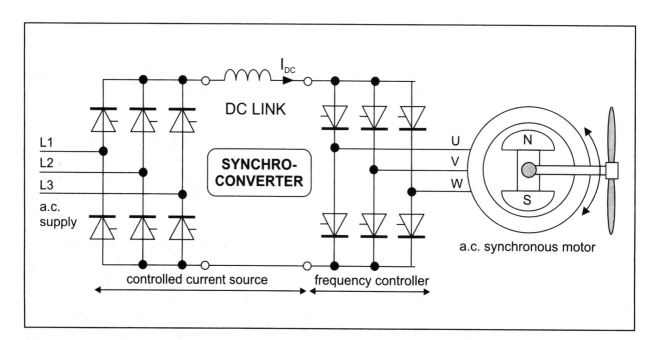

Fig. 8.15 Synchroconverter circuit.

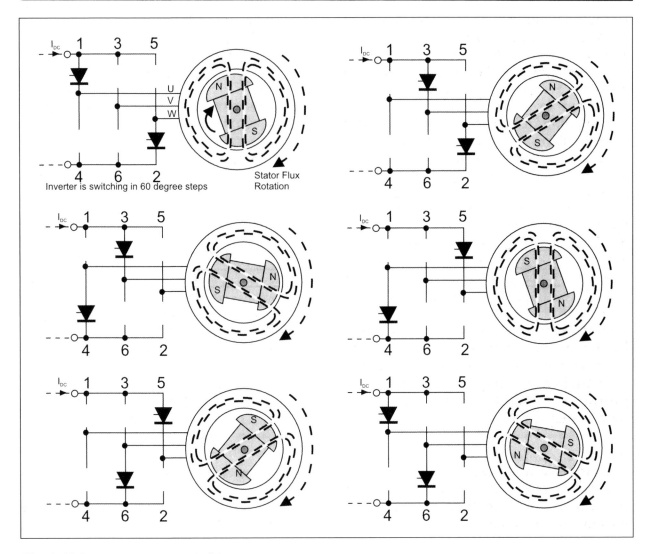

Fig. 8.16 Inverter current switching sequence.

This view considers the rectifier stage as a controlled d.c. supply and the inverter/synchronous motor combination as a d.c. motor. The switching inverter acting as a static commutator.

The combination of controlled rectifier and d.c. link is considered to be a *current source* for the inverter whose task is then to sequentially direct *blocks* of the current into the motor windings as shown in Fig. 8.16.

The *size* of the d.c. current is set by the controlled switching of the rectifier thyristors. Motor supply *frequency* (and hence its speed) is set by the *rate* of inverter switching. The six inverter

thyristors provide six current pulses per cycle (known as a six-pulse converter).

A simplified understanding of synchroconverter control is that the current source (controlled rectification stage) provides the required motor torque and the inverter stage controls the required speed. To provide the motor e.m.f. which is necessary for natural commutation of the inverter thyristors, the synchronous motor must have rotation and magnetic flux in its rotor poles. During normal running, the synchronous motor is operated with a power factor of about 0.9 *leading* (by field excitation control) to assist the line commutation of the inverter thyristors. The d.c. rotor field excitation is obtained from a separate controlled thyristor rectification circuit.

As the supply (network) and machine bridges are identical and are both connected to a three-phase a.c. voltage source, their *roles* can be switched into *reverse*. This is useful to allow the *regeneration* of motor *power* back into the mains power supply which provides an electric braking torque during a *crash stop* of the ship.

• a.c.→a.c. cycloconverter

While a synchroconverter is able to provide an output frequency range typically up to twice that of the mains input (e.g. up to 120 Hz), a cyclo-converter is restricted to a much lower

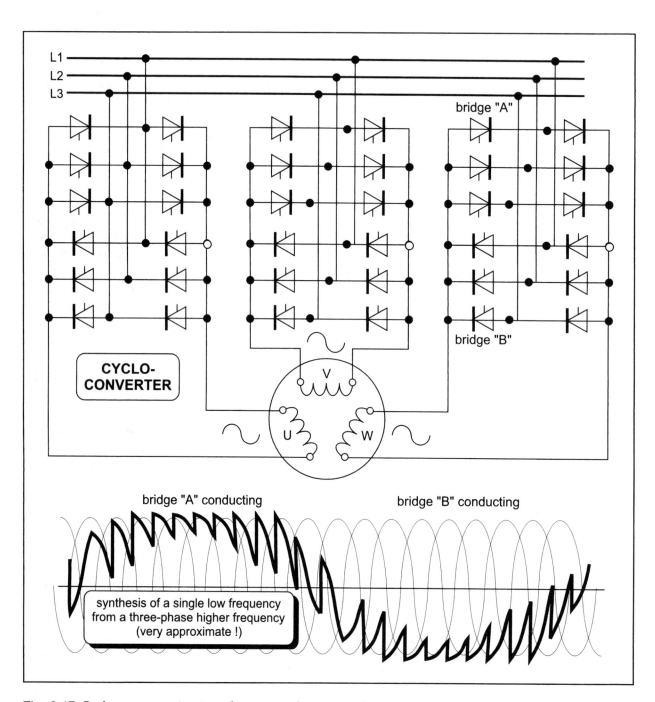

Fig. 8.17 Cycloconverter circuit and output voltage waveform.

range. This is limited to less than one third of the supply frequency (e.g. up to 20 Hz) which is due to the way in which this type of converter produces the a.c. output voltage waveform. Ship propulsion shaft speeds are typically in the range of 0-145 rev/min which can easily be achieved by the low frequency output range of a cycloconverter to a multi-pole synchronous motor. Power regeneration from the motor back into the main power supply is available.

A conventional three phase converter from a.c. to d.c. can be controlled so that the average output voltage can be increased and decreased from zero to maximum within a half-cycle period of the sinusoidal a.c. input. By connecting two similar converters back-to-back in each line an *a.c.* output frequency is obtained. The switching pattern for the thyristors varies over the frequency range which requires a complex computer program for converter control.

The diagram in Fig. 8.17 gives a basic circuit arrangement for a cycloconverter together with an approximate *voltage waveform* for the low frequency output. The corresponding *current* waveform shape (not shown) will be more sinusoidal due to the smoothing effect of motor and line inductance.

The output voltage has a significant *ripple* content which gets larger (worse) as the output frequency is raised and it is this feature that limits the maximum useful frequency.

There is no connection between the three motor windings because the line converters have to be isolated from each other to operate correctly to obtain line commutation (natural) switching of the thyristors.

The converters may be directly supplied from the HV line but it is more usual to interpose step-down transformers. This reduces the motor voltage and its required insulation level while also providing additional line impedance to limit the size of prospective fault current and harmonic voltage distortion at the main supply bus-bar.

8.6. Propulsion System Operation

This section describes the overall operation of a propulsion system and is based on a diesel-electric arrangement with *synchroconverter* frequency control. For a large ship, the power system will employ high voltage (HV) generation as in the diagram in Fig. 8.18.

In this example each 12 MW, 3 kV propulsion motor has two separate 6 MW stator windings and each *half* winding is supplied from a 6.6/3.0 kV propulsion transformer and a static six-pulse synchroconverter. The 24 pole motors have a shaft speed range of 0-145 rev/min controlled from the converter output frequency range of 0-29 Hz.

By using two converters feeding two separate stator windings fitted 30° apart, a 12-pulse shaft *torque* is achieved to minimise shaft vibration. A more complicated arrangement of supply transformers and converters can produce a 24-pulse shaft torque.

Motor *brushless* excitation is also obtained from the HV bus-bars via a 6.6/0.44 kV static transformer, a thyristor controller, an a.c.→a.c. rotary transformer (inside the motor) and a set of shaft mounted diodes for the final conversion to d.c. A third (standby) static excitation supply and controller is available but not shown in the diagram.

The related *physical* arrangement of the main components in the propulsion system are shown in Fig. 8.19.

Control *throttle* stations for both shafts are installed on the bridge (in wheelhouse and on the wings), engine control room and local (in HV switchboard room) positions. At sea the shaft speed commands are set from the bridge and repeated in the ECR. In port the control position is transferred to the ECR. The *local* control position is mainly used for

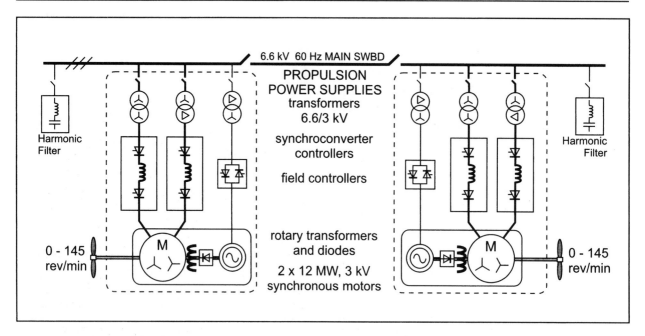

Fig. 8.18 HV propulsion power system.

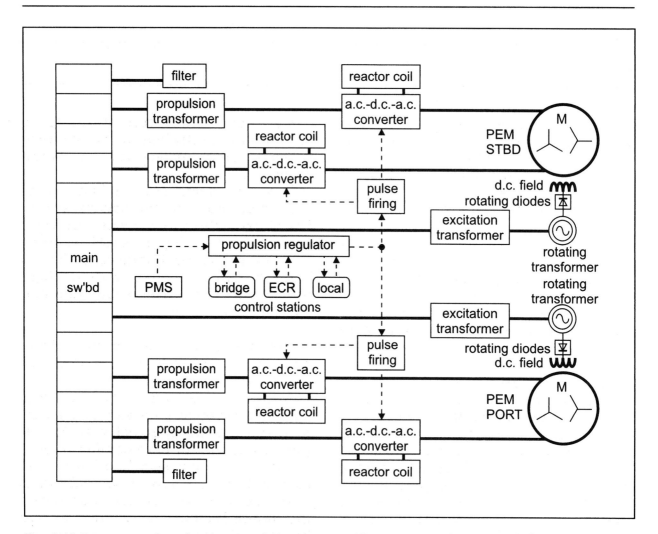

Fig. 8.19 Interconnection of main propulsion components.

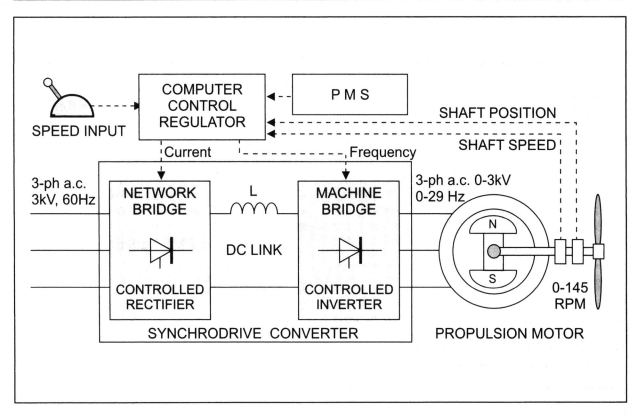

Fig. 8.20 Propulsion motor control scheme.

testing and maintenance duties but also acts as an emergency control station. Selection of the command position is determined by a switch on the propulsion console in the ECR.

An emergency push-button telegraph giving *set* speed commands (dead-slow, half-ahead etc.) is available at each control station. The ship propulsion regulator and side-thruster regulators can be combined into a master *joy-stick* controller to give overall directional control for accurate manoeuvring in port.

In a synchrodrive system as shown in Fig. 8.20, the computer receives a command (set speed) input and many feedback signals (voltage, current, power, frequency etc.) but the obvious regulating item is the actual shaft speed feedback forming a *closed* control loop. The principal parameters to be controlled are the size of motor stator current (to set motor torque) and the motor frequency to set the shaft speed. In addition,

the d.c. motor field current has to be continually controlled from the propulsion regulator via the excitation converter.

In normal running and full-away with both propulsion motor speeds within 5% of each other, the bridge can select a *shaft synchro-phasing* mode which applies momentary acceleration/deceleration to bring the propeller blades into an alignment which minimises shaft vibration into the hull.

Speed and position are derived from detectors on the non-drive end of the motor shaft.

At speeds of less than 10%, the motor does not generate sufficient *back* e.m.f. to cause automatic thyristor switch-off (line commutation) Remember that a thyristor can only switch off when its current becomes zero. This problem is overcome by *pulse-mode* operation where the current is momentarily forced to zero by the thyristors in the controlled *rectifier* stage. This allows the inverter thyristors to turn-off so that the controller can regain control. The decision is now *which* thyristor and which *sequence* of switching is required to maintain the required shaft direction of rotation. It is necessary to know exactly the position of the rotor poles and this is provided by the shaft position encoder for low-speed, *pulse-mode* operation. When *kicked* above 10% speed, the motor e.m.f. will be large enough to allow the converter to revert to its normal line-commutation mode for *synchronous* operation

QUESTION

If the individual inverter thyristors are not switched off (commutated) at the necessary instant a serious problem arises. Explain the likely consequences.

ANSWER

If two or more inverter thyristors are unable to be switched-off naturally they will apply a full short-circuit fault path across the d.c. link.

For normal running, above about 10% speed, the operation is switched to *synchronous mode* where the thyristors in both bridges are switched off naturally (line commutated) by their live a.c. voltages from supply and motor

To reverse the shaft rotation the forward/ ahead *phase sequence* of motor supply currents is reversed by the inverter thyristors. This reverses the *direction* of stator flux rotation and hence shaft direction to astern. The rate of deceleration to zero speed must be carefully controlled before a shaft reversal to avoid large power surges in the system.

For a motor braking operation, the inverter bridge can be considered as a rectifier bridge when viewed from the *live* a.c. supply produced by the motor emf. If the network (rectifier) bridge

thyristors are switched with a delay angle greater than 90° the d.c. link voltage *reverses* causing power flow from the motor back to the supply (motor braking). In this mode the roles of the network and machine bridges are swapped over.

Overall system power control is provided by a computer controlled power management system (PMS) which effectively co-ordinates power demand with its supply.

Broadly, the PMS functions are:

☐ Control of:

• Automatic power limitation for propulsion motors

• Auto-start, synchronising and load sharing of standby generators

• Control of re-generation from the propulsion motors during braking and reversing manoeuvres

• Power limitation for main generators

• Load shedding by preferential tripping

• Dynamic limitation of propulsion motor acceleration

☐ Monitoring of:

• Load sharing

• Diesel performance

• Proposal to start/stop a generator

• Running time for generators and propulsion motors

• Status and data display

8.7. Harmonics

The input current to a static power converter has, in general, a high harmonic content due to the way the current is switched (*chopped*) from phase to phase. Harmonic currents are important

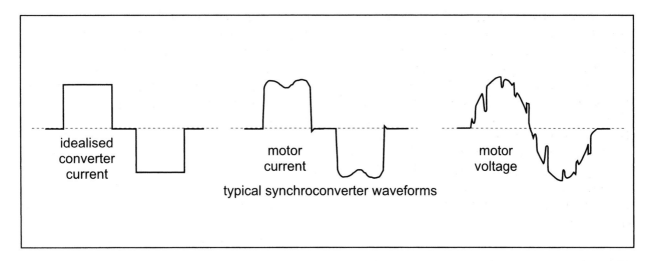

Fig. 8.21 Waveforms for synchrodrive converter.

because they cause distortion of the supply *voltage* waveform which may result in the malfunction and additional heating of other equipment connected to the supply system.

The size and frequencies of the harmonic currents and voltages depend on the converter type, the pulse number and method of control (e.g. synchroconverter, cycloconverter or PWM).

Typical waveforms for a six-pulse synchroconverter is shown in Fig. 8.21.

In general, *harmonic frequencies* are integer multiples (e.g. 3, 5, 7, 11, 13, etc.) of the fundamental (supply) frequency. Hence, a 7th harmonic in a 60 Hz a.c. voltage has a frequency of 420 Hz and an 11th has a frequency of 660 Hz. Harmonic amplitudes are roughly the reciprocal of the harmonic number, i.e. 20% (1/5) for the fifth, 14.3% for the seventh, 9.1% for the eleventh, etc. The particular shape of the resulting supply voltage will depend on harmonic currents causing additional harmonic voltages in the supply reactance (inductive and/or capacitive). See example in Fig. 8.22.

Some harmonics are eliminated by careful system design e.g. by adding more circuit inductance, using phase-shifting transformers (star-star and star-delta) and increasing the converter

pulse number. The 30° phase-shifted transformers effectively double the current pulses drawn by the motor so a 6-pulse converter system appears to be 12 pulse as viewed from the supply point.

For a generator sinusoidal a.c. voltage waveform with identical positive and negative shapes, all even numbered harmonics are cancelled out. In a three-phase a.c. system, all harmonics that are a multiple of three are also automatically cancelled. That leaves harmonic numbers of 5th, 7th, 11th, 13th, 17th, etc. as potential problems. For a pair of six-pulse synchroconverters supplied by a pair of phase-shifted transformers the significant harmonic problem is reduced to the 5th, 11th and 17th.

The actual voltage waveshape can be examined with an oscilloscope or calculated into its harmonic content with a harmonic/spectrum analyser. To accurately measure the useful level of voltage or current in a non-sinusoidal a.c. supply it is necessary to use *true rms* (root-mean-square) indicating instruments.

The harmonic content of the a.c. input to a synchroconverter also has components that are related to the motor operating frequency. The d.c. link reactor coil reduces the ripple in the link current so that the effect on the a.c. supply side is reduced.

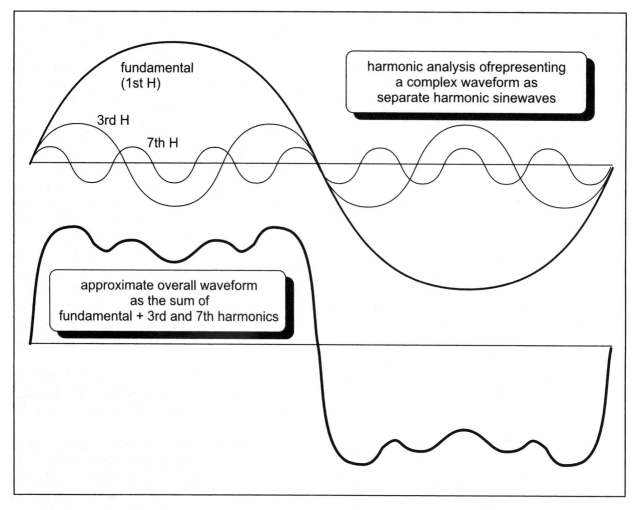

Fig. 8.22 Harmonic analysis of waveforms.

The total heating effect of distorted (non-sinusoidal) current waveform is calculated from the rms sum of all harmonics including the fundamental (or 1st harmonic). e.g. total rms value is:

$I = \sqrt{I_1^2 + I_5^2 + I_{11}^2 + I_{17}^2}$ for a waveform with three significant harmonics.

The % total harmonic distortion (THD) is found from the ratio of the sum of rms harmonics to the rms value of the fundamental.

QUESTION

A distorted 440 V, 60 Hz voltage waveform is found to include harmonics of: 20% 5th; 9% 11th; and 6% 17th.

Determine the rms size of each harmonic voltage and the overall THD.

ANSWER

The 1st harmonic rms level is 440 V. The 5th harmonic is 20% of 440 = 88 V. Similarly the 11th harmonic is 40 V and the 17th harmonic is 26 V.
The overall rms value of the three harmonics is

$$V_H = \sqrt{88^2 + 40^2 + 26^2} = 100 \text{ V}$$

So the THD = 100/440 = 0.227 per unit or 22.7%

Most ship classification societies demand that the THD of the mains voltage is less than 10% but in practice this is usually less than 5%.

To minimise the size of voltage distortion it is necessary to connect *filters* which are *tuned* to the troublesome harmonics. The filters are combination sets of inductance (L) and capacitance (C) each resonantly tuned to a particular frequency in a series/parallel circuit. Additionally, some resistance (R) is included to act as a harmonic current limiting (damping) effect.

The simplest way to view the overall system is to consider that the converter injects harmonics while the filter *absorbs* them. Filtering is not perfect over the variable frequency range so the harmonic problem is not completely solved but *is* minimised.

Practical harmonic installations in power systems are physically large and will create power losses and heat in the components.

A cycloconverter drive employs complex thyristor switching to create a variable low frequency output. The associated harmonics range is wide, variable and difficult to predict so static filtering is difficult. With large cycloconverter drives (e.g. on a cruise ship) it is usual to employ a pair of motor-generator sets (instead of transformers) between the 6.6 kV and 440 V switchboards. This arrangement provides a *clean* (harmonic-free) supply which does not transmit HV voltage variations to the LV side due to the rotational mechanical inertia of the M-G sets.

Where *clean* LV supplies are essential (e.g. 230 V, 50 Hz and 110 V, 60 Hz for instrument power on ocean survey ships with d.c. converters) it is usual to provide separate diesel-generator sets for that purpose. In this case, the main power system would probably not employ harmonic filters but is likely to use capacitive voltage surge suppression to minimise over-voltage *spikes* on the main bus-bar supply.

The general problem of *interference* (noise) in electrical systems is how to minimise it at source and/or limit its transmission into adjacent susceptible equipment to prevent circuit malfunction. Consider the interference to TV reception caused by the nearby operation of an electric power tool or unsuppressed motor bike ignition. The coupling between source and reception devices can be inductive (magnetic), electric (capacitive) or conductive (directly through the conductors). All of this is the subject of electromagnetic compatibility or *EMC* which is a complicated analysis due to the wide range of possibilities for interference coupling. Manufacturers of electrical/communication equipment have to test their designs to prove and declare acceptable levels of compatibility.

Harmonic *filtering* and circuit *screening* are two methods of limiting interference effects but no single method can be perfect.

The most important factor that compromises a screen performance is its coverage of the circuit. Think of radiated noise as visible light. A light bulb that is enclosed in a full metal box with no holes or gaps in any of the seams ensures that no light escapes from the box, (in electrical terms this is a *faraday cage* or fully screened room). If any holes exist in the box for cable entry/exit or the box seams are not perfect then light energy will escape. The amount of energy which can escape is dependent on the maximum linear dimension (L) of any aperture and the wavelength (λ) of the radiation (which is the principle used in microwave oven doors where visible light which has a short wavelength can pass through the door but microwaves with a longer wavelength cannot).

Apertures can occur in door fittings, gaskets, ventilation holes, spaces for instruments, seams on boxes, cable entry and exit points etc.

An important issue for interference is the coverage of screened and armoured cables, which is often far from ideal and allows *leakage* of radiation from the effective apertures caused by the braid *knitting,* and by the connection at either end of the screen/armour. The more expensive screened/armoured cables do have a better coverage and are to be preferred, but the effect can be negated by poor screen/armour termination.

8.8. Propulsion Auxiliaries and Protection

The electric propulsion motors and its shaft bearings, converters, control regulators, transformers reactor coils and harmonic filters all generate heat which must be continually removed by auxiliary cooling services. An over-temperature condition must be managed by load limitation or disconnection.

High current electrical components are generally cooled by forced air or by forced air/water circulation. In a large propulsion motor, see Fig. 8.23, an internal shaft mounted fan circulates air through the rotor and stator spaces. This air is forced by electric fans to flow through a fresh water cooler, usually mounted on top of the machine, which removes the heat into the main cooling system.

The motor enclosure will be typically rated as IP56 up to the shaft line and IP44 above.

Stator winding, cooling air and water temperatures are monitored for display in the ECR. It is essential that general and hot-spot temperature limits are not exceeded.

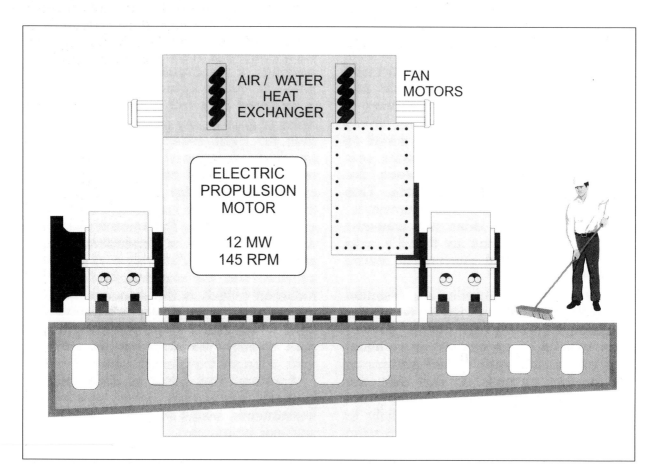

Fig. 8.23 Propulsion motor construction outline.

QUESTION

Which major feature of an electrical machine is principally degraded by over-temperature?

ANSWER

The *insulation* around the stator and rotor windings. Large HV machines are generally insulated with class F materials which have a maximum permitted temperature of 130°C but will be normally operated well below this limit.

Large motors and generators have internal electric heaters that are activated when the machine is disconnected. The requirement is to raise the internal temperature to about 3°C above ambient which will prevent condensation settling on the motor insulation. Typically, an anti-condensation heater rated at about 4 kW at 220 V would be fitted in a large HV machine.

Semiconductor components are particularly sensitive to temperature. In particular, the temperature of large-current switching thyristors in the converters must be carefully managed. A *perfect* closed switch has no voltage drop across it so its power loss is zero when conducting. A thyristor, however, develops a small voltage drop (typically up to 2 V) when conducting its current. For a thyristor carrying an average current of, say, 2000 A its power loss could be up to 4000 W which would rapidly destroy the device unless the internal heat is efficiently removed.

Fig. 8.24 shows how large power thyristors are clamped between large area metal heat sinks which conduct the internal heat away from the device. The heat sink is itself cooled by clean and dry forced air which is circulated through the converter cubicle, air filters and an air/water heat exchanger. A more effective method is to pump de-mineralised fresh water directly through the thyristor heat sinks and then circulate it through an external water/water heat exchanger.

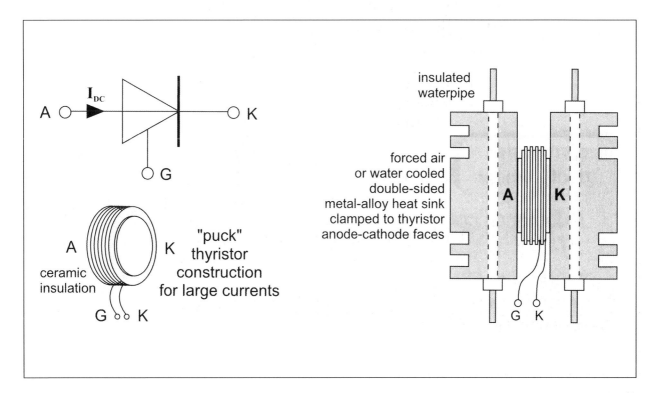

Fig. 8.24 Thyristor cooling arrangements.

QUESTION

The water used for heat sink cooling must be of exceptionally high purity. Why?

ANSWER

The metal alloy heat sinks form the electrical connections to anode and cathode so are *live* at a high voltage level. Insulated, plastic, piping is used and the electrical resistance of the water must be extremely high to avoid accidental connection between adjacent thyristors via the cooling medium.

The instrument used to measure the conductivity is similar to that used in a salinometer. *Conductivity* is measured in the units of micro-Siemen (μS) with acceptable values of less than 5 μS for thyristor cooling duty. If the set conductivity limit is exceeded the test instrument will signal alarm and trip conditions depending on the severity of the fault.

Protection of electrical power components requires that they be operated within their normal current, voltage and temperature ratings. A special case arises for the protection of large semiconductors, e.g. thyristors, which can additionally be destroyed by a fast *rate-of-change* of voltage and current caused by rapid switching. Fig. 8.25 shows thyristor protection.

To suppress a rapid overvoltage rise (dv/dt) across a thyristor an R-C *snubber* circuit is used. Its action is based on the fact that *voltage* cannot change instantaneously across a capacitor. The series resistor limits the corresponding current surge through the capacitor while it is limiting the voltage across the thyristor. Significant heat will be produced by the resistor which, in some applications, is directly cooled by a water jacket.

An in-line inductive effect will limit the rate-of-change of current (di/dt) through the thyristor. Special fast-acting line *fuses* may be used as *back-up* over-current protection for the thyristors.

Circuit protection for the electric propulsion units (including excitation and harmonic filters) principally employs co-ordinated *protective* relays which

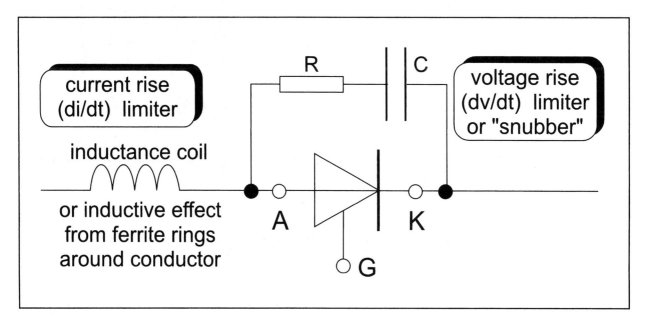

Fig. 8.25 Thyristor protection components.

monitor current, voltage, earth leakage and temperature. See Chapter Two for protective relay functions and operation.

The settings of relay parameter level (overcurrent, undervoltage etc.) and their tripping times are *critical* to the circuit protection under fault conditions. Such settings have been very carefully matched to the circuit and its components. Confirmation testing of protective relays requires calibrated current and voltage injection which is generally regarded as a specialist task for an outside contractor. Such testing is normally performed during a major survey during a dry-docking period.

8.9. High Voltage on Ships

For ships with a large electrical power demand it is necessary to utilise the benefits of a high voltage (HV) installation. For marine practice, HV means >1000 V. The design benefits relate to the simple ohms law relationship that current size (for a given power) is reduced as the voltage is increased. Working at high voltage significantly reduces the relative overall size and weight of electrical power equipment. HV

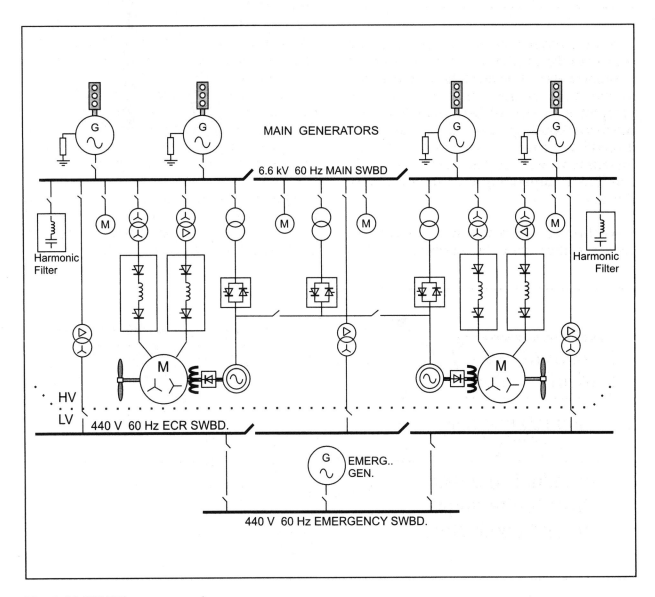

Fig. 8.26 HV/LV power supply system.

levels of 3.3 kV, 6.6 kV and 11 kV are regularly employed ashore for regional power distribution and industrial motor drives.

The main disadvantage perceived by the user/maintainer, when working in an HV installation, is the very necessary adherence to stringent safety procedures.

In the ships power network shown in Fig. 8.26, all of the equipment indicated above the dotted line is considered as HV. For the purposes of safety, this includes the LV field system for a propulsion motor as it is an integrated part of the overall HV equipment. From the HV generators, the network supplies HV motors (for propulsion, side thrusters and air conditioning compressors) and the main transformer feeders to the 440 V switchboard. Further distribution links are made to interconnect with the emergency switchboard.

• HV Circuit breakers and contactors

Probably the main difference between a HV and an LV system occurs at the HV main switchboard. For HV, the circuit breaker types may be air-break, oil-break, gas-break using SF6 (sulphur hexafluoride) or vacuum-break. Of these types, the most popular and reliable are the vacuum interrupters, which may also be used as contactors in HV motor starters. See Fig. 8.27.

Each phase of a vacuum circuit breaker or contactor consists of a fixed and moving contact within a sealed, evacuated envelope of borosilicate glass. The moving contact is operated via flexible metal bellows by a charging motor/spring or solenoid operating mechanism. The high electric strength of a vacuum allows a very short contact separation, and a rapid restrike-free interruption of the arc is achieved.

When an alternating current is interrupted by the separating contacts, an arc is formed by a metal vapour from the material on the contact surfaces and this continues to flow until a current zero is approached in the a.c. wave form. At

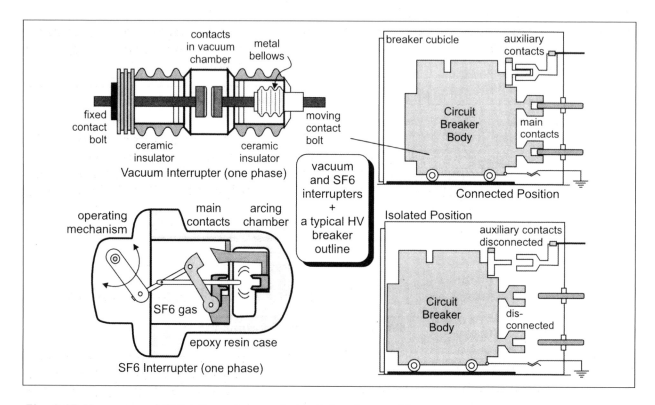

Fig. 8.27 Vacuum and SF6 interrupters and circuit breaker positions.

this instant the arc is replaced by a region of high dielectric strength which is capable of withstanding a high recovery voltage. Most of the metal vapour condenses back on to the contacts and is available for subsequent arcing. A small amount is deposited on the shield placed around the contacts which protects the insulation of the enclosure. As the arcing period is very short (typically about 15 ms), the arc energy is very much lower than that in air-break circuit-breakers so vacuum contacts suffer considerably less wear.

Because of its very short contact travel a vacuum interrupter has the following advantages:

🗸 compact quiet unit

🗸 minimum maintenance

🗸 non-flammable and non-toxic

The life of the unit is governed by contact erosion but could be up to 20 years.

In the gas-type circuit breaker, the contacts are separated in an SF6 (sulphur hexafluoride) gas which is typically at a sealed pressure chamber at 500 kPa or 5 bar (when tested at 20°C).

QUESTION

Some HV systems have the neutral point of a generator earthed to the ships hull via a neutral earthing resistor (NER). What is this connection for?

ANSWER

To minimise the size of earth fault current. A *hard* (zero resistance) earth fault causes a short-circuit across a generator phase winding, so the fault current is V_{PH}/R_{NER}. e.g. in a 6.6 kV system with a 200 Ω NER, ER, the V_{PH} = 6600/√3 = 3810 V and the maximum E/F current is 3810/200 = 19 A.

• HV Insulation Requirements

The HV winding arrangements for generators, transformers and motors are similar to those at LV except for the need for better insulating materials such as Micalastic or similar.

The HV windings for transformers are generally insulated with an epoxy resin/powdered quartz compound. This is a non-hazardous material which is maintenance free, humidity resistant and tropicalised.

Conductor insulation for an HV cable requires a more complicated design than is necessary for an LV type. However, less copper area is required for HV conductors which allows a significant saving in space and weight for an easier cable installation. Where the insulation is air (e.g. between bare-metal live parts and earth within switchboards and in terminal boxes) greater clearance and creepage distances are necessary in HV equipment.

QUESTION

Would a 500 V *megger* test be suitable to determine the insulation integrity of a 6.6 kV motor?

ANSWER

No. It would give a rough guide to the IR value but at 500 V, the tester is not properly stressing the insulation. For 6.6 kV equipment, a 5000 V IR tester is required.

8.10. High Voltage Safety

Making personal contact with any electric voltage is potentially dangerous. At high voltage (>1000 V) levels the electric shock potential is lethal. Body resistance decreases with increased voltage level which enhances the current flow. Remember that an electric shock current as low as 15 mA can be fatal.

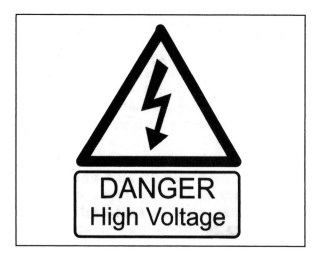

Fig. 8.28 HV warning notice.

The risk to people working in HV areas is greatly minimised by the diligent application of sensible general and company safety regulations and procedures. Personnel who are required to routinely test and maintain HV equipment should be *trained* in the necessary *practical* safety procedures and certified as qualified for this duty. Approved safety clothing, footwear, eye protection and hard hat should be used where danger may arise from arcs, hot surfaces and high voltage etc.

The access to HV switchboards and equipment must be strictly controlled by using a permit-to-work scheme and isolation procedures together with *live-line* tests and *earthing-down before any* work is started. The electrical permit requirements and procedures are similar to permits used to control access in any *hot-work* situation, e.g. welding, cutting, burning etc. in a potentially hazardous area.

All work to be carried out on HV equipment is subject to an *Electrical Permit to Work (EPTW)*.

✳ EPTW

The format of a permit will vary for different companies and organisations. The broad guidelines for the necessary declarations and procedures are outlined below:

Before work is commenced on HV equipment an EPTW must be issued. This permit is usually the last stage of a planned maintenance task which has been discussed, prepared and approved by the *authorising* officer to be carried out by the *responsible* person. The carbon-copied permit, signed by the responsible person, usually has at least five sections with the first stating the work to be carried out. The next section is a *risk assessment* declaring where electrical isolation and earthing has been applied and where danger/caution notices have been displayed then the permit is signed as authorised by the Chief Electrotechnical Officer (CETO) or Chief Engineer. In the third section, the person responsible for the work (as named in section one) signs to declare that he/she is satisfied with the safety precautions and that the HV circuit has been isolated and earthed. Section four relates to the suspension or completion of the designated work. Finally, the last section cancels the permit with a signature from the authorising officer. A Permit-to-Work is usually valid only for 24 hours.

Some marine and offshore companies will also require an associated *Electrical Isolation Certificate* to declare and record exactly where the circuit isolation and earthing has been applied *before* the EPTW can be authorised. A *Sanction-to-Test* safety certificate may also be required when an electrical test (e.g. an electrical insulation test) is to be applied. This is necessary as the circuit earth generally has to be removed during such testing.

Before *earthing-down* the particular circuit or equipment declared in the EPTW

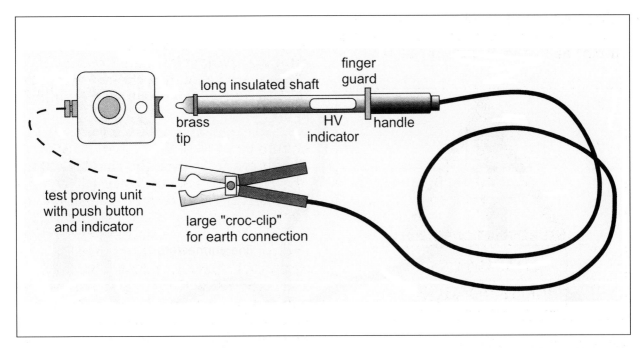

Fig. 8.29 HV live-line testing components.

it must be *tested* and *proved dead* after disconnection and isolation. This can only be carried out by using an approved live-line tester as shown in Fig. 8.29. The tester itself must be *proven* before *and* after such a test. This is checked by connecting the tester to a known HV source (supplied either as a separate battery operated unit or included as an internal self-test facility).

Two people should always be together when working on HV equipment.

✳ Earthing-down

Before work can be allowed to commence on HV equipment it must be *earthed* to the hull for operator safety.

As an example, consider the earthing arrangements at an HV *switchboard*. Here, the earthing-down method is of two types:

▼ Circuit Earthing:

After disconnection from the live supply, an incoming or outgoing feeder cable is connected by a manually operated switch to connect all three conductors to earth. This action then releases a *permissive-key* to allow the circuit breaker to be withdrawn to the TEST position. The circuit breaker cannot be re-inserted until the earth has been removed and the key restored to its normal position.

▼ Bus-bar Earthing:

When it is necessary to work on a section of the HV switchboard bus-bars, they must be isolated from *all* possible electrical sources. This will include generator incomers, section or bus-tie breakers and transformers (which could *back-feed*) on that bus-bar section. Earthing down is carried out at a bus-section breaker compartment after satisfying the permissive key exchanges. In some installations the application of a bus-bar earth is by a special earthing circuit breaker which is temporarily inserted into the switchboard solely for the bus-bar earthing duty.

For extra confidence and operator safety, *additional* earthing can be connected local to the work task with approved *portable* earthing straps and an insulated extension tool, e.g. at the terminals of an HV motor as shown in Fig. 8.30.

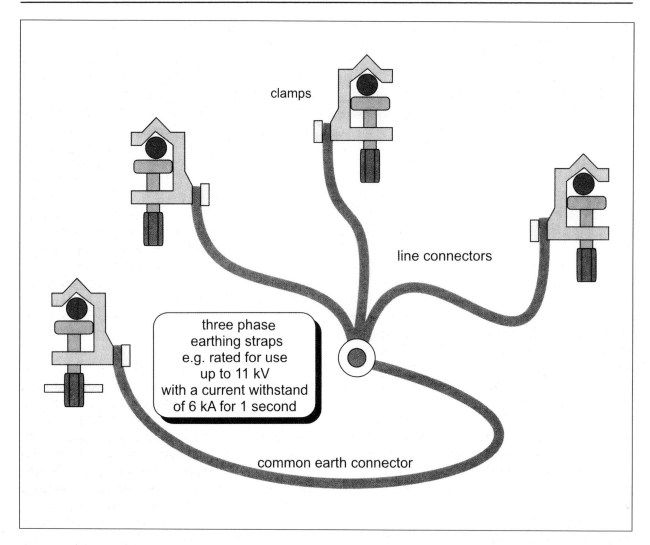

clamps

line connectors

three phase
earthing straps
e.g. rated for use
up to 11 kV
with a current withstand
of 6 kA for 1 second

common earth connector

Fig. 8.30 Portable earthing connectors.

Remember to always connect the common wire to earth *first* before connecting the other wires to the three phase connections. When removing the earthing straps, always remove the earth connection *last*.

voltage because the earth connection *bonds* the circuit to earth (zero volts).

QUESTION

Why is *earthing down* considered essential during HV maintenance?

ANSWER

So that the worker can be assured that the equipment (and himself) *cannot* experience any accidentally applied

8.11. High Voltage Equipment Testing

The high voltage (e.g. 6.6 kV) installation covers the generation, main supply cables, switchgear, transformers, electric propulsion (if fitted) and a few large motors e.g. for side-thrusters and air conditioning compressors. For all electrical equipment the key indicator to its safety and general condition is its insulation resistance (IR) and this is particularly so for HV apparatus. The IR must be tested periodically between phases and between phases and earth. HV equipment that is well designed and maintained, operated within its power and temperature ratings should have a useful insulation life of 20 years.

An IR test is applied with a high d.c. voltage which applies a reasonable stress to the dielectric material (insulation). For 6.6 kV rated equipment, a periodical 5000 V d.c. insulation resistance (*megger*) test is recommended. The IR test should be applied for one minute and temperature corrected to a standard of 40°C. The minimum IR value is usually recommended as $(kV + 1)$ MΩ where kV is the equipment voltage rating. e.g. 7.6 MΩ would be an acceptable IR value for a 6.6 kV machine. For machines with healthy insulation, an IR test result may indicate a value up to 100 times greater than the recommended minimum.

A more involved IR test (the *polarisation index* or P.I.) is used when the insulation value may be suspect or recorded during an annual survey. The P.I. value is the ratio of the IR result after 10 minutes of testing to the value recorded after one minute. For class F insulation materials the recommended P.I. value is 2.0. To apply a P.I. test over a ten minute period requires a special IR tester that has a motor-driven generator or an electronic converter powered from a local 220 V a.c. supply.

The condition of HV insulation is governed by many factors such as temperature, humidity, surface condition and operating voltage level. Be guided by the manufacturers recommendations when testing and maintaining HV insulation.

Before applying an IR test to *HV* equipment its power supply must be switched off, isolated, confirmed dead by an approved live-line tester and then *earthed* for complete safety in accordance with the current EPTW regulations.

The correct procedure is to connect the IR tester to the circuit under test with the safety earth connection *ON*. The safety earth may be applied through a switch connection at the supply circuit breaker or by a temporary earth connection local to the test point. This is to ensure that the operator never touches a unearthed conductor. With the IR tester now connected, the safety earth is disconnected (using an insulated extension tool for the temporary earth). Now the IR test is applied and recorded. The safety earth is now reconnected *before* the IR tester is disconnected. This safety routine must be applied for each separate IR test.

Large currents flowing through machine windings, cables, bus-bars and main circuit breaker contacts will cause a temperature rise due to I^2R resistive heating. Where overheating is suspected, e.g. at a bolted bus-bar joint in the main switchboard, the local *continuity* resistance may be measured and checked against the manufacturers recommendations or compared with similar equipment that is known to be satisfactory. A normal ohmmeter is not suitable as it will only drive a few mA through the test circuit. A special low resistance tester or micro-ohmmeter (traditionally called a *ducter*) must be used which drives a calibrated current (usually $I = 10$ A) through the circuit while measuring the volt-drop (V) across the circuit. The meter calculates R from V/I and displays the test result. For a healthy bus-bar joint a continuity of a few mΩ would be expected.

Normally the safe testing of HV equipment requires that it is disconnected from its power supply. Unfortunately, it is very difficult, impossible and unsafe to closely observe the on-load operation of internal components within HV enclosures. This is partly resolved by temperature measurement with an recording infra-red camera from a safe

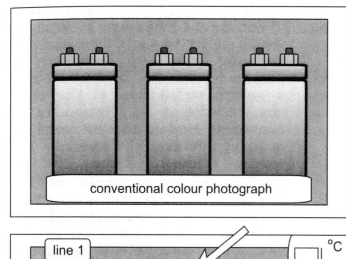

location/identification	
area:	6.6 kV main board
equipment:	Gen 2 breaker
component:	copper bus-bars
date/time:	22/03/99/15:45

fault diagnosis and recommendation

copper temperature on middle phase much higher than adjacent bars.

Check copper connections for tightness, clean and re-check

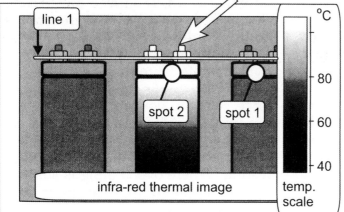

label	temperature °C
spot 1	55.2
spot 2	100.3
line 1: max.	99.0
line 1: min.	50.6

Fig. 8.31 Infrared image testing.

distance. The camera is used to scan an area and the recorded infra-red image is then processed by a computer program to display hot-spots and a thermal profile across the equipment. To examine internal components, e.g. bus-bar joints, a camera recording can be made immediately after the equipment has been switched off and isolated in accordance with an EPTW safety procedure. Alternatively, some essential equipment, e.g. a main switchboard, can be monitored *on-line* using specially fitted and approved enclosure *windows* suitable for infra-red testing. These *windows* are small apertures with a permanently fixed steel mesh through which the camera can view the internal temperature from a safe position. An outer steel plate fixed over the window mesh maintains the overall enclosure performance during normal operation.

A conventional photograph of the equipment is taken simultaneously to match the infra-red image and both are used as part of a test report. Such testing is usually performed by a specialist contractor who will prepare the test report and propose recommendation/repair advice to the ship operator.

Fig. 8.31 (unfortunately not in colour like the original) gives typical results from an infra-red camera test on a bus-bar connection.

In this on-line test, the camera recorded hot-spot temperatures up to 100°C and the report recommended that this copper connection is checked for tightness as it is running very hot compared to that on the neighbouring copper-work.

To test the insulating integrity of an HV vacuum-type circuit breaker requires a special high voltage impulse test. The tester produces a short duration voltage pulse, of typically 10 kV for a 6.6 kV circuit, which is connected across the open breaker contacts. Any weakness in the insulating strength of the vacuum in the interrupter chamber will be detected as a current flow and the tester will display the condition as a *pass* or *fail*.

Gas (SF6) HV circuit breakers rely on the quality and pressure of the gas acting as the insulation between the contacts. A falling gas pressure can be arranged to initiate an alarm from pressure switches fitted to each switching chamber. Normal gas pressures are typically 500 kPa or 5 bar.

Overall *circuit* protection of HV equipment is supervised by co-ordinated protective relays. These must be periodically tested to confirm their level settings (for current, voltage, frequency etc.) and their tripping times. This requires the injection of calibrated values of current and voltage into the protective relays which is usually performed by a specialist contractor during a main ship survey while in dry-dock.

Index